About the Author

Before becoming a professional entertainer, songwriter, verse
writer and singer in 1988, Jim Haynes taught writing, literature,
history and drama in schools and universities from outback
New South Wales to Britain and back again! He has two
masters degrees in Literature, from the University of Wales
(UK) and New England University (NSW).

Jim has won 'Comedy Song of the Year' four times at the
Tamworth Festival, including the hits, 'Don't Call Wagga
Wagga Wagga' and 'Since Cheryl Went Feral', which topped the
Country Charts for five weeks in 1997. He has toured
extensively both here and overseas as a comic and singer and
has appeared regularly on television and worked for some time
in radio.

In 1990 Jim originated the idea of morning shows based on
bush verse and humour at the Tamworth Festival. His 'Big
Bush Brekky' shows now attract huge audiences each morning
of the ten-day festival.

Jim has released many successful albums of his own songs, verse
and humour, and has produced albums of verse for the ABC.
His collection of verse, *I'll Have Chips*, won the inaugural Bush
Laureate Book of the Year Award and he is the author of a
successful volume of stories, *Memories of Weelabarabak –
Stories of a Bush Town*.

An Australian

Heritage of
Verse

Jim Haynes

ABC
BOOKS

For Sylvia, Jillian, Katherine and Alison ... and their descendants.

Published by ABC Books for the
AUSTRALIAN BROADCASTING CORPORATION
GPO Box 9994 Sydney NSW 2001

Copyright © Jim Haynes 2000

First published October 2000

National Library of Australia
Cataloguing-in-Publication entry
An Australian heritage of verse.

Includes index.
ISBN 0 7333 0898 8.

1. Australian poetry. I. Haynes, Jim. II. Australian
Broadcasting Corporation.

A821.008

Designed by Robert Taylor
Set in 10/14 pt Garamond by Midland Typesetters,
Maryborough, Victoria
Colour separations by Finsbury, Adelaide
Printed and bound in Australia by
Griffin Press, Adelaide

5 4 3 2 1

Contents

Thanks

This collection would not have been near as good as it is without the input and quality control of many people – it's good to have mates!

Special thanks must go to Frank Daniel – the master of the world wide web – who was a tower of strength, a tireless collaborator and kept finding stuff when I was stuck. Russell Hannah was a mine of information (mostly useless), as he always is, and Robyn was a great listener and proofreader, as she always is. Ted Egan, Joy McKean and John Derum also provided help beyond the call of duty.

The Mitchell Library was pretty useful too – along with Patricia Rolfe's history of the *Bulletin*, *The Journalistic Javelin*, and previous wonderful anthologies of various kinds including those by Keesing and Stewart, Banjo Paterson, Bill Scott and David Mulhallen.

Also, thanks to Stuart Neal and Matthew Kelly for giving me the chance to devote three whole months of my life to this project – I'm a better person for it I know!

Editor's Note

This selection is designed to demonstrate what Australian rhymed verse is all about. It was made on the basis that these poems are representative of the genre in its many moods and styles. Hopefully they are also the most entertaining poems written in this style over the past two hundred years or so. While half the poems chosen are from contemporary writers, I have, at the same time, attempted to make this collection as definitive as possible. I have tried to keep in mind that this should be an essential collection for reciting and performing as well as reading. No matter what mood you wish to experience or create, or what emotion you wish to stir in yourself or your audience, it's here somewhere in this collection.

My other task was to make the collection a social documentary of the past two hundred years, while making it as universal as possible. I wanted to demonstrate, as the title says, our *heritage* of rhymed verse at its most representative and diverse. One of the purposes of this type of literature has always been to document, and comment on, contemporary issues – whether it be Phar Lap, mini skirts, chainsaws, rural hardship or city life. The thirteen sections were chosen with a view to making each one wide enough to cover different eras and attitudes to the subject material.

Some fine verse has been omitted simply because I had many examples covering a certain topic, theme, opinion or attitude. Many are here because they fitted the bill when I needed a particular viewpoint or mood – or some essential part of our heritage appeared to be missing from the collection.

I have also included, in several cases, verse originally written as song lyrics. While there is a major difference today between popular song lyrics and verse, the distinction was certainly not apparent before the advent of the popular song and the 'Tin Pan Alley' tradition, which began late in the nineteenth century. Rhymed verse was traditionally sung in both the folk and classical musical traditions right up to that time – as indeed it is today. In her history of the *Bulletin* Patricia Rolfe comments that bush verse 'had antecedents in the bush songs as well as

Gordon.' In his introduction to Chris Kempster's authoritative work, *Songs of Henry Lawson*, Professor Manning Clark notes that Lawson 'wrote with a passion that clamours for music'.

Many songwriters in the folk, country and popular music fields have put music to the works of 'bush' poets. The works of many 'bush' poets were originally written to tunes – this is especially true of Morant and Ogilvie (and Paterson in several notable cases). Thus, it is very difficult, if not impossible, to draw the line between 'bush verse' and the 'bush ballad'. My only rule for including these 'lyrics' was that they had to stand the test of reading as verse on the page. I have included them because they were, in my opinion, the best examples I found to cover a certain topic or theme.

Finally, to all the experts in this area who have an alternative selection half-formulated somewhere in the back of their mind, all I can say is this:

> I'm on a hiding to nothing – no matter what I do,
> This book will displease many and maybe please a few
> My right-wing country mates will say, 'There's too much
>   left-wing stuff!'
> My left-wing folkie friends, of course, will say there's not
>   enough.
> 'Too much old stuff', 'Too much new stuff' – everyone will
>   moan,
> 'Not enough of Paterson', 'Too many of his own'.
> 'Not enough of people', 'Not enough of places',
> And, 'Far too many silly poems about the bloody races'.
> 'I didn't like the crude ones', 'It was all too sanitised',
> 'What small integrity he had has now been compromised.'
> So I'm sorry, just a little, if you don't like my collection.
> And you can be sure, when you do yours, I won't like *your*
>   selection!

Introduction

Rhymed verse has many purposes apart from fulfilling our emotional needs as poetry. It can document history, heroics and current events, tell stories, comment on social issues and satirise. At its best it is as subtle and satisfying as any form of literature can be, but its primary purpose is entertainment – whether it be for reading, reciting, performing or listening.

Rhymed verse for entertainment, information and social comment flourished in Australia in the early nineteenth century for the same reasons that it flourished in other countries and cultures from Ancient Greece to Elizabethan England – the population was far-flung, isolated and largely illiterate. Verse was used extensively to document local events and, by the middle of that century, it had become a major part of each colony's literary tradition. There is a vast amount of localised, occasional verse from this period in the archives of local newspapers of the time – most of it is pure doggerel and of no interest today. (Indeed most of it would have been of no interest outside the district or settlement it was written in at the time!)

Then along came the *Bulletin* – established in 1880 by JF Archibald and John Haynes (no relation, to the best of my knowledge), and the rhymed verse tradition was well and truly confirmed and established as part of our 'national' heritage. The first 'bush ballad' the *Bulletin* published was 'Sam Holt', in March 1881. A parody of a popular song of the time, 'Sweet Alice Ben Bolt', the poem, by GH Gibson ('Ironbark') is a series of complaints addressed to a bushman who has struck it lucky and become a city 'toff'. The poem reminds him of his sinful days in the bush. The fact that it is a parody full of the jargon and racism of its day make it fairly meaningless today but it certainly contained the themes of 'city versus the bush' and what we now call the 'tall poppy' syndrome.

> Say don't you remember that fiver, Sam Holt, you borrowed
> so frank and so free . . .
> I guess I may whistle a good many times 'fore you think of
> that fiver or me.

The *Bulletin* introduced Paterson and Lawson to the Australian public, along with Victor Daley, Mary Gilmore, CJ Dennis, Will Ogilvie, Harry Morant, WT Goodge, 'John O'Brien' and the rest. The *Bully* regularly published the work of over sixty verse writers. It is interesting to note that, in publishing thousands of ballads and verses, the *Bulletin* actually published less than two per cent of the verse submitted. That is a telling figure to me – and confirms my experience over the last twenty years – for every one or two writers of verse you hear of in Australia there are another hundred out there, writing away for themselves and their mates and family.

At first the *Bulletin* struggled and payment was sometimes late. Victor Daley once wrote on the wall of John Haynes' office: 'He parts his coin with childbirth pains – his name is Haynes.' (No relation I tell you!) Soon, however, the *Bulletin* became the chief source of income for our best writers of verse. It was the *Bulletin* that sent Lawson on his inspirational trip to Bourke and supported many writers, as well as artists like the Lindsays, for many years. The importance of the *Bulletin* to our rhymed verse heritage cannot be overestimated.

In the twentieth century rhymed verse became a bastion of 'Australian-ness' in a sea of foreign influences – both in literature and culture generally. This was no doubt partly due to the *Bulletin's* long-standing anti-British and 'White Australia' editorial policies. Improved communication and developments in mass media accelerated this trend as the century unfolded. Rural lifestyles and traditional values are more and more represented by rhymed verse as they cease to be the norm in a modern, multicultural society.

There are cycles of popularity throughout the history of Australian rhymed verse. At times the education system was very aware of 'Australian-ness' and emphasised our rhymed verse tradition. At other times school curricula in verse and song were dominated by non-Australian material and fiercely Australian approaches were seen as parochial or embarrassing. There were movements like the Jindyworobaks and the rising and falling popularity of 'folk', 'bush' and Australian 'country' music – all based to a certain extent on a verse tradition. Through all these trends Aussies kept writing rhymed verse about the things that they related to in their everyday lives. The latest surge in popularity for rhymed verse began in the late 1980s (after a fairly lean time following a boom in the 'folk' scene in the 1960s) and it continues today.

This resurgence of rhymed verse over the past decade has, I'm sure, given thousands of Australians much pleasure and satisfaction. Rhymed verse has always given me pleasure. As a child my mother would read and quote Paterson, Lawson and others whose names she didn't even know, and these fragments and images have stayed with me all my life. I heard a lot of verse about characters, racehorses and tall tales as a kid and, when I went west as a young man of nineteen, bushmen in the pub or around the campfire would recite bush ballads at length for entertainment or to make a point. I first heard 'That Day at Boiling Downs' and 'My Hat!' in the bar of Maiden's Hotel, Menindee.

The art of writing and reciting rhymed verse was still alive back then but it appeared to be dying. Television was spreading into the bush bringing American music and entertainment, and British comedy routines. People stopped making their own fun and sharing their stories and heritage around the campfire or on the verandah. Bush verse was down – but not out. Then, in the lead up to the Bicentenary, the 1980s saw a revival in 'bush' music, led by The Bushwackers. This was accompanied by a revived interest in bush verse; each bush band had someone who recited a verse or two between songs or dances. The Bushwackers had the very talented Dobe Newton, The Bush Bandicoots had the wonderful Ted Simpson – Bandy Bill & Co only had me! In the bicentennial year of 1988 I quit teaching and returned to Sydney, after twenty years of 'bush finishing school', to work on 'Australia All Over'. It was then that I began writing and collecting contemporary 'bush verse' in earnest.

My association with the folk movement (through being a member of Bandy Bill & Co Bush Band from 1978) had led to meeting bush poets and collectors like the late Ted Simpson and Alan Scott. I also met collectors and historians like Warren Fahey and Bill Scott, folk poets like Denis Kevans, John Dengate and Keith McKenry and characters steeped in the bush verse tradition like Ted Egan and Russell Hannah. Working on Australia All Over' led to making the acquaintance of people like the late Leonard Teale, John Derum and my dear friend Col 'Blue the Shearer' Wilson.

It was through 'doing the poetry' on 'Australia All Over' that I realised the art form of bush verse was still alive out there – but it was mostly happening in isolation. People like Grahame Watt in Victoria and the late Charlee Marshall in Queensland were writing for the local market and sending stuff off to ABC Radio. South Australia had Bob Magor and the Central West had 'Blue the Shearer'. (Many of these poets thought nobody else wrote bush verse! Frank Daniel said that, until he met Col Wilson and myself at Stuart Town one night, he thought he was the only bloke silly enough to be bothered putting yarns and memories to verse.)

Parallel to all this the likes of 'Mac' Cormack, Kelly Dixon, Ray Rose, Bruce Simpson, Joe Daly and Tony Brooks were writing rhymed verse which was being turned into ballads by artists like Slim Dusty and Ted Egan. And Slim, Ted, Joy McKean, Harold and Wilga Williams and others were reworking older verse and writing some wonderful folk poetry of their own.

I was aware of all these different aspects of Australian rhymed verse by 1991. Yet, when I was asked to produce an album of collected contemporary bush verse in that year, there was a mere handful of entertaining poets and performers to call on. Now there is more 'bush' verse around the country than you can poke a stick at. Whether this is just another part of a cyclical phenomenon, one can't really say just yet but, at present, rhymed verse is certainly booming. It is a staple entertainment at folk and country music events, and has many festivals and events all its own; and there are many competitions based on performances and unpublished verse.

Significantly there is now also an established set of recognised national awards, the Australian Bush Laureate Awards*, for

* For information on the Australian Bush Laureate Awards write to PO Box 298 Tamworth 2340

published and recorded verse, organised along similar lines to music and arts industry awards. The trophies themselves are known as 'Golden Gumleaf' trophies and they are presented in Tamworth each January. Although these awards are only five years old as this book goes to press, twelve writers represented here are already 'Bush Laureate' winners (Frank Daniel, Kelly Dixon, Slim Dusty, Murray Hartin, Jim Haynes, Mark Kleinschmidt, Bob Magor, Keith McKenry, Bob Miller, Carmel Randle, Ray Rose and Bruce Simpson), many others have been finalists. More importantly, perhaps, the number of good quality publications and albums released increases annually.

Let's hope that – whether it's ebbing or flowing, flavour of the decade or not – the great Australian tradition of rhymed verse as social documentary and entertainment will live as long as there are Aussie words to rhyme. After all, this is a nation where, according to Henry Lawson, 'every third bushman is a poet, with a big heart that keeps his pockets empty'.

Galleries of Pink Galahs

Places & Pictures

*F*rom Henry Lawson right through to Denis Kevans, John Williamson and Joy McKean, Australia's native-born writers of descriptive verse have had an ongoing love affair with the incredible beauty and variety of Australia's landscape. No other land or nation is defined by its visual imagery the way this beautiful old continent is.

Australia has two very different histories – an Aboriginal one so ancient and strange to Europeans – and a European one very brief in Western terms. This sometimes makes it hard to present a strong, simple image or cultural perspective to other nations. Often Australia tends to be presented to the world visually – defined by natural landscapes like Uluru, Sydney Harbour, gum trees and the Barrier Reef – or man-made landscapes like wheatfields, coastal cities and little outback towns. These images have always been very powerful to Australians themselves too; they are something tangible to recognise as 'ours'. They help us define ourselves and remember who we are.

Galleries of Pink Galahs / John Williamson
The Blue Mountains / Henry Lawson
Moss's Gentle Fingers / Denis Kevans
The Australian Sunrise / James Cuthbertson
Waratah, My Mountain Queen / Henry Lawson
Wide Horizons / Mark Kleinschmidt
The Min Min Light / Joy McKean

Galleries of Pink Galahs

John Williamson

Galleries of pink galahs
Crystal nights with diamond stars
Apricots preserved in jars
That's my home

Land of oceans in the sun
Purple hazes, river gum
Breaks your heart when rain won't come
It breaks your heart

It takes a harsh and cruel drought
To sort the weaker saplings out
It makes room for stronger trees
Maybe that's what life's about

Winter's come, the hills are brown
Shops are closed, the blinds are down
Everybody's leavin' town
They can't go on

The south wind through verandah gauze
Whines and bangs the homestead doors
A mother curses dusty floors
And feels alone

Trucks and bulk bins filled with rust
Boy leaves home to make a crust
A father's dreams reduced to dust
But he must go on

Tortured red gums, unashamed
Sunburnt country wisely named
Chisel-ploughed and wire-claimed
But never, never, never tamed

Whirlwind swirls a paper high
Same old news of further dry
Of broken clouds just passing by
That's my home

The Blue Mountains

Henry Lawson

Above the ashes straight and tall,
    Through ferns with moisture dripping,
I climb beneath the sandstone wall,
    My feet on mosses slipping.

Like ramparts round the valley's edge
    The tinted cliffs are standing,
With many a broken wall and ledge,
    And many a rocky landing.

And round about their rugged feet
    Deep ferny dells are hidden
In shadowed depths, whence dust and heat
    Are banished and forbidden.

The stream that, crooning to itself,
  Comes down a tireless rover,
Flows calmly to the rocky shelf,
  And there leaps bravely over.

Now pouring down, now lost in spray
  When mountain breezes sally,
The water strikes the rock midway,
  And leaps into the valley.

Now in the west the colours change,
  The blue with crimson blending;
Behind the far Dividing Range,
  The sun is fast descending.

And mellowed day comes o'er the place,
  And softens ragged edges;
The rising moon's great placid face
  Looks gravely o'er the ledges.

Moss's Gentle Fingers

Denis Kevans

Where the moss's gentle fingers paint the sleeping boulders green,
I'll walk, in all my wisdom, where no mortal's ever been,
And where immortal trees stretch up their fingers to the sky,
The moss will cool the water for the lyre-bird and I,
                    the lyre-bird and I.

Sing out, happy lyre-bird, your song for everyone,
The parrot in the treetop, the quail that likes to run,
The whistler in the canopy, the honey-eater's call,
Sing out, happy lyre-bird, beside the waterfall,
                    beside the waterfall.

Like octopus's tentacles, the roots of trees have grown,
With steel embrace, they vainly try to crush the hearts of stone,
And stone from stone, and tree from stone, or is it stone from tree?
They wrestle, in the half-light, for the lyre-bird and me,
                    the lyre-bird and me.

I see the pythons writhing, and the Titans fighting, too,
And a sudden shaft of sunlight trying Cinderella's shoe,
And, where the half-light weakens, and the roots are tangled wild,
I seem to see a carving of Madonna and her child,
                                    Madonna and her child.

But the lyre-bird has found me, and he's trying out my air,
He sends his voice out mocking me, from here, and over there,
So I'll bluey up my blankets, where no mortal's ever been,
And the moss's gentle fingers paint the sleeping boulders green,
                                    the sleeping boulders green.

The Australian Sunrise

James Cuthbertson

The Morning Star paled slowly, the Cross hung low to the sea,
And down the shadowy reaches the tide came swirling free,
The lustrous purple blackness of the soft Australian night
Waned in the grey awakening that heralded the light;
Still in the dying darkness, still in the forest dim,
The pearly dew of the dawning clung to each giant limb,
Till the sun came up from the ocean, red with the cold sea mist,
And smote on the limestone ridges, and the shining tree-tops kissed;

Then the fiery Scorpion vanished, the magpie's note was heard,
And the wind in the sheoak wavered and the honeysuckles stirred;
The airy golden vapour rose from the river breast,
The kingfisher came darting out of his crannied nest,
And the bulrushes and reed-beds put off their sallow grey
And burnt with cloudy crimson at the dawning of the day.

Waratah, My Mountain Queen

Henry Lawson

Waratah, my Mountain Queen,
Grandest flower ever seen,
Glorious in shade or sun,
Where our rocky gullies run.
There is nothing, near or far,
Like our Mountain Waratah.

Wide Horizons

Mark Kleinschmidt

Majestic those wild rugged summits,
How noble these gums reaching high,
But give me the far wide horizons
And contented I'll be when I die,
For I love the huge sky and the distance
Of the plains that roll to the west,
Though I see the beauty of elsewhere,
Wide horizons are all I request.

The Min Min Light

Joy McKean

Have you ever heard the story of the Queensland Min Min Light,
Heard the old folks tell in whispers how it beckons thru' the night;
How your horse will rear in terror, and your dog will howl in fright,
For there's somethin' mighty eerie in that dancin' Min Min Light.

There's a couple living westward on a lonely station camp,
Each night they keep their vigil by the glimmer of a lamp;
They keep their watch together till they see it glowing bright,
And they sometimes rise and follow that misty Min Min Light.

Years ago they had a youngster, the laughter of their life,
Always he would ask them to see that pretty light;
One night when all were sleeping, the lad awoke and so,
Looking out the window, he saw that Min Min glow.

It seemed that he could touch it and it moved off far ahead,
He ran and laughed behind it, and followed where it led;
Across the darkened ridges far into the night,
The lad was lost for ever to that cruel Min Min Light.

His resting place is hidden, his parents hope and pray
Some night that ghostly light may come and show to them the way;
But it quivers and it dances through the cold and lonely night,
But for ever keeps its secret, that cruel Min Min Light.

Now I've told to you the story of the Queensland Min Min Light,
How the old folk tell in whispers how it beckons through the night;
And your horse will rear in terror, and your dog will howl in fright,
And there's something mighty eerie in that dancing Min Min Light.

The Stringy-bark Tree

Henry Lawson

There's the whitebox and pine on the ridges afar,
Where the iron-bark, blue-gum, and peppermint are;
There is many another, but dearest to me,
And the king of them all was the stringy-bark tree.

Then of stringy-bark slabs were the walls of the hut,
And from stringy-bark saplings the rafters were cut;
And the roof that long sheltered my brothers and me
Was of broad sheets of bark from the stringy-bark tree.

And when sawn timber homes were built out in the West,
Then for walls and for ceilings its wood was the best;
And for shingles and palings to last while men be,
There was nothing on earth like the stringy-bark tree.

Far up the long gullies the timber-trucks went,
Over tracks that seemed hopeless, by bark hut and tent;
And the gaunt timber-finder, who rode at his ease,
Led them on to a gully of stringy-bark trees.

Now still from the ridges, by ways that are dark,
Come the shingles and palings they call stringy-bark;
Though you ride through long gullies a twelve months you'll see
But the old whitened stumps of the stringy-bark tree.

Blue Gums Calling Me Back Home

Harry & Wilga Williams

Blue Gum trees I hear you calling me,
Back to where I always feel so free,
To the land where kangaroos and emus roam,
The bush will always be my home.
Cooee, cooee,
I can hear you calling me back home.

I can hear the ripple of a mountain stream,
See the sunsets in my every dream,
I can smell the scent of fresh cooked johnny cake,
And hear the cooee of a mate.
Cooee, cooee,
I can hear you calling me back home.

I can hear the click sticks tapping out a song,
Of my Waradgery Tribe as I dance along,
I can taste the honey of the wild bush bee,
From the blue gum tree that's calling me.
Cooee, cooee,
I can hear you calling me back home.

Sydney-Side

Henry Lawson

Where's the steward? – Bar-room steward? Berth? Oh, any berth will do –
I have left a three-pound billet just to come along with you.
Brighter shines the Star of Rovers on a world that's growing wide,
But I think I'd give a kingdom for a glimpse of Sydney-Side.

Run of rocky shelves at sunrise, with their base on ocean's bed;
Homes of Coogee, homes of Bondi, and the lighthouse on South Head;
For in loneliness and hardship – and with just a touch of pride –
Has my heart been taught to whisper, 'You belong to Sydney-Side.'

Oh, there never dawned a morning, in the long and lonely days,
But I thought I saw the ferries streaming out across the bays –
And as fresh and fair in fancy did the picture rise again
As the sunrise flushed the city from Woollahra to Balmain:

And the sunny water frothing round the liners black and red,
And the coastal schooners working by the loom of Bradley's Head;
And the whistles and the sirens that re-echo far and wide –
All the life and light and beauty that belong to Sydney-Side.

And the dreary cloud line never veiled the end of one day more,
But the city set in jewels rose before me from 'The Shore'.
Round the sea-world shine the beacons of a thousand ports o'call,
But the harbour-lights of Sydney are the grandest of them all!

Wheat

CJ Dennis

'Sowin' things an' growin' things, an' watchin' of 'em grow;
That's the game,' my father said, an' father ought to know.
'Settin' things an' gettin' things to grow for folks to eat:
That's the life,' my father said, 'that's very hard to beat.'
For my father was a farmer, as his father was before,
Just sowin' things an' growin' things in far-off days of yore,
In the far-off land of England, till my father found his feet
In the new land, in the true land, where he took to growin' wheat.
    Wheat, Wheat, Wheat! Oh, the sound of it is sweet!
    I've been praisin' it an' raisin' it in rain an' wind an' heat
        Since the time I learned to toddle, till it's beatin' in my noddle,
    Is the little song I'm singin' you of Wheat, Wheat, Wheat.

Plantin' things – an' grantin' things is goin' as they should,
An' the weather altogether is behavin' pretty good –
Is a pleasure in a measure for a man that likes the game,
An' my father he would rather raise a crop than make a name.
For my father was a farmer, an' 'All fame,' he said, 'ain't reel;
An' the same it isn't fillin' when you're wantin' for a meal.'
So I'm followin' his footsteps, an' a-keepin' of my feet,
While I cater for the nation with my Wheat, Wheat, Wheat.
    Wheat, Wheat, Wheat! When the poets all are beat
    By the reason that the season for the verse crop is a cheat,
        Then I comes up bright an' grinnin' with the knowledge that I'm winnin',
    With the rhythm of my harvester an' Wheat, Wheat, Wheat.

Readin' things an' heedin' things that clever fellers give,
An' ponderin' an' wonderin' why he was meant to live –
Muddlin' through an' fuddlin' through philosophy an' such
Is a game I never took to, an' it doesn't matter much.
For my father was a farmer, as I might 'a' said before,
An' the sum of his philosophy was, 'Grow a little more.
For growin' things,' my father said, 'it makes life sort o' sweet
An' your conscience never swats you if your game is growin' wheat.'
  Wheat, Wheat, Wheat! Oh, the people have to eat!
  An' you're servin', an' deservin' of a velvet-cushion seat
    In the cocky-farmers' heaven when you come to throw a seven;
  An' your password at the portal will be, 'Wheat, Wheat, Wheat.'

Now, the preacher an' the teacher have a callin' that is high
While they're spoutin' to the doubtin' of the happy by an' by;
But I'm sayin' that the prayin' it is better for their souls
When they've plenty wheat inside 'em in the shape of penny rolls.
For my father was a farmer, an' he used to sit an' grieve
When he thought about the apple that old Adam got from Eve.
It was foolin' with an orchard where the serpent got 'em beat,
An' they might 'a' kept the homestead if they'd simply stuck to wheat.
  Wheat, Wheat, Wheat! If you're seekin' to defeat
  Care an' worry in the hurry of the crowded city street,
    Leave the hustle all behind you; come an' let contentment find you
  In a cosy little cabin lyin' snug among the wheat.

In the city, more's the pity, thousands live an' thousands die
Never carin', never sparin' pains that fruits may multiply;
Breathin', livin', never givin'; greedy but to have an' take,
Dyin' with no day behind 'em lived for fellow-mortals' sake.
Now my father was a farmer, an' he used to sit and laugh
At the 'fools o' life', he called 'em, livin' on the other half.
Dyin' lonely, missin' only that one joy that makes life sweet –
Just the joy of useful labour, such as comes of growin' wheat.
  Wheat, Wheat, Wheat! Let the foolish scheme an' cheat;
  But I'd rather, like my father, when my span o' life's complete,
    Feel I'd lived by helpin' others; earned the right to call 'em brothers
  Who had gained while I was gainin' from God's earth His gift of wheat.

When the settin' sun is gettin' low above the western hills,
When the creepin' shadows deepen, and a peace the whole land fills,
Then I often sort o' soften with a feelin' like content,
An' I feel like thankin' Heaven for a day in labour spent.
For my father was a farmer, an' he used to sit an' smile,
Realizin' he was wealthy in what makes a life worth while.
Smilin', he has told me often, 'After all the toil an' heat,
Lad, he's paid in more than silver who has grown one field of wheat.'
Wheat, Wheat, Wheat! When it comes my turn to meet
Death the Reaper, an' the Keeper of the Judgment Book I greet,
Then I'll face 'em sort o' calmer with the solace of the farmer
That he's fed a million brothers with his Wheat, Wheat, Wheat.

Little Towns

Jim Haynes

Today let's take our hats off to Australia's little towns,
In the heartland of Australia where they have their ups and downs.
Like Wirrabarra and Werris Creek and lots of towns between,
With pubs and halls and shops and schools – you know the kind I mean.
Wheat silos and a railway yard that's not used anymore,
Tennis courts, a garage, maybe just a general store.
West Wyalong and Walla Walla, Winkie, Wallaroo,
Woodenbong, Wandiligong, Wondoan, Wee Waa too,
Weethalle and Wilcannia, Wingalee and Wallaroo –
And lots of other little towns without a 'W'!
Don't you go driving past 'em, pull up and look around,
Buy some petrol, have a cuppa, and enjoy a little town!

Old Tiboob'ra

Joe Daly & Slim Dusty

When I'm too old to earn a quid
And my roving days are o'er,
There's a little stretch of New South Wales
That I'll be headin' for.
To rest my weary bones until
The good Lord calls my name,
Back home in old Tiboob'ra,
The place from where I came.

Now I've been around in many towns
In Australia's seven states;
And many a cheque I've busted up.
And I've met with many mates
Then for a while I'd settle down,
Until my itching toes
Drew me back to old Tiboob'ra
Where friendship fairly flows.

I know someday when I get back
To that little old town of mine,
What I have searched the country for
Has been there all the time.
I know my mates will take me back
And treat me just the same,
Back home in old Tiboob'ra
The place from where I came.

The Railway Hotel

WG Howcroft

When Joe was a young 'un, his cheeks flecked with down,
He drew his first pay cheque to head into town.
Then up spoke his father: 'Son, heed my words well –
Keep clear of the girls at the Railway Hotel.

'Those harpies will fleece you of all that you own,
They're wicked and wanton with hearts hard as stone.
Believe me, young fella, the road straight to hell
Begins at the door of the Railway Hotel.

'They'll ply you with whisky, with beer, rum and gin,
Then when you're half sozzled they'll lead you to sin.
They're skilled at seduction, at this they excel –
Those trollops who tempt at the Railway Hotel.'

'Gee whiz!' cried our hero, with awe on his face,
'So *that's* what goes on in that old wooden place!
Our parson has warned me of women who dwell
In dens of ill-fame like the Railway Hotel.

'It seems I can still hear that old preacher's words
On drinking and gambling, bad language and birds.
But where did he gain such vast knowledge, pray tell,
Of girls like the ones at the Railway Hotel?'

Joe caught a fast pony and girthed it up tight,
Then, bidding his father a hasty goodnight,
He sprang in the saddle and galloped pell-mell
For his destination – *the Railway Hotel!*

Daintree

Greg Champion

There was a town called Daintree – and Daintree was its name.
The locals all knew it as Daintree – but it was Daintree just the same.
On the map it was known as Daintree – in the Daintree region it lay,
Just near the Daintree River, smack bang on the Daintree Highway.

And everything around Daintree was in Daintree, more or less,
And why they called it Daintree was anybody's guess.
Everyone who came to Daintree thought it was really good,
And when asked if they thought they might like to come back . . .
Most of them usually said they probably would . . .!

And all the people of Daintree, they loved their little town,
And the fame and the legend of Daintree spread for several miles around.
It was a grouse little place that Daintree – and that's why it's such a shame,
That every time I've been to Daintree . . . I can never think of its name!

Send Her Down!

Jim Haynes

We used to say, 'Send her down Hughie,'
'Send her down,' that's what we'd say.
After straining our eyes
At endless blue skies,
When we saw the clouds gather – we'd pray.

We'd crack the old jokes – 'Get Don Talbot,
Teach the frogs how to swim once again.'
'We'd love to see showers,
For the kids' sake not ours,
Well, the missus and me have seen rain.'

'It's the sheep that I worry about,
They'll faint 'cos they've never seen rain,
To revive 'em you must
Get a bucket of dust
And throw on 'em to wake 'em again!'

And then there'd be ants in the sugar
And there'd be a ring round the moon –
And there would be smiles
Round the country for miles,
'Cos we knew it was gonna rain soon.

And then, when it came, you could smell it,
A scent as the cool breeze unfurled –
A wonderful smell
As the first big drops fell –
The most beautiful smell in the world.

And boy, that tin roof took a beating,
Couldn't hear yourself talk for the sound,
But still you would pray
In that strange outback way,
'Thanks Hughie – keep sending her down.'

We used to say, 'Send her down Hughie,'
'Send her down,' that's what we'd say –
After straining our eyes
At endless blue skies,
When we saw the clouds gather – we'd pray.

Where the Bush School Used to Be

James Mangan

There's a dozen different places round the district where you'll see
A pepperina growing and a camphor laurel tree,
And a pine tree, not a native, and a fence which leans in need,
Round a garden bed that struggles 'neath a wilderness of weed.
There's a flagpole still upstanding, but no flag to flutter free,
Not a soul to stand saluting where the bush school used to be.

Gone the schools, but not forgotten, written now in history,
And those bush folk who were pupils have a clinging memory –
Yes, the bush folk, they remember, here their future hopes were born,
Here they heard the lilting birdsong on a spring or summer morn.
And those cold and frosty mornings when their feet were numb and bare,
And their ponies just like dragons puffing steam-clouds in the air.

Oh! the news which passed amongst them 'standing easy' on the line,
How someone's dad was cutting chaff and someone's cutting pine,
And the piebald mare at Jones's, she had piebald twins last night,
The Martin kids have measles and the Smith kids have the blight;
And when the flag was hoisted, to attention at command,
Then the teacher spoke with feeling of a noble Motherland.

Oh! the tang of sandwich dinners underneath the 'dinner tree',
Where I swapped a 'jam' with Mary and she gave a 'meat' to me,
Drab those schools I now remember, though in youth we thought them fine,
Each one painted as the other, each one of the same design,
And those teachers, bless the teachers, write their wondrous deeds in stone,
Far from home and friends and family, yet they called these schools their own.

Now the school bus, warm or chilly, and it's never running late,
Does a pick-up in the morning and delivery at the gate –
Yes the whirring and the buzzing on macadam-coated roads,
Of the flashing cars and motorbikes and trucks with heavy loads,
Drown the jingle of the buckles and the creak of saddle straps,
Spoil the scent of sweating ponies and the sheen of saddle flaps.

When you're driving down the highway and you see a vacant spot,
See a flagpole and a pine tree and neglected garden plot,
Hear the glory of the trilling of the early morning song,
See a pony saddled ready where the grass is growing long;
Pause, and listen for a moment by the pepperina tree,
Hear the phantom songs of children, where the bush school used to be.

Going to School

CJ Dennis

Did you see them pass to-day, Billy, Kate and Robin,
All astride upon the back of old grey Dobbin?
Jigging, jogging off to school, down the dusty track –
What must Dobbin think of it – three upon his back?
Robin at the bridle-rein, in the middle Kate,
Billy holding on behind, his legs out straight.

Now they're coming back from school, jig, jog, jig.
See them at the corner where the gums grow big;
Dobbin flicking off the flies and blinking at the sun –
Having three upon his back he thinks is splendid fun:
Robin at the bridle-rein, in the middle Kate,
Little Billy up behind, his legs out straight.

The Indian Pacific

Joy McKean

From coast to coast by night and day
Hear the clickin' of the wheels,
The hummin' of the diesel
On her ribbons of steel;
Carryin' the mem'ries
Of a nation built by hand,
See the Indian Pacific span the land.

She's the pride of all the railway men
'Cross country where she flies,
From the blue Pacific waters
To where the mountains rise;
By lakes and wide brown rivers,
Through desert country dry,
See the Indian Pacific passin' by.

Beside the line a drover waves
His battered old grey hat,
And kids are catchin' yabbies
Down by the river flat,
And a woman hangs her washing
In the backyard near the line,
As the Indian Pacific's rollin' by.

Hear the whistle blowin' lonely
'Neath the Nullarbor starlight,
Salutin' those who walked across
The track she rides tonight;
Callin' to the railway camp
And the fettlers on the line,
I'm the Indian Pacific right on time.

From the silver of the Broken Hill
To old Kalgoorlie gold,
She mirrors all the colours
Of a land so hard and old;
Then the western flowers are blooming,
And the air is just like wine,
And the Indian Pacific's makin' time.

Oh, the Indian Pacific
She goes rollin' down the track,
Five thousand miles to travel,
Before she's there and back.
From the waters of the western sea
To the eastern ocean sand,
The Indian Pacific spans the land.

I Knew I Knew Him

Characters & Caricatures

Australian society is the kind of melting pot that has always produced a large number of eccentrics and larger-than-life characters, and once you get beyond the Great Divide they seem to become more eccentric, perhaps due to isolation and the rigours of pioneering life! We all know these characters but Ted Egan knows more characters than anyone else I know – but then Ted knows more people than anyone else in the world so it's not surprising!

It's true, I was with Ted in Rome when he met the Pope, I waited down in St Peter's square while they chatted on the balcony. I wasn't surprised that Ted managed to get an audience with the Pope – Ted knows everyone after all – but I was a bit surprised when a little Italian bloke stopped his pushbike next to me and asked, 'Hey mate, who's that up there with Ted?'

I Knew I Knew Him

Kelly Dixon

Well, he sits a little different to the fellow that I knew –
And he walks a little slower than the way he used to do –
Yet, he looks a lot like someone – and I bet he is the same.
Can't remember where I knew him, and I can't recall his name.

But I know him and those moleskins, and the way they fitted him
With those two top buttons missing. Was it Tom, or Joe, or Jim?
I'm not sure so go and ask him – say he's like a bloke to me
I used to know somewhere in Queensland. Ask him where he used to be.

Did he ever work in stockcamps 'down the Cooper' years ago
Did I meet him in some shanty, on some stockroute we both know?
There you are! I knew I knew him! and those missing buttons, too –
But I'm sure the bugger's lying – he was never known as Blue!

Just as cheeky too, as ever, fancy claiming I'm the bloke
Owes him fifty bloody dollars, got from him when I was broke!
Ah well son, go back and tell him, bring his horses over here –
He can camp with us this evening, he might even have a beer.

When you rode across all friendly, like all dinkum bushies do,
Are you sure you heard him clearly, he claimed his name was Blue?
And the cheek of him suggesting I'd forget a debt I owe
Old mates' faces might elude me; but their nicknames never – no!

'Skew-Wiff' Kelly

Grahame Watt

His name was 'Skew-Wiff' Kelly,
And everything he built
Was either at an angle,
Or leaning at a tilt!

On all of his construction jobs
He used the rule of thumb.
He'd close one eye and line it up
And reckon it was plumb.

He would use the best of timber
And take a lot of care,
But every job completed
Was a little bit off-square.

His reputation grew and grew
As 'Skew-Wiff' moved around.
The cockies over-looked his faults
For his workmanship was sound!

So as you travel round the place
You can see where 'Skew-Wiff's' been.
That hay-shed leaning side-ways.
That verandah with a lean!

You've seen his good old tank-stands,
They've a wind-blown look with time.
His fences have a stagger,
And wander just off line.

You've seen a 'skew-wiff' chimney
And you've seen a 'skew-wiff' door.
His buildings stand – defiant
Of the gravitation law.

Yet a funny thing about it,
Though his buildings aren't quite straight,
They always look so comfortable
As if they'd time to wait!

Now 'Skew-Wiff' died some years ago,
But I reckon he'd be pleased
For his tombstone's got a lean on –
About forty-five degrees!

The Boy from Tech

Milton Taylor

A Sydney lad, he went out West,
To work in the shearing game.
He thought he'd show the bushies how,
And earn great wealth and fame.
He knew quite well he'd be a star,
What else could one expect.
For they were simple country hicks,
And he was fresh from Tech.

He got a job with Grazcos,
They sent him to a shed.
He strode up Monday morning,
Prepared to knock 'em dead.
He made one gun quite snarly,
When he sneered and said, 'By heck,
You've got this hand piece loaded wrong,
Not like we did at Tech.'

They put him on the table,
He was far too flaming slow,
He skirted wool the college way,
And didn't stand a show.
So they tried him out at picking up,
He made each fleece a wreck.
He wouldn't try the local way,
It wasn't taught at Tech.

Well, the presser was a bit behind,
And the Sydney lad was sent,
To help him catch the shearers up,
So 'round our hero went.
He pressed the pins and the presser roared,
'I'll break your stupid neck,
If you ever touch my press again
You presser from the Tech!'

They tried him out at every job
But all to no avail,
With his college way of doing things,
Most dismally he'd fail,
Until at last the boss strolled up
And handed him his cheque.
'You can go and roll your swag,' he said,
'Like they taught you to – at Tech!'

Happy Jack
A `Mac' Cormack & Slim Dusty

I once knew a feller, a trav'lling mate,
Not bad as fellers go;
He was happiest when he was mis'rable,
If ever that could be so.
He would wake up ev'ry mornin'
With the world upon his back,
And so for the want of a better name
We called him Happy Jack.

If ever you've travelled on outback tracks,
As most of us sometimes do,
With anxious eyes on the petrol gauge
In the hope it will see you through,
And you're a hundred miles from nowhere
And eighty still to go,
You'll hear his voice like the crack of doom
'Petrol's gettin' low.'

And when you're out on the black soil flats
You know what some rain can do,
You hope for the best as you head for the West
And you whisper a prayer or two;
And just when you're half way over
And starting to breathe again
He'll say with a sigh and a mournful eye,
'I think we're in for rain.'

And when on a long and lonely run,
With nothing in between,
The town you left is away in the past,
The next one a distant dream.
Oh he'll pick up his ears and listen
And then in accents low:
'I don't like the noise she's makin', Boss,
The diff's about to go.'

When you've bumped over corrugations
So deep you could bury a cow,
You say to yourself, 'It's pretty bad,
But the worst must be over now.'
Then he'll look at you with a woeful look
And furrows on his brow:
'The last fifty miles of this road, they say,
Is the worst in Australia now.'

Oh I wonder where he is today,
This trav'lling mate I had.
Wherever he is it's safe to say
That things are really bad.
If it's not the diff it's something else,
Or the petrol's gettin' low;
It's pounds to peanuts and that's a bet –
Something's about to go.

Fencing Wire

Frank Daniel

Big Bill was not the creator, he was just an innovator,
Changing things around as need desired.
He was capable of shaping anything that needed making,
Just from a length of good old fencing wire.

He could modify inventions far beyond MacKay's intentions.
His skill by all was very much admired.
He could swing a sagging gate, or repair a fire-grate,
With dexterous use of lengths of fencing wire.

39

Repair the beaters on his Binder, lace a belt up on the grinder,
Or sew a crack up in his tractor tyre,
He was as skilful as could be, and everywhere you'd see
Where Bill had been with bits of fencing wire.

He used it 'til he died, and though his kids all wailed and cried,
It was observed by all when he expired,
That his coffin, sleek and tan, was made by a handy-man,
And the lid was tied on tight with fencing wire.

Bruce

Col Wilson ('BLUE THE SHEARER')

This is the tale of a man called 'Bruce',
Who was hopelessy hooked on chocolate mousse.
For other foods, he had no use.
Not meat, nor fish, nor orange juice,
Nor vegetables – just chocolate mousse.
His wife said one day: 'Tell me Bruce.
Why do you just eat chocolate mousse?
Are you trying to reduce?'
He answered: 'Darling. You're a goose.
Don't you know that chocolate mousse
Acts upon me like Mateus?
As the saying goes. I just hang loose.'
His wife remarked: 'THAT'S you're excuse.'
His use of mousse became profuse.
Addiction held him like a noose.
He lived like some old-world recluse,
With facial features turning puce,
Until from life, he did vamoose.
His coffin's made of polished spruce.
And on his tombstone? 'HERE LIES BRUCE,
WHO DIED OF CHOCOLATE MOUSSE ABUSE.'

The Man from Ironbark

AB Paterson ('THE BANJO')

It was the man from Ironbark who struck the Sydney town,
He wandered over street and park, he wandered up and down.
He loitered here, he loitered there, till he was like to drop,
Until at last in sheer despair he sought a barber's shop.
''Ere! shave my beard and whiskers off, I'll be a man of mark,
I'll go and do the Sydney toff up home in Ironbark.'

The barber man was small and flash, as barbers mostly are,
He wore a strike-your-fancy sash, he smoked a huge cigar:
He was a humorist of note and keen at repartee,
He laid the odds and kept a 'tote', whatever that may be.
And when he saw our friend arrive, he whispered 'Here's a lark!
Just watch me catch him all alive this man from Ironbark.'

There were some gilded youths that sat along the barber's wall,
Their eyes were dull, their heads were flat, they had no brains at all;
To them the barber passed the wink, his dexter eyelid shut,
'I'll make this bloomin' yokel think his bloomin' throat is cut.'
And as he soaped and rubbed it in he made a rude remark:
'I s'pose the flats is pretty green up there in Ironbark.'

A grunt was all reply he got; he shaved the bushman's chin,
Then made the water boiling hot and dipped the razor in.
He raised his hand, his brow grew black, he paused a while to gloat,
Then slashed the red-hot razor-back across his victim's throat;
Upon the newly-shaven skin it made a livid mark –
No doubt it fairly took him in – the man from Ironbark.

He fetched a wild up-country yell might wake the dead to hear,
And though his throat, he knew full well, was cut from ear to ear,
He struggled gamely to his feet, and faced the murderous foe.
'You've done for me! you dog, I'm beat! one hit before I go!
I only wish I had a knife, you blessed murdering shark!
But you'll remember all your life the man from Ironbark.'

He lifted up his hairy paw, with one tremendous clout
He landed on the barber's jaw, and knocked the barber out.
He set to work with nail and tooth, he made the place a wreck;
He grabbed the nearest gilded youth, and tried to break his neck.
And all the while his throat he held to save his vital spark,
And 'Murder! Bloody Murder!' yelled the man from Ironbark.

A peeler man who heard the din came in to see the show;
He tried to run the bushman in, but he refused to go.
And when at last the barber spoke, and said ''Twas all in fun –
'Twas just a little harmless joke, a trifle overdone.'
'A joke!' he cried. 'By George, that's fine; a lively sort of lark;
I'd like to catch that murdering swine some night in Ironbark.'

And now while round the shearing-floor the listening shearers gape,
He tells the story o'er and o'er, and brags of his escape.
'Them barber chaps what keeps a tote, by George, I've had enough,
One tried to cut my bloomin' throat, but thank the Lord it's tough.'
And whether he's believed or no, there's one thing to remark,
That flowing beards are all the go way up in Ironbark.

The Man from Waterloo

Henry Lawson (WITH KIND REGARDS TO 'BANJO')

It was the Man from Waterloo,
　　When work in town was slack,
Who took the track as bushmen do,
　　And humped his swag out back.
He tramped for months without a bob,
　　For most the sheds were full,
Until at last he got a job
　　At picking up the wool.
He found the work was rather tough,
　　But swore to see it through,
For he was made of sterling stuff –
　　The Man from Waterloo.

The first remark was like a stab
  That fell his ear upon,
'Twas – 'There's another something scab
  The boss has taken on!'
They couldn't let the towny be –
  They sneered like anything;
They'd mock him when he'd sound the 'g'
  In words that end in 'ing'.

There came a Man from Ironbark,
  And at the shed he shore;
He scoffed his victuals like a shark,
  And like a fiend he swore.
He'd shorn his flowing beard that day –
  He found it hard to reap –
Because 'twas hot and in the way
  While he was shearing sheep.

His loaded fork in grimy holt
  Was poised, his jaws moved fast,
Impatient till his throat could bolt
  The mouthful taken last.
He couldn't stand a something toff,
  Much less a jackaroo;
And swore to take the trimmings off
  The Man from Waterloo.

The towny saw he must be up
  Or else be underneath,
And so one day, before them all,
  He dared to clean his teeth.

The men came running from the shed,
  And shouted, 'Here's a lark!'
'It's gone to clean its tooties!' said
  The Man from Ironbark.
His feeble joke was much enjoyed;
  He sneered as bullies do,
And with a scrubbing-brush he guyed
  The Man from Waterloo.

The jackaroo made no remark
　But peeled and waded in,
And soon the Man from Ironbark
　Had three teeth less to grin!
And when they knew that he could fight
　They swore to see him through,
Because they saw that he was right –
　The Man from Waterloo.

Now in a shop in Sydney, near
　The Bottle on the Shelf,
The tale is told – with trimmings – by
　The jackaroo himself.
'They made my life a hell,' he said;
　'They wouldn't let me be;
They set the bully of the shed
　To take it out of me.

'The dirt was on him like a sheath,
　He seldom washed his phiz;
He sneered because I cleaned my teeth –
　I guess I dusted his!
I treated them as they deserved –
　I signed on one or two!
They won't forget me soon,' observed
　The Man from Waterloo.

Pushin' Time

Tony Brooks & Slim Dusty

I've got this big Mack rollin',
She's screamin' down the line,
I see the guide posts clickin' by,
I'm a truckie pushin' time.
There's black tar down beneath me
And a blue sky overhead,
And while there's one more load to move
I'm pushin' till I'm dead.

We're rollin' and we're pushin'
From the Gulf down to the Bight,
From Perth across to Sydney
The trucks roll day and night.
Oh, the log book may be out of date,
But hell, that ain't a crime,
We dodge the weights and measure boys,
And we're always pushin' time.

I may have a general cargo,
Or a load of prime Gulf beef,
A swag of kegs of Southern beer
To bring some town relief.
I'll haul in tons of mining gear
To open some new mine,
But no matter what I carry,
You can bet I'm pushin' time.

If you see this big rig comin',
You can bet she's trackin' wide,
You'd better move it over
And give us room to ride.
I've logged a million miles or two
And may be past my prime,
But I'm still a wizard at the wheel
When I'm pushin' time.

The Weather Prophet

AB Paterson ('THE BANJO')

''Ow can it rain,' the old man said, 'with things the way they are?
You've got to learn off ant and bee, and jackass and galah;
And no man never saw it rain, for fifty years at least,
Not when the blessed parakeets are flyin' to the east!'

The weeks went by, the squatter wrote to tell his bank the news.
'It's still as dry as dust,' he said, 'I'm feeding all the ewes;
The overdraft would sink a ship, but make your mind at rest,
It's all right now, the parakeets are flyin' to the west.'

45

Mickety Mulga

T Ranken

He worked wid us at Wantigong –
Old Mickety Mulga Jim.
We'd all a-gone blue mouldy if
It 'adn't bin for him.
He'd keep us yarnin' at the fire,
An' laughin' be the hour
At 'is amusin' anecdotes,
Be George, he 'ad a power.
'E told us up in Queensland, where
'E'd never go again,
He come to some dry water-'ole
Upon a ten-mile plain.
The tank was dry, and Jim was dry,
But be a 'appy thought,

He wrung 'is empty water-bag
An' got about a quart;
But couldn't find a stick o' wood
To bile his billy by,
So stuck a match into the grass,
Which then was pretty dry.
He 'eld the billy to the flame
Wid a bit of fencing-wire,
But 'ad to go to foller it,
So rapid run the fire.
Five miles acrost that flamin' plain
He raced that fire, did he,
But when at last the billy biled,
He 'ad forgot the tea!

The Big White Bullock

T Ranken

Under a guidin' providence
Is Mickety Mulga Jim,
For nothink yet of serious 'arm
'As ever come to him.

A big white bullick charged him once,
But never gored 'is pelt,
Because the animal's two 'orns
Run just inside 'is belt.
The bullick bucked, and tossed, and roared,
But couldn't shake him loose;
Jim tried to slip the buckle free,
But found it was no use.
For days and days, so Mulga says,
He was suspended so,
And then became unconscious
Wid swinging to and fro.

46

In this suspensive attitude
He hung, he thinks, a week,
Until the bullick went to drink
And soused him in the creek.
The water brought his senses back,
And made him kick and cough;
Till wid his frantic strugglin's
The bullick's 'orns broke orf.

If to convince his hearers
This anecdote should fail,
He shows 'em both, the 'orns and belt,
To certify his tale!

He Said

Helen Avery

'The wind's a bastard today,' he said,
Pushed his hat to the back of his head,
Reached for the worn tobacco tin,
Fumbled the pungent weed within.
'From the bowels of hell,' he said.

'Straight from the bowels of hell,' he said,
Spat from his lips a tobacco shred,
Leant on the old verandah rail,
Tough as leather, straight as a nail.
'Cloud's in the north,' he said.

'Clouds are around in the north today.'
He scanned where the distant cloud bank lay,
Rolled the smoke with a languid air,
Bent to the dog and scratched its hair,
'It'll make a mistake one day . . .

'It'll make a mistake and rain, it will,'
Put the smoke to his lips, his eyes grew still,
Cupped his hands 'round a gleam of flame,
Drew on the roll till a red glow came,
'. . . And maybe the dams will fill.

47

'Yeah, the dams might fill, and the grass might grow,
And the feathers wash white on that miserable crow.
The frogs'll drown, and the ducks'll bog . . .'
He reached again to the patient dog,
And he turned on his heel to go!

Whalan of Waitin' a While

JW Gordon (JIM GRAHAME)

Long life to old Whalan of Waitin' a While;
Good luck to his children and wife;
They gain all the pleasure and gladness that come
And miss all the worries of life.
They do not complain if the season is dry.
They go into debt with a smile.
'It's no use of moaning, it might have been worse,'
Says Whalan of Waitin' a While.

The gates on the boundary fences are down
And buried in rubbish and dust;
The white ants and weevils have eaten the rungs,
The hinges are rotting with rust.
The sheep wander in, and the sheep wander out
And ramble for many a mile:
'I must take a day off and fix up those gates,'
Says Whalan of Waitin' a While.

The pigs roam at large, but they come home at night
And sleep head and tail by the door,
And sometimes a sow has a litter of pigs
That sleep with her under the floor.
They suckle and squabble around her all night,
The odours arising are vile;
'We'll sell them right out when a buyer comes up,'
Says Whalan of Waitin' a While.

The brand on the calves is as big as a plate
And looks like a slash or a wale,
And sometimes it reaches from shoulder to hip,

And sometimes it reaches the tail.
'Twas made from the side of a square iron tank,
Cut out with a chisel or file,
'It's not very neat, but it might have been worse,'
Says Whalan of Waitin' a While.

The boys and the girls all at riding excel,
They stick to a saddle like glue,
And follow a bullock through low mulga scrub
As straight as a die and as true.
They're no good at figures and can't read at all,
Nor write in an elegant style.
'We'll give them a bit of a schooling some day,'
Says Whalan of Waitin' a While.

The tanks and the dams very seldom get full,
No matter how heavy it rains;
They've a halo of bones of the sheep that have bogged,
And the dust-storms have silted the drains.
Storm-water is wasted and sweeps down the flat –
A flood that would fill up the Nile –
'We'll clean out those drains when the weather gets cool,'
Says Whalan of Waitin' a While.

The sulky and buggy stand out in the sun,
The woodwork is gaping with cracks,
The leather is wrinkled and perishing fast,
And pulling away from the tacks.
The wheels are all loose and the paint's falling off
And the cushions have long lost their pile;
'I'd put up a shed, but I cannot find time.'
Says Whalan of Waitin' a While.

Good luck to old Whalan of Waitin' a While.
He'll live just as long as the rest,
And smile at the things that make most people frown,
And his health is as good as the best.
Good luck to the mother at Waitin' a While,
Who waddles along with a smile;
She'll have a fine time when the good seasons come,
And she doesn't mind Waitin' a While.

49

Me and My dog

Anon

Me and my dog
   have tramped together
   in cold weather
   and hot.

Me and my dog
   don't care whether
   we get any work
   or not.

Are You the Cove?

Joseph Furphy (TOM COLLINS)

'Are you the Cove?' he spoke the words
As swagmen only can;
The Squatter freezingly inquired,
'What do you mean, my man?'

'Are you the Cove?' his voice was stern,
His look was firm and keen;
Again the Squatter made reply,
'I don't know what you mean.'

'O! dash my rags! let's have some sense –
You ain't a fool, by Jove,
Gammon you dunno what I mean;
I mean – are you the Cove?'

'Yes, I'm the Cove,' the Squatter said;
The Swagman answered, 'Right,
I thought as much: show me some place
Where I can doss tonight.'

Eh!

Richard Magoffin

Y'reckon, eh? Well, so do I –
It's like their flamin' hide
T'say we all talk different, eh? –
Fair churns me up inside!
They reckon, eh, in Queensland, eh,
Y'know eh like they say –
They reckon we talk slower
An' we use a lot of 'eh'.

Eh, bullshit, eh? Y'reckon, eh?
Yair, course it is, eh Joe?
There's no doubt in my mind, y'know –
At least we 'ave a go!
Eh? No mistake! Eh – watch me beer!
Eh – 'oo the 'ell ar you?
Aw – all the way from Melbourne, eh?
Well, sport, how do you do?

We mightin' 'ave an 'Arbour Bridge.
Eh! Watch me bloody beer!
But eh, we got – eh, ridgy-didge –
The min-min light up 'ere.
An' wot about the bloody Reef,
Eh Joe? Y'reckon, eh?
Well like, y'know – beyond belief –
Yair, eh – that's what I say!

Well like, y'know, in Queensland, eh,
There goes me bloody beer!
Eh yair – another Fourex, mate –
'Oo is that bloody queer?
At least we're not the Garden State –
Eh? Not all pansies gay?
Yair, sure y'come from Melbourne, mate –
Eh, lay orf mate – EH! EH!

The Swagman

CJ Dennis

Oh, he was old and he was spare;
His bushy whiskers and his hair
Were all fussed up and very grey
He said he'd come a long, long way
And had a long, long way to go.
Each boot was broken at the toe,
And he'd a swag upon his back.
His billy-can, as black as black,
Was just the thing for making tea
At picnics, so it seemed to me.

'Twas hard to earn a bite of bread,
He told me. Then he shook his head,
And all the little corks that hung
Around his hat-brim danced and swung
And bobbed about his face; and when
I laughed he made them dance again.
He said they were for keeping flies –
'The pesky varmints' – from his eyes.
He called me 'Codger' ... 'Now you see
The best days of your life,' said he.
'But days will come to bend your back,
And, when they come, keep off the track.
Keep off, young codger, if you can.'
He seemed a funny sort of man.

He told me that he wanted work,
But jobs were scarce this side of Bourke,
And he supposed he'd have to go
Another fifty miles or so.
'Nigh all my life the track I've walked,'
He said. I liked the way he talked.
And oh, the places he had seen!
I don't know where he had not been –
On every road, in every town,
All through the country, up and down.
'Young codger, shun the track,' he said.
And put his hand upon my head.

I noticed, then, that his old eyes
Were very blue and very wise.
'Ay, once I was a little lad,'
He said, and seemed to grow quite sad.
I sometimes think: When I'm a man,
I'll get a good black billy-can
And hang come corks around my hat,
And lead a jolly life like that.

The Man Who Always Runs to Catch the Tram
WT Goodge ('THE COLONEL')

He's the latest evolution of a prehistoric type –
  The man who always runs to catch the tram!
He's never got the time to light his after-breakfast pipe –
  The man who has to run to catch the tram!
He is all a ball of energy and vigour; couldn't wait!
It is worse to be too early than it is to be too late!
He'll be rushing up the garden path when Peter slams the gate –
  The man that has to run to catch the tram!
You can take him in his business; I'll bet you ten to one –
  The man who has to run to catch the tram!
That he's always in a hurry, and there's mighty little done –
  The same as when he's running for the tram!
Doesn't matter if a lawyer at the starting of the term,
Or the 'I'll-be-there-directly!' of a tea and sugar firm –
It is still to-day the early bird that gathers in the worm;
  Not the bird who has to run to catch the tram!

The Man from Balmain

Anon

There was a young man from Balmain
Who was thought to be slightly insane.
  When his sweetheart said, 'Kiss me,
  and mind you don't miss me,'
He asked for a fortnight to train.

53

The Silent Member

CJ Dennis

He lived in Mundaloo, and Bill McClosky was his name,
But folks that knew him well had little knowledge of that same;
For he some'ow lost his surname, and he had so much to say –
He was called 'The Silent Member' in a mild, sarcastic way.

He could talk on any subject – from the weather and the crops
The astronomy and Euclid, and he never minded stops;
And the lack of a companion didn't lay him on the shelf,
For he'd stand before a looking-glass and argue with himself.

He would talk for hours on lit'rature, or calves, or art, or wheat;
There was not a bally subject you could say had got him beat;
And when strangers brought up topics that they reckoned he would baulk,
He'd remark, 'I never heard of that.' But all the same – he'd talk.

He'd talk at christ'nings by the yard; at weddings by the mile;
And he used to pride himself upon his choice of words and style.
In a funeral procession his remarks would never end
On the qualities and virtues of the dear departed friend.

We got quite used to hearing him, and no one seemed to care –
In fact, no happ'ning seemed complete unless his voice was there.
For close on thirty year he talked, and none could talk him down,
Until one day an agent for insurance struck the town.

Well, we knew The Silent Member, and we knew what he could do,
And it wasn't very long before we knew the agent, too,
As a crack long-distance talker that was pretty hard to catch;
So we called a hasty meeting and decided on a match.

Of course, we didn't tell them we were putting up the game;
But we fixed it up between us, and made bets upon the same.
We named a time-keep and a referee to see it through;
Then strolled around, just casual, and introduced the two.

The agent got first off the mark, while our man stood and grinned;
He talked for just one solid hour, then stopped to get his wind.
'Yes; but –' sez Bill; that's all he said; he couldn't say no more;
The agent got right in again, and fairly held the floor.

On policies, and bonuses, and premiums, and all that,
He talked and talked until we thought he had our man out flat.
'I think –' Bill got in edgeways, but that there insurance chap
Just filled himself with atmosphere, and took the second lap.

I saw our man was getting dazed, and sort of hypnotized,
And they oughter pulled the agent up right there, as I advised.
'See here –' Bill started, husky; but the agent came again,
And talked right on for four hours good – from six o'clock to ten.

Then Bill began to crumple up, and weaken at the knees,
When all at once he ups and shouts, 'Here, give a bloke a breeze!
Just take a pull for half a tick and let me have the floor,
And I'll take out a policy.' The agent said no more.

The Silent Member swallowed hard, then coughed and cleared his thoat,
But not a single word would come – no; not a blessed note.
His face looked something dreadful – such a look of pained dismay;
Then he gave us one pathetic glance, and turned, and walked away.

He's hardly spoken since that day – not more than 'Yes' or 'No'.
We miss his voice a good bit, too; the town seems rather slow.
He was called 'The Silent Member' just sarcastic, I'll allow;
But since that agent handled him it sort o' fits him now.

The Last of the Hand Cutters

Bill Scott

In the bar of the White Horse one Saturday night
There were lavender bugs round the overhead light.
The rain belted down on the footpath outside
When an old drunk leapt up on a table and cried:
'Farewell to the days of the file and the knife
And the wandering canecutters' trouble-filled life,
Farewell to the guns and the Saturday sprees
When the gang was eight men, and the cook was Chinese!

'I've cut down at Childers where the cockies are mean,
They grizzle and moan if you don't top it clean.
I've sweated at Bingera through the hot days
For plantation bosses with tabletop drays.
I've cut out at Marion, cursing my lot,
In Q44 that was tied in a knot,
But the worst place of all was at Condong, my boys,
For a fat Cane Inspector, all bullshit and noise!

'I've spent my slack seasons at ringing out West,
And I'll swear for big tallies, the North is the best,
For from Ingham to Mossman as everyone knows
Are the best little towns where the sugarcane grows.
But the old days are gone with the good times we've seen,
For the cutters are stuffed by this harvest machine
That thrashes along through the furrows and ruts
In a cloud of blown trash with hot gas in its guts.

'Now there's nothing much left for a cutter like me
But the pension and just the occasional spree!'
Then he fell from the table and flat on the floor
When a canecocky present let out his loud roar:
'Oh, die, you old bastard, and stop your complaining!'
So he snuffed it. Outside the rain just went on raining.
Next morning at dawn when the sky was pale grey,
A harvester clanked in and took him away.

Vale, Rusty Reagan

Bruce Simpson

Old Rusty Reagan's cashed his chips,
No more he'll go on droving trips,
And no more grog will pass the lips
Of drunken Rusty Reagan.
He died of drink, or so they say,
Or pure neglect, but anyway
The sands of time have slipped away
For luckless Rusty Reagan.

Although he camped upon the flat
The bar was his true habitat,
And home was underneath the hat
Of drifter Rusty Reagan.
There's none to say from whence he came,
Not sure in fact if that's his name;
To Rusty though it's all the same –
Dead finish Rusty Reagan.

No relatives with reddened eyes
Will weep at Rusty's sad demise;
No lowered flag at half-mast flies
To honour Rusty Reagan.
We'll miss perhaps his ugly dial,
His raucous voice and toothy smile,
We'll miss him for a little while,
Then forget Rusty Reagan.

Perhaps somewhere someone will wait –
A mother, sister, brother, mate –
Who'll wonder as they vainly wait
For absent Rusty Reagan.
I'd like to think some tears might fall
For Rusty's ilk, no-hopers all,
Who answer that last trumpet call
Unmourned like Rusty Reagan.

Red Jack

Mary Durack

She rises clear to memory's eye
From mists of long ago,
Though we met but once, in '98 –
In the days of Cobb and Co.

'Twas driving into Hughenden
With mail and gold for load
That I saw Red Jack, the wanderer,
Come riding down the road.

Red Jack and Mephistopheles –
They knew them far and wide,
From Camooweal to Charters Towers,
The route they used to ride.

They knew them round the Selwyns where
The Leichhardt has its source,
Along the winding cattle ways –
A woman and a horse.

And strange the tales they told of them
Who ranged the dusty track:
The great black Mephistopheles
And the red-haired witch Red Jack.

She claimed no name but that, they said,
And owned no things but these:
Her saddle, swag and riding-kit
And Mephistopheles.

And often travellers such as I
Had seen, and thought it strange,
A woman working on the line
That crossed McKinlay Range.

Had seen her in the dreary wake
Of stock upon the plains,
Her brown hand quick upon the whip
And light upon the reins.

With milling cattle in the yard
Amid the dust-fouled air,
With rope and knife and branding iron –
A girl with glowing hair.

'Red Jack's as good as any man!'
The settlers used to own;
And some bold spirits sought her hand,
But Red Jack rode alone.

She rode alone, and wise men learned
To set her virtue high,
To weigh what skill she plied her whip
With the hardness of her eye.

I saw Red Jack in '98,
The first time and the last,
But her face, brown-gaunt, and her hair, red-bright,
Still haunt me from the past.

The coach drew in as she rode in sight;
We passed the time of day;
Then shuffled out the mail she sought
And watched her ride away.

And oh! her hair was living fire,
But her eyes were cold as stone:
Red Jack and Mephistopheles
Went all their ways alone.

'He Isn't Long for This World'

Henry Lawson

He isn't long for this world,
   His cares are nearly past;
He isn't long for this world,
   He'll find his rest at last.

He isn't long for this world,
   His griefs are nearly o'er;
He isn't long for this world –
   He's only four foot four.

The Reverend James

Quendryth Young

The Reverend James, so the record book claims,
Hailed from Ireland, high minded and pious.
Though kindly his roar, he would lay down the law
With a definite Methodist bias.

He wrote many tracts plainly stating the facts,
That the wages of drink were quite frightful:
'The pleasure of sin that gets innocents in –
Is the Devil disguised as delightful.'

He'd bellow with rage if you mentioned the stage:
'Brazen hussies just cause a sensation!
They're nothing but flirts who go raising their skirts,
And invite our young men to temptation.'

He guided his kin through a life free from sin,
And with goodness they tried to repay him.
'Be kind, be discreet, be polite and be neat.'
And they wouldn't have dared disobey him.

'At meals bow your head as there's grace to be said,'
Which went on, in a monotone, slowly.
They acted as told as their dinner grew cold,
But at least it was blessed and holy.

Through dust and through mud, even rivers in flood,
On his horse he trekked roads far outreaching;
He answered the call to bring succour to all,
And no weather could hinder his preaching.

One night, goes the tale, was a terrible gale,
But his duty surpassed all his fears,
(Was gallant of him as he'd not learnt to swim)
But his mare had some other ideas.

In river bank sludge she stood firm, wouldn't budge,
Though at no other time had been nervous:
'My flock is at prayer in the church over there,
And it won't rise till I start the service.'

James spurred on his steed but she just wouldn't heed:
'Bend your knees, bend your knees when I tell you!'
And never before did a creature ignore
His command, which could always compel you.

There flashed through his mind a great curse of the kind
Used by men whose base morals he doubted.
He thought of his cloth and he held back his wrath;
It was 'Bother!' he vehemently shouted.

At dawn the next day, with the storm cleared away,
They found damaged so much that they cherished.
The banks had submerged as the river flood surged,
So that all who would cross it had perished.

Now everyone knew the respect that was due
To the pastor, for naught terrified him;
Excepting of course for his life-saving horse,
And he thanked the good Lord she'd defied him.

Holy Dan

Anon

It was in the Queensland drought;
And over hill and dell,
No grass – the water far apart,
All dry and hot as hell.
The wretched bullock teams drew up
Beside a water-hole
They'd struggled on through dust and drought
For days to reach this goal.

And though the water rendered forth
A rank, unholy stench,
The bullocks and the bullockies
Drank deep their thirst to quench.

Two of the drivers cursed and swore
As only drivers can.
The other one, named Daniel,
Best known as Holy Dan,

Admonished them and said it was
The Lord's all-wise decree;
And if they'd only watch and wait,
A change they'd quickly see.

'Twas strange that of Dan's bullocks
Not one had gone aloft,
But this, he said, was due to prayer
And supplication oft.
At last one died but Dan was calm,
He hardly seemed to care;
He knelt beside the bullock's corpse
And offered up a prayer.

'One bullock Thou has taken, Lord,
And so it seemeth best.
Thy will be done, but see my need
And spare to me the rest!'

A month went by. Dan's bullocks now
Were dying every day,
But still on each occasion would
The faithful fellow pray,
'Another Thou has taken, Lord,
And so it seemeth best.
Thy will be done, but see my need,
And spare to me the rest!'

And still they camped beside the hole,
And still it never rained,
And still Dan's bullocks died and died,
Till only one remained.
Then Dan broke down – good Holy Dan –
The man who never swore.
He knelt beside the latest corpse,
And here's the prayer he prore.

'That's nineteen Thou has taken, Lord,
And now You'll plainly see
You'd better take the bloody lot,
One's no damn good to me.'

The other riders laughed so much
They shook the sky around;
The lightning flashed, the thunder roared.
And Holy Dan was drowned.

A Cowyard Romeo

JW Gordon (JIM GRAHAME)

Young Billy Riley was in love with pretty Kate McBride,
Their parents both had dairy farms out on the Lachlan side;
Modest and innocent the maid, and shy the youthful swain,
Who mostly worshipped from afar, and lilted his refrain:

'You're more to me than all the cream that Mum has ever churned,
And dearer than the biggest cheque that Dad has ever earned,
Just like a lonely poddy calf I am when we're apart,
For you're the Jersey heifer in the cowyard of my heart.

Your eyes are bluer than the bloom that crowns the lucerne patch,
Your bosom's whiter than the chicks that snowy leghorns hatch,
This farm will rival Paradise if you will be my wife,
And place your little head within the cowbail of my life.

Your cheek is smooth as rabbit skin, your hair is soft as silk,
And white your teeth as foam that floats on separated milk,
To me your smiles are like the rills I see on little streams,
And I'd imprison you beyond the sliprails of my dreams.

No sapling grows as straight as you, or kurrajong as neat,
The bush can boast no fairer flower, or honey quite as sweet;
Oft, when the cows are obstinate and I am in despair,
I think of you and then I build a dairy in the air.

Oh, when I'm driving out with you, the world seems good to me,
The magpies' songs are like a flood of silver melody,
I would not swap the old spring cart for fleets of motor cars,
Or change the winding bush track for a roadway to the stars.

I think I hear it from the milk that gurgles in the pail
(E're break of day when I am crouched half-frozen at the bail)
The old cows seem to know it too, though we're so far apart,
That you're the little Jersey in the cowyard of my heart.'

Such a Good Boy

Alistair Morrison ('AFFERBECK LAUDER')

He never said 'Die' to the living.
He never said 'Scat' to a cat.
He never said 'Boo' to a kangaroo.
He never did this – or that.

He always kept clear of propellers;
Never spoke to the man at the wheel.
He always said 'Thanks' to people in banks,
And always took food with his meal.

He never took umbrage, or opium,
Or ran round the rugged rocks.
He never missed school, or acted the fool,
And always wore woollen socks.

He never sat on a tuffet,
Or pulled out a plum with his thumb;
And never, in churches, left ladies in lurches;
Or opened the OP rum.

He never pinched little girls' bottoms,
Or peered down the front of their necks;
Considered it folly to covet a dolly,
Or think of the opposite sex.

He never did anything nasty.
He never got stinking, or cried;
Unmarred by one speckle, a permanent Jekyll
With never a shadow of Hyde.

He never called anyone 'Drongo',
Or even ate peas with a knife.
He never crossed swords with the overlords;
Such a good boy all his life.

When he finally died and was buried
His loving ones tried to mourn;
They put at his head a tablet which read,
'Here he lies, but why was he born?'

Mrs Polkinghorne

Hal Gye (JAMES HACKSTON)

Mrs Polkinghorne – I see her yet.
  For company two cats,
Driving her rattling wagonette,
  Her horses wearing hats.

Straight as a poker was her back,
  Her face stern as the sphinx –
No friendly nods or jokes to crack
  And, oh, no passing winks.

We'd hear her coming miles away
  And Mum, with happy face,
Would set our cracked cups on a tray,
  And tidy up the place.

Mrs Polkinghorne, so lean and strong
  (In her the soil had roots),
Wore number nines and we (so wrong)
  Laughed at her hobnailed boots.

She brought us mutton down the years,
  For which we seldom paid,
And some weeks Mum came close to tears
  As her excuse she made.

You might have thought her wagonette
  Lopsided or would break,
The way it leaned when up she'd get
  And give the reins a shake.

Each week she came, always the same,
  Way down the Bungo Flats,
Driving her bays adown the days.
  With daisies in their hats.

65

Two Gossips

Harry Morant ('THE BREAKER')

One fox-faced virgin, word for word, repeats each sland'rous thing she's heard,
And sourly smiles as scandal slips with gusto from her thin white lips.
She's bad enough! – but list a minute, beside her mate she isn't in it!
This latter lady, 'pon my word, repeats things ... she has never heard!

Ballad Of The Totems

Oodgeroo Noonuccal (KATH WALKER)

My father was Noonuccal man and kept old tribal way,
His totem was the Carpet Snake, whom none must ever slay;
But mother was of Peewee clan, and loudly she expressed
The daring view that carpet snakes were nothing but a pest.

Now one lived right inside with us in full immunity,
For no one dared to interfere with father's stern decree:
A mighty fellow ten feet long, and as we lay in bed
We kids could watch him round a beam not far above our head.

Only the dog was scared of him, we'd hear its whines and growls,
But mother fiercely hated him because he took her fowls.
You should have heard her diatribes that flowed in angry torrents
With words you never see in print, except in D. H. Lawrence.

'I kill that robber,' she would scream, fierce as a spotted cat;
'You see that bulge inside of him? My speckly hen make that!'
But father's loud and strict command made even mother quake;
I think he'd sooner kill a man than kill a carpet snake.

That reptile was a greedy-guts, and as each bulge digested
He'd come down on the hunt at night as appetite suggested.
We heard his stealthy slithering sound across the earthern floor,
While the dog gave a startled yelp and bolted out the door.

Then over in the chicken-yard hysterical fowls gave tongue,
Loud frantic squawks accompanied by the barking of the mung,
Until at last the racket passed, and then to solve the riddle,
Next morning he was back up there with a new bulge in his middle.

When father died we wailed and cried, our grief was deep and sore,
And strange to say from that sad day the snake was seen no more.
The wise old men explained to us: 'It was his tribal brother,
And that is why it done a guy' – but some looked hard at mother.

She seemed to have a secret smile, her eyes were smug and wary,
She looked as innocent as the cat that ate the pet canary.
We never knew, but anyhow (to end this tragic rhyme)
I think we all had snake for tea one day about that time.

Tumba-Bloody-Rumba

Will Carter

I was down in the Riverina, knockin' 'round the towns a bit,
And occasionally resting with a schooner in me mitt.
And, on one of these occasions, when the bar was pretty full,
And the local blokes were arguin' assorted kind of bull,
I heard a conversation, most peculiar in its way.
It's only in Australia you would hear a joker say:
'How ya bloody been, ya drongo? Haven't seen ya fer a week.
And yer mate was lookin' for ya when ya come in from the creek.
'E was lookin' up at Ryan's and around at bloody Joe's,
And even at the Royal, where 'e bloody NEVER goes.'
And the other bloke says, 'Seen 'im. Owed 'im half a bloody quid.
Forgot to give it back to him, but now I bloody did,
Could've used the thing me bloody self, been off the bloody booze,
Up at Tumba-bloody-rumba shootin' kanga-bloody-roos.'

Now the bar was pretty quiet and everybody heard
The peculiar integration of this adjectival word.
But no-one there was laughing – and me – I wasn't game.
So I just sits back and lets them think I spoke the bloody same.
Then someone else was interested to know just what he got,
How many kanga-bloody-roos he went and bloody shot.
And the shooting bloke says, 'Things are crook, the droughts too bloody tough.
I got forty-two by seven and that's not good-e-bloody-nough.'
And, as this polite rejoinder seemed to satisfy the mob,
Everyone stopped listening and got on with the job,
Which was drinkin' beer and arguin', and talkin' of the heat,
Of boggin' in the bitumen in the middle of the street.
But as for me, I'm here to say the interesting news
Was 'Tumba-bloody-rumba – shootin' kanga-bloody-roos.'

The Durkins

PJ Hartigan (JOHN O'BRIEN)

Have you ever seen the Durkins at the Sunday morning Mass
    At the little old St Peter's week by week,
Since Old Man and Granny Durkin, then an Irish lad and lass,
    Made their home upon the farm along the creek?

There've been Durkins and more Durkins ranged sedately in a row,
    Thumbing prayer-books with the pictures through the text.
When the bench was filled with Durkins then the Durkin overflow
    Had to take up fresh allotments in the next.

Years ago came Old Man Durkin when the world and he were young,
    And the colleen wife he brought across the sea
With the dimples and the blushes and the brogue upon the tongue
    And a little Durkin cooing on her knee.

Then another, and another as the years went marching on
    And turned them into sturdy lad and lass,
But whatever were the changes, you could always count upon
    Another Durkin cooing at the Mass.

Faith, Old Man and Granny Durkin left a string of them behind,
    Splendid men and splendid women, loved and prized.
And the Durkins that came after kept the lesson well in mind
    Till St Peter's, so 'tis said, was Durkinized.

Yes, and some were Durkinesses, and they wouldn't be outshone,
    But of course they had to change the honoured name,
So we've Walshes and McCarthys and O'Connors, and so on,
    But we reckon them as Durkins just the same.

There are little toddling Durkins lisping sweet phonetic prayer,
    There are Durkins in the First Communion class,
There are Durkins for confirming, and as everyone's aware,
    There's a further Durkin cooing at the Mass.

Yes, the altar-boy's a Durkin, proper, pious and sedate,
    And the choir is mostly Durkin kith and kin,
While a sober-sided Durkin, faith, he takes around the plate,
    And it's Durkin, Durkin, Durkin putting in.

Now, then, hold your tongue a minute, I know what you're hinting at –
    'Tis that everyone's a Durkin but the priest.
You can leave that to the Sisters, for they all have noticed that,
    And their wonderment at such has never ceased.

Now they're making a novena that the Durkin altar-boy
    Will develop leanings that way; and if so
There could be no heavenly gesture which would bring a greater joy
    To a loyal band of mortals here below.

If the Bishop will ordain him in the little church out here
    There'll be Durkins! – ha-esh, it's looking far ahead,
But begobs I'd love to see it. See them come from far and near,
    I'll be looking forward to it though I'm dead.

Well, Old Man and Granny Durkin take their sleep in holy ground
    Where the Durkin plot is filling up, alas!
If a monument you're seeking, well, then, take a look around,
    Count the Durkins at the Sunday morning Mass.

Encore

Neil Carroll ('HIPSHOT')

'It seems to me.' The teacher said, to little Encore Smith,
'That "Encore" is a funny name to be labelled with.
Are you the second on the list?' And Encore answered, 'No, Ma'am!
My Mother called me "Encore" 'cause I wasn't on the programme!!!!'

The Eye of the Beholder

Opinions & Beliefs

Most Australians are never short of an opinion or two, although one Aussie's view of the world is rarely the next person's view and, again, the very individual way of seeing things tends to be more apparent west of the Great Divide.

It didn't surprise me to find that, when Aussies became philosophical, they often chose rhymed verse to say what they were thinking or feeling. Sometimes there's a moral to the story, sometimes it's just an expression of the joy they find in their daily life. Some of these poems are straight from the heart, some are sarcastic and others are expressions of outright disapproval.

Of course many Aussies, like the boy in the little ditty that follows, don't feel the need to express an opinion at all, especially if nothing's wrong!

The boy had never said a word, his mother was distraught,
He'd been at school almost a year – how could the lad be taught?
A mute for all of his six years – not one word had he spoken,
He seemed OK in other ways but his mother's heart was broken.
Then one morning from his breakfast plate he slowly raised his head,
Flexed his lips a few times and ... 'This toast is burnt,' he said.
'Why did you never speak?' his mother cried, 'if you knew how?'
'Well,' he observed, 'everything has been all right 'till now!'

The Eye of the Beholder / Col Wilson ('BLUE THE SHEARER')

One Lifetime's Not Enough / Ray Rose

G'Day / Grahame Watt   71

The Eye of the Beholder

Col Wilson ('BLUE THE SHEARER')

Three men on a mountain peak,
Gazed in silent awe,
On the scenic grandeur spread beneath the skies.
On the mist above the treetops.
The sun on silver streams,
And each man saw the scene through different eyes.

One man was a Preacher.
He sank down on his knees,
And thanked his God for nature's beauties grand,
Confessed his own humility,
The puny lot of man,
And gloried in the sight his eyes had scanned.

One man was an Artist.
A painter of renown.
He saw the scene surrounded by a frame.
He knew if he could find the skill
To capture what he saw,
Then he would be assured of wealth and fame.

The third man was a Farmer.
He stood and let his gaze
Range as far as vision would allow.
O'er rugged hills and valleys,
And he murmured to himself:
'What a lousy place to lose a cow.'

One Lifetime's Not Enough

Ray Rose

We may think we'll live forever,
While we're young we cut it rough.
Too late, too soon, it's over,
One lifetime's not enough!

'G'day'

Grahame Watt

'G'day! How are ya? How'd ya be?'
It's the same all day when people meet me.
They ask the same question, like a form of address,
They say, 'How're ya goin'?' When they couldn't care less.

One of these days I vow and declare,
I'll tell 'em the truth – that'll give 'em a scare.
When they say, 'How're ya goin'?', not wanting to know,
I'll give 'em a talking for an hour or so.

'I'm no bloomin' good thanks, I'm no good at all,
The bank's got me farm and me back's to the wall,
The drought's killed me stock, then, just for a change,
The bushfires went through and me dog got the mange.

All I've got in me pocket is a dirty big hole,
And because of some reason I can't get the dole.
Then me missus shot through with some shearer named Jack.
Now, to add to me troubles, she wants to come back.

Things are real crook, I think that I'm done.
I'd shoot meself if I could borrow a gun.'
So next time you see me for Gawd's sake don't say,
'How're ya goin'?' – Just say, 'G'day!'

In & Out

Anon

Into life the male child comes – short on hair and long on gums.
Out of life he goes when useless, in the same shape, bald and toothless!

Tact

Anon

In between 'truth' and 'fiction' there lies a word of fact,
The path that goes between the two is the gentle path of tact.

I Am

Mary Duroux

I am
the river,
   gently flowing,
   as I wind my way to the sea.

I am
the breeze,
   softly blowing,
   through the leaves of a
   mighty tree.

I am
the snowcapped mountain,
   the frost, the wind, the rains.

I am
a misty fountain,
   the dry and dusty plains.

I am
the sparkle,
   of the early morning dew.

I am
the dream,
   of my mother's dreaming,

Who are you?

Preaching

Victor Daley ('CREEVE ROE')

I learnt the language of the birds.
   A new St Francis I would be;
But, when I understood their words –
   The birds were preaching unto me.

The Men Who Come Behind

Henry Lawson

There's a class of men (and women) who are always on their guard –
Cunning, treacherous, suspicious – feeling softly – grasping hard –
Brainy, yet without the courage to forsake the beaten track –
Cautiously they feel their way behind a bolder spirit's back.

If you save a bit of money, and you start a little store –
Say, an oyster-shop for instance, where there wasn't one before –
When the shop begins to pay you, and the rent is off your mind,
You will see another started by a chap that comes behind.

So it is, and so it might have been, my friend, with me and you –
When a friend of both and neither interferes between the two;
They will fight like fiends, forgetting in their passion mad and blind,
That the row is mostly started by the folk who come behind.

They will stick to you like sin will, while your money comes and goes,
But they'll leave you when you haven't got a shilling in your clothes.
You may get some help above you, but you'll nearly always find
That you cannot get assistance from the men who come behind.

There are many, far too many, in the world of prose and rhyme,
Always looking for another's 'footsteps on the sands of time'.
Journalistic imitators are the meanest of mankind;
And the grandest themes are hackneyed by the pens that come behind.

If you strike a novel subject, write it up, and do not fail,
They will rhyme and prose about it till your very own is stale,
As they raved about the region that the wattle-boughs perfume
Till the reader cursed the bushman and the stink of wattle-bloom.

They will follow in your footsteps while you're groping for the light;
But they'll run to get before you when they see you're going right;
And they'll trip you up and baulk you in their blind and greedy heat,
Like a stupid pup that hasn't learned to trail behind your feet.

Take your loads of sin and sorrow on more energetic backs!
Go and strike across the country where there are not any tracks!
And – we fancy that the subject could be further treated here,
But we'll leave it to be hackneyed by the fellows in the rear.

Question Not
(A fragment from *Ye Wearie Wayfarer*)

Adam Lindsay Gordon

Question not, but live and labour till yon goal be won,
Helping every feeble neighbour, seeking help from none;
Life is mostly froth and bubble, two things stand like stone,
Kindness in another's trouble, courage in your own.
Courage, comrades, this is certain, all is for the best –
There are lights behind the curtain – Gentles, let us rest.

Patches

Grahame Watt

'The trouble with the world,' said Dad, as he reached for pipe and matches,
'The trouble with the world today, is no-one uses **patches**.
Back in those days, those early days when payin' crops were few,
We had to fix the things we had, we had to just 'make do'.
If harness broke we fixed it up, we never missed a beat,
Patched it up with rivet strap and we were on our feet.
Some fencin' wire, a pair of pliers did wonders on the track,
'The cockies' friend' in times of need – a friend to all outback.
And no-one threw a thing away, like flour bags and such,
They were handy for all sorts of things, and the cost was not too much.
Kero tins and kero boxes, they were treasures to us folk,
For buckets and for furniture, and to fix the things that broke.
Newspaper wasn't thrown away, we'd keep it for ourselves,
All cut in fancy patterns to brighten up the shelves.
We never threw a thing away, and we mended what we had.
I reckon that it stood us well, we could teach a few,' said Dad.
'When as families we had arguments we didn't throw it all away.
We'd wait a while and patch it up – not like they do today.
Nowadays it's "throw away", "get a new one", "no expense",
We settled for the old one, and I reckon that made sense.
We were satisfied with what we had and stayed together longer,
We never threw it all away – and the patches made us stronger!'

Ribbons
(To the Show Ring Children)

Will Ogilvie

When the crowds are collected to cheer you,
  O'er the fences in front of the stand.
And when heaven itself would seem near you,
  And the ribbons are placed in your hand.
Your throne is not Caesar's or Nero's,
  The world is not all at your feet.
You're really no gallanter heroes,
  Than half of the others you've beat.

All the glory, be pleased to remember,
  Was never intended to last;
It will soon be no more than an ember,
  In the faded-out fires of the past.
There are lights that are brighter to borrow,
  There are flames that are finer to fan
When you wake in the world of the morrow,
  And grow to be woman and man.

Be courtly to girls you have beaten,
  Be kindly to fellows who fall;
Disappointment's ill food to be eaten
  Defeat can be bitter as gall.
Don't allow all those ribbons to spoil you
  But behave as good breeding demands.
And never let selfishness soil you
  Or greed; they have dirt on their hands.

Be sportsmen and carry your honours,
  With pride, but with modesty too
And so be beloved by the donors
  Who have handed their trophies to you.
Be kind to the rest you've outridden,
  Be glad you've prevailed in the strife.
And let jealousy die and be hidden
  And you'll win the blue ribbons of life!

A Mate Can Do No Wrong

Henry Lawson

We learnt the creed at Hungerford,
   We learnt the creed at Bourke;
We learnt it in the good times,
   And learnt it out of work.
We learnt it by the harbour-side
   And on the billabong:
'No matter what a mate may do,
   A mate can do no wrong!'

He's like a king in this respect
   (No matter what they do),
And, king-like, shares in storm and shine
   The Throne of Life with you.
We learnt it when we were in gaol,
   And put it in a song:
'No matter what a mate may do,
   A mate can do no wrong!'

They'll say he said a bitter word
   When he's away or dead.
We're loyal to his memory,
   No matter what he said.
And we should never hesitate,
   But strike out good and strong.
And jolt the slanderer on the jaw –
   A mate can do no wrong!

Coolgardie

Anon

Damn Coolgardie, damn the track;
Damn the road both there and back.
Damn the water, damn the weather,
   Damn Coolgardie altogether.

A Bachelor's View

Harry Morant ('THE BREAKER')

'Just a kiss for the baby,' the fond mother said,
As she bent o'er the babe in her arms;
But the philistine bachelor, shaking his head,
Seemed oblivious of babyhood's charms
'Baby-girls doubtless are pretty,' said he,
With a cynical shrug of his shoulder,
'But for kissable purposes, Madam, you see
I prefer 'em some twenty years older!'

To a City Cousin

Mary Duroux

Can you hear the whisper
    In the grass beneath your feet?

Can you taste the flavour
    Of wild honey, pure and sweet?

Can you see the wonder
    Of the moon, the earth, and sky?

Can you feel the pleasure
    In a stream rippling by?

Can you smell the perfume
    From the wattle, golden hue?

Can you touch the gum trees
    Reaching up towards the blue?

Can you accomplish all of this,
    If not, then it's a pity,

You have lost a paradise
    In moving to the city.

Ned Kelly

Anon

Ned Kelly was born in a ramshackle hut,
  He'd battled since he was a kid:
He grew up with bad men and duffers and thieves,
  And learnt all the bad things they did.

Now down at Glenrowan they held up the pub,
  And were having a drink and a song,
When the troopers rolled up and surrounded the place:
  The Kellys had waited too long.

Some say he's a hero and gave to the poor.
  While others, 'A killer,' they say;
But to me it just proves the old saying is true,
  The saying that crime doesn't pay.

Yet, when I look round at some people I know.
  And the prices of things that we buy;
I just think to myself, well perhaps, after all,
  Old Ned wasn't such a bad guy.

Lullaby

Victor Daley ('CREEVE ROE')

Oh, hush thee, my baby, the time it has come,
For the nuisance to pass here with trumpet and drum.
Oh, fear not the bugle, though loudly it blows –
'Tis the Salvation Army disturbs thy repose.

West

Anon

Have you ever been droving out West,
Where the flies are a terrible pest?
The mosquitoes at night, by the Jesus they bite!
I reckon you'll know that you're earning your dough,
If you ever go droving out West!

I Whistle Through the Bush

Anon

My traps are all a-jangle in an easy-swinging tangle,
And I'm setting in a circle, keeping round a fringe of trees.
Yes I am a rabbit-trapper – a canny bunny-snapper,
And I whistle through the bushland though I'm wet up to me knees.

While other blokes are courtin' tabbies I'm out among the rabbies,
I can hear 'em buckin', squealin' 'bout a dozen traps ahead.
While other blokes are flirtin' at the last trap I am certain,
To be baggin' up those bunnies, keepin' tally as I tread.

And I'm under no man's orders and I recognize no borders,
There's a welcome everywhere for me in my old dungarees.
Though I'm muck-and-gory-spattered and me clobber's torn and tattered,
I'm as carefree as those bunnies 'til they fall for one of these.

If I make the railway early there's a shy and dinkum girlie,
Who'll juggle with the cream cans as she writes cheques out for me.
Yes I am a rabbit-trapper – a canny bunny-snapper,
And I whistle through the bushland like the birds up in the trees.

Western Australians

Anon

Oh, we've just blown across from the West,
We're all forty-two round the chest.
Fremantle and Perth are the best towns on earth
And we don't give a stuff for the rest.
We'll take off our coats and our vests
Whenever we're put to the test.
We've all got good throttles for emptying bottles
And we reckon Swan beer is the best.

Son of Mine
(To Denis)
Oodgeroo Noonuccal (KATH WALKER)

My son, your troubled eyes search mine,
Puzzled and hurt by colour line.
Your black skin as soft as velvet shine;
What can I tell you, son of mine?

I could tell you of heartbreak, hatred blind,
I could tell of crimes that shame mankind,
Of brutal wrong and deeds malign,
Of rape and murder, son of mine;

But I'll tell instead of brave and fine
When lives of black and white entwine,
And men in brotherhood combine –
This would I tell you, son of mine.

My Son

Neil McArthur

The teacher rang the other day, and sounded most upset
My son was caught out back of school, with a lighted cigarette
I said, 'I'll come and pick him up, the stupid, little bloke
I'll be there soon, I'll just drop in and buy myself some smokes.'

I picked him up and brought him home and kicked him up the bum
'Cigarettes will kill you quick, you ought to know that son
And tell me where you got them from, you sneaky little grub!'
He said from the cigarette machine, when I took him to the pub!

The teacher rang again next day, and sounded rather mean
My son was caught out back of school, with a dirty magazine
I said, 'I'll come and get him, and bring the bugger home
I'll just drop this porno movie back, that I've had out on loan.'

I picked him up and brought him home and kicked him up the bum
'You're too young to read that smut, you ought to know that son.
And tell me where you purchased it, that magazine you read.'
He said he found it lying under my side of the bed!

Well the teacher rang again next day, and said he'd had enough
My son was drinking cans of beer and passing 'round the stuff
I said, 'I'd come and get him, but I really shouldn't drive
'Cause I've been watching cricket, and I'm over .05.

'So send the little bugger home, and I'll kick him up the bum
I'll just have another can or two, while I wait for you to come.'
The teacher dropped him home and said, to him it seemed quite sane
That if my son played up again, that I should get the cane!

To Jim

Henry Lawson

I gaze upon my son once more,
　　With eyes and heart that tire,
As solemnly he stands before
　　The screen drawn round the fire;
With hands behind clasped hand in hand,
　　Now loosely and now fast –
Just as his fathers used to stand
　　For generations past.

A fair and slight and childish form,
　　And big brown thoughtful eyes –
God help him! for a life of storm
　　And stress before him lies:
A wanderer and a gipsy wild,
　　I've learnt the world and know,
For I was such another child –
　　Ah, many years ago!

But in those dreamy eyes of him
　　There is no hint of doubt –
I wish that you could tell me, Jim,

The things you dream about.
Dream on, my son, that all is true
    And things not what they seem –
'Twill be a bitter day for you
    When wakened from your dream.

You are a child of field and flood,
    But with the gipsy strains
A strong Norwegian sailor's blood
    Is running through your veins.
Be true, and slander never stings,
    Be straight, and all may frown –
You'll have the strength to grapple things
    That dragged your father down.

These lines I write with bitter tears
    And failing heart and hand.
But you will read in after years.
    And you will understand:
You'll hear the slander of the crowd,
    They'll whisper tales of shame,
But days will come when you'll be proud
    To bear your father's name.

But Oh! beware of bitterness
    When you are wronged, my lad –
I wish I had the faith in men
    And women that I had!
'Tis better far (for I have felt
    The sadness in my song)
To trust all men and still be wronged
    Than to trust none and wrong.

Be generous and still do good
    And banish while you live
The spectre of ingratitude
    That haunts the ones who give.
But if the crisis comes at length
    That your future might be marred,
Strike hand, my son, with all your strength!
    For your own self's sake, strike hard!

The Play

CJ Dennis

'Wot's in a name?' she sez ... And then she sighs,
An' clasps 'er little 'ands, an' rolls 'er eyes.
'A rose,' she sez, 'be any other name
Would smell the same,
Oh, w'erefore art you Romeo, young sir?
Chuck yer ole pot an' change yer moniker!'

Doreen an' me, we bin to see a show –
The swell two-dollar touch. Bong tong, yeh know
A chair apiece wiv velvit on the seat;
A slap-up treat.
The drarmer's writ be Shakespeare, years ago,
About a barmy goat called Romeo.

'Lady, be yonder moon I swear!' sez 'e.
An then 'e climbs up on the balkiney;
An' there they smooge a treat, wiv pretty words,
Like two love-birds.
I nudge Doreen. She whispers, 'Ain't it grand!'
'Er eyes is shinin'; an' I squeeze 'er 'and.

'Wot's in a name?' she sez. 'Struth, I dunno.
Billo is just as good as Romeo.
She may be Juli-er or Juli-et –
'E loves 'er yet.
If she's the tart 'e wants, then she's 'is queen,
Names never count ... But ar, I like 'Doreen!'

A sweeter, dearer sound I never 'eard;
Ther's music 'angs around that little word,
Doreen! ... But wot was this I starts to say
About the play?
I'm off me beat. But when a bloke's in love
'Is thorts turn 'er way, like a 'omin' dove.

This Romeo 'e's lurkin' wiv a crew –
A dead tough crowd o' crooks – called Montague.
'Is cliner's push – wot's nicknamed Capulet –
They 'as 'em set.
Fair narks they are, jist like them back-street clicks.
Ixcep' they fights wiv skewers 'stid o' bricks.

Wot's in a name? Wot's in a string o' words?
They scraps in ole Verona wiv the'r swords,
An' never give a bloke a stray dog's chance,
An' that's Romance.
But when they deals it out wiv bricks an' boots
In Little Lon., they're low, degraded broots.

Wot's jist plain stoush wiv us, right 'ere to-day,
Is 'valler' if yer fur enough away.
Some time, some writer bloke will do the trick
Wiv Ginger Mick,
Of Spadger's Lane. *'E'll* be a Romeo,
When 'e's bin dead five 'undred years or so.

Fair Juli-et, she gives 'er boy the tip.
Sez she: 'Don't sling that crowd o' mine no lip;
An' if you run agin a Capulet,
Jist do a get,'
'E swears 'e's done wiv lash; 'e'll chuck it clean.
(Same as I done when I first met Doreen.)

They smooge some more at that. Ar, strike me blue!
It gimme Joes to sit an' watch them two!
'E'd break away an' start to say good-bye,
An' then she'd sigh
'Ow, Ro-me-o!' an' git a strangle-holt,
An' 'ang around 'im like she feared 'e'd bolt.

Nex' day 'e words a gorspil cove about
A secrit weddin'; an' they plan it out.
'E spouts a piece about 'ow 'e's bewitched:
Then they git 'itched ...
Now, 'ere's the place where I fair git the pip:
She's 'is for keeps, an' yet 'e lets 'er slip!

Ar! but 'e makes me sick! A fair gazob!
'E's jist the glarsey on the soulful sob,
'E'll sigh and spruik, an' 'owl a love-sick vow –
(The silly cow!)
But when 'e's got 'er, spliced an' on the straight,
'E crools the pitch, an' tries to kid it's Fate.

Aw! Fate me foot! Instid of slopin' soon
As 'e was wed, off on 'is 'oneymoon,
'Im an' 'is cobber, called Mick Curio,
They 'ave to go
An' mix it wiv that push o' Capulets.
They look fer trouble; an' it's wot they gets.

A tug named Tyball (cousin to the skirt)
Sprags 'em an' makes a start to sling off dirt.
Nex' minnit there's a reel old ding-dong go –
'Arf round or so.
Mick Curio, 'e gets it in the neck,
'Ar, rats!' 'e sez, an' passes in 'is check.

Quite natchril, Romeo gits wet as 'ell.
'It's me or you!' 'e 'owls, an' wiv a yell,
Plunks Tyball through the gizzard wiv 'is sword,
'Ow I ongcored!
'Put in the boot!' I sez. 'Put in the boot!'
'Ush!' sez Doreen ... 'Shame!' sez some silly coot

Then Romeo, 'e dunno wot to do.
The cops gits busy, like they allwiz do,
An' nose around until 'e gits blue funk
An' does a bunk.
They wants 'is tart to wed some other guy.
'Ah, strike!' she sez. 'I wish that I could die!'

Now, this 'ere gorspil bloke's a fair shrewd 'ead.
Sez 'e, 'I'll dope yeh, so they'll *think* yer dead.'
(I tips 'e was a cunnin' sort, wot knoo
A thing or two).
She takes 'is knock-out drops, up in 'er room:
They think she's snuffed, an' plant 'er in 'er tomb.

Then things gits mixed a treat an' starts to whirl.
'Ere's Romeo comes back an' finds 'is girl
Tucked in 'er little coffing, cold an' stiff,
An' in a jiff
'E swallers lysol, throws a fancy fit,
'Ead over turkey, an' 'is soul 'as flit.

Then Juli-et wakes up an' sees 'im there,
Turns on the water-works an' tears 'er 'air,
'Dear love,' she sez, 'I cannot live alone!'
An', wif a moan,
She grabs 'is pockit knife, an' ends 'er cares ...
'*Peanuts or lollies!*' sez a boy upstairs.

Moderation

Victor Daley ('CREEVE ROE')

I do not wish for wealth
   Beyond a livelihood;
I do not ask for health
   Uproariously good.

I do not care for men
   To point with pride at me;
A model citizen
   I do not wish to be.

I have no dream bizarre
   Of strange erotic joy;
I want no avatar
   Of Helena of Troy.

I do not crave the boon
   Of Immortality;
I do not want the moon,
   Not yet the rainbow's key.

I do not yearn for wings,
   Or fins to swim the sea;
I merely want the things
   That are not good for me.

If I Was Prime Minister

Jim Haynes

If I Was Prime Minister by gee, by gosh, by golly,
I'd pass a law that every day each kid must get a lolly.
And you could choose your lolly from a lovely Lolly Trolley.

If I Was Prime Minister by gum, by gee, by gosh,
I'd say that every Saturday kids didn't have to wash,
Unless their parents served them fish and chips and lemon squash.

If I Was Prime Minister by gosh, by gum, by gee,
I'd say that every kid must have a tree house and a tree.
And if you didn't then the army had to build you one for free.

If I Was Prime Minister by gee, by gosh, by gum,
I'd pass a law that everyone would have to help my mum.
Then she could put her feet up and she wouldn't look so glum.

If I Was Prime Minister by gee, by gosh by gad,
I reckon that Australia wouldn't be too bad,
And kids would say I was the best Prime Minister we'd had!

Darwin

Anon

We've flying ants with frilly pants
And stinging, stinking wogs;
Clammy slugs and poison bugs
And bloated, croaking frogs.

We've crocodiles and miles and miles
Of snake-infested scrub;
We've fish that bite throughout the night
Outside the flaming pub.

We've fever, bogs and dingo dogs
And places fraught with vice;
Steaming days that wilt our ways
And lousy little lice.

The mozzies croon a songless tune
Around our tortured heads;
The sandflies bite throughout the night,
They're hatching in our beds.

Big ants and flies with avid eyes
Eat every mortal thing.
Our Christmas cheer is third-rate beer.
Oh Death, where is Thy sting?

Social Comment

Anon

The people of Melbourne are frightfully well-born.
Of much the same kidney is the 'beau-monde' of Sydney.
Adelaide's forte is culture –
But in Brisbane the people insult ya and don't even know they've been rude,
They're that ignorant, common and crude!
It's hardly worth . . . mentioning . . . Perth.

Ode To Westralia

Anon

Land of forests, fleas and flies, blighted hopes and blighted eyes,
Art thou hell in earth's disguise, Westralia?
Art thou some volcanic blast big volcanoes spurned, outcast?
Art thou unfinished, made the last, Westralia?

Was thou once the chosen land where Adam broke God's one command,
And he, in wrath, changed thee to sand, Westralia?
Land of politicians silly, home of wind and willy-willy,
Land of blanket, tent and billy – Westralia!

Home to brokers, bummers, clerks, nests of sharpers, mining sharks,
Dried up lakes and desert parks – Westralia!
Land of humpies, brothels, inns, old bag huts and empty tins.
Land of blackest, grievous sins – Westralia!

A Bushman's Farewell to Queensland

Anon

Queensland, thou art a land of pests,
From flies and fleas one never rests,
Even now mosquitoes around me revel,
In fact they are the very devil.

Sand flies and hornets just as bad,
They nearly drive a fellow mad;
The scorpion and the centipede
With stinging ants of every breed.

Fever and ague with the shakes,
Triantelopes and poisonous snakes,
Goannas, lizards, cockatoos,
Bushrangers, logs and jackaroos.

Bandicoots and swarms of rats,
Bull-dog ants and native cats,
Stunted timber, thirsty plains,
Parched-up deserts, scanty rains.

There's Barcoo rot and sandy blight,
There's dingoes howling half the night,
There's curlews' wails and croaking frogs,
There's savage blacks and native dogs.

There's scentless flowers and stinging trees,
There's poison grass and Darling peas
Which drive the cattle raving mad
– Make sheep and horses just as bad.

And then it never rains in reason,
There's drought one year and floods next season,
Which wash the squatters' sheep away
And then there is the devil to pay.

To stay in thee, O land of Mutton,
I would not give a single button!
But bid thee now a long farewell,
Thou scorching, sunburnt land of hell!

Stanzas in Praise of South Australia

'W'

Hail South Australia! blessed clime,
  Thou lovely land of my adoption:
(I never meant to see the spot
  If I had had the slightest option).

Hail charming plains of bounteous growth!
  Where tufted vegetation smiles,
(Those dull atrocious endless flats,
  And no plain less than thirteen miles).

Hail tuneful choristers of air!
  Who open wide your tiny throats.
(There's not a bird on any tree
  Can twitter half-a-dozen notes).

Hail glorious gums of matchless height!
  Whose heads the very skies pervade;
Whose tops and trunks yield vast supplies,
  (But not a particle of shade).

Hail far-famed *Torrens*, graceful stream!
  On whose sweet banks I often linger,
Sooth'd by the murmur of thy waves,
  (And plumb the bottom with my finger).

Hail *June*, our grateful *winter* month!
  Which never bring'st us wintry rigours.
And when *sweet February* comes
  (It finds us steaming like the niggers).

Hail balmy rains! in showers come down,
  To do both town and country good;
(And give to each on reaching home
  The blessings of a ton of mud).

Hail land! where all the wants of life
  Flow in cheap streams of milk and honey;
Where all are sure of daily bread
  (If they can fork out ready money).

Hail *South Australia*! once more hail!
  That man indeed is surely rash
Who cannot live content in thee,
  Or wants for anything (but cash).

93

The Riders in the Stand

AB Paterson ('THE BANJO')

There's some that ride the Robbo style, and bump at every stride;
While others sit a long way back, to get a longer ride.
There's some that ride like sailors do, with legs, and arms, and teeth;
And some ride on the horse's neck, and some ride underneath.

But all the finest horsemen out – the men to beat the band –
You'll find amongst the crowd that ride their races in the stand.
They'll say, 'He had the race in hand, and lost it in the straight.'
They'll show how Godby came too soon, and Barden came too late.

They'll say Chevalley lost his nerve, and Regan lost his head;
They'll tell how one was 'livened up' and something else was 'dead' –
In fact, the race was never run on sea, or sky, or land,
But what you'd get it better done by riders in the stand.

The rule holds good in everything in life's uncertain fight:
You'll find the winner can't go wrong, the loser can't go right.
You ride a slashing race, and lose – by one and all you're banned!
Ride like a bag of flour, and win – they'll cheer you in the stand.

Taking a Turn

Pauline Quaife

Don't raise your voice or shout at me – and please don't be so stern.
Feed me up and pamper me or I might 'take a turn'.
I've got this pain around my heart, my gastric juices burn!
It isn't the buns or the big cheese tart, I'm going to 'take a turn'.
I didn't mess the kitchen floor, the toast I didn't burn.
So don't you blame me anymore – I don't want to 'take a turn'.
It's very lonely roundabout, for company I yearn.
I can't stay home so take me out, or I know I'll 'take a turn'.
Hold my hand and kiss my cheek, some patience you must learn,
Just be gentle, kind and meek – then I won't 'take a turn'.

On the Night Train

Henry Lawson

Have you seen the bush by moonlight, from the train, go running by?
Blackened log and stump and sapling, ghostly trees all dead and dry;
Here a patch of glassy water; there a glimpse of mystic sky?
Have you heard the still voice calling – yet so warm, and yet so cold:
'I'm the Mother-Bush that bore you! Come to me when you are old'?

Did you see the Bush below you sweeping darkly to the Range,
All unchanged and all unchanging, yet so very old and strange!
While you thought in softened anger of the things that did estrange?
(Did you hear the Bush a-calling, when your heart was young and bold:
'I'm the Mother-Bush that nursed you; come to me when you are old'?)

In the cutting or the tunnel, out of sight of stock or shed,
Have you heard the grey Bush calling from the pine-ridge overhead:
'You have seen the seas and cities – all is cold to you, or dead –
All seems done and all seems told, but the grey-light turns to gold!
I'm the Mother-Bush that loves you – come to me now you are old'?

Taking His Chance

Heroes & Heroines

H ere are verses in praise of those who dared the unknown, those whose spirit of adventure paved the way for others – 'role models' they call them these days! Sportsmen and women who excelled by playing the game fairly and for the right reasons (where are they now?), people brave enough to speak out and act on their convictions.

You'll notice that many of the role models written about in this section actually had the wrong kind of convictions! Nearly half the Aussie 'heroes' here were considered 'criminals' by the establishment in one way or another. What does that say about Aussies and the people they admire and remember? Well, criminal stock played a large part in the nation's history. Perhaps that gave us a healthy kind of hybrid vigour! Migrants tend to be the non-conformist, forward-thinking minority of the country they leave anyway – and perhaps that's all a lot of these 'criminals' were.

An old Darling River cockie I knew was once told by the police to be on his guard because some blokes had escaped from Wentworth Prison and were believed to be heading up the river. 'I'll be all right Sergeant,' said Old Jack, 'I'm not that worried about the ones who get out – I'm a lot more worried about the ones who oughta be in there! I'll take me chance.' And I fancy 'taking me chance' is pretty much what Aussies see as 'heroic behaviour'. (Old Jack was a hero to me!)

Just plodding along and conforming to some well-established ritual never seems as much fun as 'having a go'. It has been noted that, unlike our American cousins, Aussies prefer the underdog to the successful champion. Well, the poems I found tell me that we love a champion too, but it's not just success we admire. We love those who overcome adversity and, win or lose in the end, we love those who 'ave a go! **97**

Taking His Chance

Henry Lawson

They stood by the door of the Inn on the rise;
May Carney looked up in the bushranger's eyes:
'Oh! why did you come? – it was mad of you, Jack;
You know that the troopers are out on your track.'
A laugh and a shake of his obstinate head –
'I wanted a dance, and I'll chance it,' he said.

Some twenty-odd bushmen had come to the ball,
But Jack from his youth had been known to them all,
And bushmen are soft where a woman is fair,
So the love of May Carney protected him there.
Through all the short evening – it seems like romance –
She danced with a bushranger taking his chance.

'Twas midnight – the dancers stood suddenly still,
For hoof-beats were heard on the side of the hill!
Ben Duggan, the drover, along the hillside
Came riding as only a bushman can ride.
He sprang from his horse, to the dancers he sped –
'The troopers are down in the gully!' he said.

Quite close to the shanty the troopers were seen.
'Clear out and ride hard for the ranges, Jack Dean!
Be quick!' said May Carney – her hand on her heart –
'We'll bluff them awhile, and 'twill give you a start.'
He lingered a moment – to kiss her, of course –
Then ran to the trees where he'd hobbled his horse.

She ran to the gate, and the troopers were there –
The jingle of hobbles came faint on the air –
Then loudly she screamed: it was only to drown
The treacherous clatter of sliprails let down.
But troopers are sharp, and she saw at a glance
That someone was taking a desperate chance.

They chased, and they shouted, 'Surrender, Jack Dean!'
They called him three times in the name of the Queen.
Then came from the darkness the clicking of locks;
The crack of a rifle was heard on the rocks!
A shriek, and a shout, and a rush of pale men –
And there lay the bushranger, chancing it then.

The sergeant dismounted and knelt on the sod –
'Your bushranging's over – make peace, Jack, with God!'
The dying man laughed – not a word he replied,
But turned to the girl who knelt down by his side.
He gazed in her eyes as she lifted his head:
'Just kiss me – my girl – and – I'll chance it,' he said.

She's Australian

Ted Egan

She comes from Macedonia, Lebanon, Cambodia,
El Salvador or Chile – perhaps she's Vietnamese.
She's working in a factory, she's bringing up a family,
And she's all, she's all – all or any one of these.
Her clothes are somewhat different, she doesn't speak much English,
Worships at a different church, never tasted beer.
She works away relentlessly, she's good for the economy.
In every sense this woman's an Australian pioneer.

She's out there on the factory floor, legs are aching, feet are sore,
Mindless repetition but she hopes it's for the best.
Wondering, 'Am I pregnant? Can we afford another child?'
Longing, longing for elusive hours of rest.
The factory whistle blows, she quickly hurries for the bus.
Ignores the jibes and insults, pretends she doesn't hear.
Runs to do the shopping, cook the family dinner,
No rest for her this woman – this Australian Pioneer.

She doesn't drive a bullock wagon, crack a stockwhip, ride a horse,
But I guess if she had to she would quickly find a way.
She's nonetheless a sister to the women of another time,
Who did those things, they surely did – and are revered today.
She came out to Australia from a homeland wracked with poverty,
Hunger and oppression – a life of constant fear.
But nonetheless it's difficult, this new life so bewildering,
And the woman's never heard of crazy words like 'pioneer'.

The kids are home from school but the city's just so stifling,
She remembers all these dreams about the beaches, bush and sun.
Late at night she sits awhile, thinking of her childhood,
Reflecting, reflecting on this new life she's begun.
But her son will play for Collingwood, her daughter's Jana Wendt.
And Australia should be grateful that she came over here,
Working in the factory, bringing up a family,
Laying the foundations – this Australian pioneer.
She's here, she's here, she's living over here.
She's not an alien she's Australian – and she's a pioneer.

The Man from Snowy River

AB Paterson ('THE BANJO')

There was movement at the station, for the word had passed around
That the colt from old Regret had got away,
And had joined the wild bush horses – he was worth a thousand pound,
So all the cracks had gathered to the fray.
All the tried and noted riders from the stations near and far
Had mustered at the homestead overnight,
For the bushmen love hard riding where the wild bush horses are,
And the stockhorse snuffs the battle with delight.

There was Harrison, who made his pile when Pardon won the cup,
The old man with his hair as white as snow;
But few could ride beside him when his blood was fairly up –
He would go wherever horse and man could go.
And Clancy of the Overflow came down to lend a hand,
No better horseman ever held the reins;
For never horse could throw him while the saddle-girths would stand –
He learnt to ride while droving on the plains.

And one was there, a stripling on a small and weedy beast;
He was something like a racehorse undersized,
With a touch of Timor pony – three parts thoroughbred at least –
And such as are by mountain horsemen prized.
He was hard and tough and wiry – just the sort that won't say die –
There was courage in his quick impatient tread;
And he bore the badge of gameness in his bright and fiery eye,
And the proud and lofty carriage of his head.

But still so slight and weedy, one would doubt his power to stay,
And the old man said, 'That horse will never do
For a long and tiring gallop – lad, you'd better stop away,
Those hills are far too rough for such as you.'
So he waited sad and wistful – only Clancy stood his friend –
'I think we ought to let him come,' he said;
'I warrant he'll be with us when he's wanted at the end,
For both his horse and he are mountain bred.

'He hails from Snowy River, up by Kosciusko's side,
Where the hills are twice as steep and twice as rough,
Where a horse's hoofs strike firelight from the flint-stones every stride,
The man that holds his own is good enough.
And the Snowy River riders on the mountains make their home,
Where the river runs those giant hills between;
I have seen full many horseman since I first commenced to roam,
But nowhere else such horsemen have I seen.'

So he went; they found the horses by the big mimosa clump,
They raced away towards the mountain's brow,
And the old man gave his orders, 'Boys, go at them from the jump,
No use to try for fancy riding now.
And, Clancy, you must wheel them, try and wheel them to the right.
Ride boldly, lad, and never fear the spills,
For never yet was rider that could keep the mob in sight,
If once they gain the shelter of those hills.'

So Clancy rode to wheel them – he was racing on the wing
Where the best and boldest riders take their place,
And he raced his stock-horse past them, and he made the ranges ring
With the stockwhip, as he met them face to face.
Then they halted for a moment, while he swung the dreaded lash,
But they saw their well-loved mountain full in view,
And they charged beneath the stockwhip with a sharp and sudden dash,
And off into the mountain scrub they flew.

Then fast the horsemen followed, where the gorges deep and black
Resounded to the thunder of their tread,
And the stockwhip woke the echoes, and they fiercely answered back
From cliffs and crags that beetled overhead.
And upward, ever upward, the wild horses held their way,
Where mountain ash and kurrajong grew wide;
And the old man muttered fiercely, 'We may bid the mob good-day,
No man can hold them down the other side.'

When they reached the mountain's summit, even Clancy took a pull –
It well might make the boldest hold their breath;
The wild hop scrub grew thickly, and the hidden ground was full
Of wombat holes, and any slip was death.
But the man from Snowy River let the pony have his head,
And he swung his stockwhip round and gave a cheer,
And he raced him down the mountain like a torrent down its bed,
While the others stood and watched in very fear.

He sent the flint-stones flying, but the pony kept his feet,
He cleared the fallen timber in his stride,
And the man from Snowy River never shifted in his seat –
It was grand to see that mountain horseman ride.
Through the stringybarks and saplings, on the rough and broken ground
Down the hillside at a racing pace he went;
And he never drew the bridle till he landed safe and sound
At the bottom of that terrible descent.

He was right among the horses as they climbed the further hill,
And the watchers on the mountain, standing mute,
Saw him ply the stockwhip fiercely, he was right among them still,
As he raced across the clearing in pursuit.
Then they lost him for a moment, where two mountain gullies met
In the ranges – but a final glimpse reveals
On a dim and distant hillside the wild horses racing yet,
With the man from Snowy River at their heels.

And he ran them single-handed till their sides were white with foam;
He followed like a bloodhound on their track,
Till they halted, cowed and beaten; then he turned their heads for home,
And alone and unassisted brought them back.
But his hardy mountain pony he could scarcely raise a trot,
He was blood from hip to shoulder from the spur;
But his pluck was still undaunted, and his courage fiery hot,
For never yet was mountain horse a cur.

And down by Kosciusko, where the pine-clad ridges raise
Their torn and rugged battlements on high,
Where the air is clear as crystal, and the white stars fairly blaze
At midnight in the cold and frosty sky,
And where around the Overflow the reed beds sweep and sway
To the breezes, and the rolling plains are wide,
The Man from Snowy River is a household word today.
And the stockmen tell the story of his ride.

Namatjira

Oodgeroo Noonuccal (KATH WALKER)

Aboriginal man, you walked with pride,
And painted with joy the countryside.
Original man, your fame grew fast,
Men pointed you out as you went past.

But vain the honour and tributes paid,
For you strangled in rules the white men made:
You broke no law of your own wild clan
Which says, 'Share all with your fellow-man.'

What did their loud acclaim avail
Who gave you honour, then gave you jail?
Namatjira, they boomed your art,
They called you genius, then broke your heart.

The Women of the West

George Essex Evans

They left the vine-wreathed cottage and the mansion on the hill,
The houses in the busy streets where life is never still,
The pleasures of the city, and the friends they cherished best;
For love they faced the wilderness – the Women of the West.

The roar, and rush, and fever of the city died away,
And the old-time joys and faces – they were gone for many a day;
In their place the lurching coach-wheel, or the creaking bullock-chains,
O'er the everlasting sameness of the never-ending plains.

In the slab-built, zinc-roofed homestead of some lately taken run,
In the tent beside the bankment of a railway just begun,
In the huts on new selections, in the camps of man's unrest,
On the frontiers of the Nation, live the Women of the West.

The red sun robs their beauty and, in weariness and pain,
The slow years steal the nameless grace that never comes again;
And there are hours men cannot soothe, and words men cannot say –
The nearest woman's face may be a hundred miles away.

The wide bush holds the secrets of their longing and desires,
When the white stars in reverence light their holy altar fires,
And silence, like the touch of God, sinks deep into the breast –
Perchance He hears and understands the Women of the West.

For them no trumpet sounds the call, no poet plies his arts,
They only hear the beating of their gallant, loving hearts.
But they have sung with silent lives the song all songs above –
The holiness of sacrifice, the dignity of love.

Well have we held our fathers' creed. No call has passed us by.
We faced and fought the wilderness, we sent our sons to die.
And we have hearts to do and dare, and yet, o'er all the rest,
The hearts that made the Nation were the Women of the West.

Death of a Kelly

Charlee Marshall

The priest has been to see me, so I know me time is near,
    We knelt beside the window while we prayed:
Fruitless prayers – forgive me, Father – for the place I go from here
    Is beyond your jurisdiction, I'm afraid;
And here's Milord the Warder and his henchmen comin' down,
    They're going to teach a Kelly how to die!
But I showed 'em how, and when, and where, that night outside Glenrowan;
    The only lesson left to learn is why.
They'll never hang Ned Kelly, though the law will take its course
    With this worthless lump of clay bound up with chain;
Go out in the Warby Ranges, look at every mounted horse –
    There the Spirit of Ned Kelly rides again.

How can they hang a concept, hang a waking nation's pride,
    That will win the north and civilize the west?
There's a little bit o' Kelly fiercely beating there inside
    Every miner, every lonely settler's breast;
In the heart of every duffer, from Strathbogie to Tatong,
    And the Bushmen in the valleys further north.
The same 'Die Game' defiance of the free against the strong
    Is waitin' for the chance to gusher forth.
It will motivate the armies of this Nation-with-no-name,
    Win them honours in the battles yet to come;
For these young colonial heroes, the prospect of dyin' game
    Is a stronger spur than British fife or drum.

Well now, I guess I'm ready, there's a hangin' to be done;
    I hope ye've measured out the length of fall –
There's no need to bind me ankles, no true Kelly ever run,
    And I'd like to meet me maker standin' tall;
I'd like to say I'm sorry, but that won't bring Dan back,
    It won't lift up Trooper Scanlan from the grave,
Or put Joe Byrne beside me on some vagrant mountain track,
    Or stand me on the gallows doubly brave –
Perhaps, if I should live again, I'd walk a different ground;
    Buy a farm, and build a house, and take a wife;
Lose meself in corn and praties wi' the children runnin' round –
    But ye only get one chance ... ah-h, such is life.

King Paraway

Ted Egan

In the 80s Australia saw movements of cattle,
In the world's driest continent the drovers did battle
With Nature, and thousands of hard miles were spanned
As two hundred thousand were walked overland
Into Queensland, the Territory, and the Kimberley runs
And in the forefront was one of the land's finest sons.
There are hundreds of drovers of whom we could sing
But everyone knows Nat Buchanan was King.

The bush blacks all called him Old Paraway,
You see him tomorrow, he left yesterday.
With thousands of cattle he keeps riding on
To nowhere, from somewhere, here he comes, now he's gone,
With a bright green umbrella to shade the fierce sun.
On the Murranji, on the Murchison, on another new run,
Old Paraway's the man of whom desert tribes sing
And everyone knows Nat Buchanan was King.

People talk about drovers and who was the best,
Some give you their choice and discard all the rest.
There are books on the subject with hundreds of pages
About bullocks that rushed, and the endless dry stages.
Old timers regale you with tales of the past
Of whipping up water, and night horses fast.
There are hundreds of drovers of whom we could sing,
But everyone knows Nat Buchanan was King.

If drovers had titles, Bill Gwydir's a Prince
None better at Birdsville before him or since.
Matt Savage was the Duke of the Murranji Track,
Edna Zigenbine's Queen of the plains way out back.
Arch McLean, Teddy Sheehan and old Walter Rose
They'd be knights of the saddle as everyone knows.
There are hundreds of drovers of whom we could sing
But everyone knows Nat Buchanan was King.

Nat Buchanan, old Bluey, Old Paraway
What would you think if you came back today?
It's not as romantic as in your time, old Nat,
Not many drovers and we're sad about that.
Fences and bitumen and road trains galore.
Oh they move cattle quicker but one thing is sure
Road trains go faster, but of drovers we sing
And everyone knows Nat Buchanan was King.

Tjandamara

Ted Egan

In April 1897 Australia's whites rejoiced
For the telegram came to say that he was dead
The famous Kimberley outlaw, betrayed and shot at last
And as proof the police paraded a severed head.
The white man called him Pigeon
But no-one quite knows why,
Certainly he had a great ability to fly
But his proper name was Tjandamara
Wangarango man of the Tjilia Dreaming
Born and raised in the Kimberley
A hunter through and through.

He once was a famous tracker for the Kimberley police
And he was sent one time to capture a man
A member of his own race.
But the old man told the tracker:
'It's time to make a stand.
Don't be a white man's puppy dog,
Drive the foreigners from your land.'
So he stole the white man's rifles,
Shot the police on sight,
Freed their chained up prisoners in the middle of the night
Formed a gang of fighters,
Gave each man a gun
And Tjandamara the tracker
Became an outlaw on the run.

The police brought reinforcements
And trackers by the score
But for three long years he led them a merry chase
He tracked their trackers, stole their rifles,
Tunnelled his way through stone,
Until at last he fought them face to face.
There at a place called Tunnel Creek,
He fired his final shot,
And one of his own race killed him,
The ultimate tragic blot.
They took his head in a bag to Derby,
Evidence for the court,
The end of Tjandamara,
Or that was what they thought.

So what do you say about Tjandamara?
What's your opinion of Che Guevara?
Were they justified? Have they really died?
What did you think about Robin Hood?
Could you really call Ned Kelly 'good'?
And are you satisfied, when you speak with pride?
Were they freedom fighters or agitators?
Bloody killers or liberators?
Jokes aside
It's the people who make the legends
So let it be cut and dried
What's the verdict on Tjandamara?
The people will decide.

The Flash Stockman

Anon

I'm a stockman to my trade, and they call me ugly Dave,
I'm old and grey and only got one eye;
In a yard I'm good, of course, but just put me on a horse,
And I'll go where lots of young uns daren't try.

I lead 'em through the gidgee over country rough and ridgy,
I lose 'em in the very worst of scrub;
I can ride both rough and easy, with a dewdrop I'm a daisy,
And a right-down bobby-dazzler in a pub.

Just watch me use a whip, I can give the dawdlers gyp,
I can make the bloody echoes roar and ring;
With a branding iron, well, I'm a perfect flaming swell,
In fact, I'm duke of every blasted thing.

To watch me skin a sheep, it's so lovely you could weep.
I can act the silvertail as if my blood was blue;
You can strike me pink or dead, if I stood upon my head,
I'd be just as good as any other two.

I've a notion in my pate, that it's luck, it isn't fate,
That I'm so far above the common run:
So in every thing I do, you could cut me fair in two,
For I'm much too bloody good to be in one.

The Cattle King

Robert Raftery

The fireball of drought was loose and raged across the land.
   The station wife, twice-widowed, with the windlass in her hand,
Strained hard to raise the old drum with it's life-preserving load,
   And her blue dog barked to signify a stranger on the road.

'G'day missus,' said the stranger, as he rode up to the well.
   'Hot day', he said. 'My word it is,' came softly like a bell.
'That's hard work for a woman. Here, let me take a turn.'
   Now high above the water line, the windlass rope would burn.

'Husband away?' the stranger asked. 'No, Jack died last year.
   We've carried on, the kids and me, to make a go of here,
But the bank was out last Friday, and they took our little Skip,
   Our only saddle pony, Jack's horse, even his whip.

'My God, I hate those rotten banks, but I'll live to see them out.
   If only He would send the rain and break this cursed drought.
Oh, there's feed for both your horses sir, and something for your dog,
   And I'll be making tea and damper, I'll serve it on that log.'

The tall, dark-bearded stranger worked lithely with a will.
   He watered all her spindly stock, their troughs to overfill.
'I'm heading down to Broken Hill aboard tomorrow's train,
   There's things aboard my wagonette I'll never use again.

There's stockman's gear and blankets, and pots and pans and lids;
   There's tools and things and sundries and there's sweet things for the kids.'
She thought of him from time to time when night returned the day,
   His country gait, his kindliness and the way he said 'g'day'.

The sun brought molten blasts from hell and scorched the very air,
   As wagons forged on through her gate she cried out in despair,
'My God they've come to take the lot.' she grappled for the gun.
   'No banker's jurisdiction will drive us from our run.'

'I'm no banker missus, I hail from Broken Hill.
   I've been sent to set this pump-house up, a tank-stand and a mill.'
'Oh! There really must be some mistake, not in our wildest dreams;
   A windmill on our little run, it's far beyond our means.'

'You showed a kindness to our boss, his dog and to his stock.
   He's responded to your spirit, your vision and your flock.'
The station widow settled back against the hitching rail.
   Her thoughts were on the stranger and the mill with thrashing sails.

'Your boss?' she said, 'he's tall and dark? His beard inclined to grey?
   Good looking in his youth no doubt, and an old dog in his dray?'
'That's it ma'am, you described him well – he's made The Centre ring.
   You've described a living legend, Sydney Kidman, cattle king.'

A Racing Eight

James Cuthbertson

Who knows it not, who loves it not,
The long and steady swing,
The instant dip, the iron grip,
The rowlocks' linkèd ring,
The arrowy sway of hands away,
The slider oiling aft,
The forward sweep, the backward leap
That speed the flying craft?

A racing eight of perfect mould,
True to the builder's law,
That takes the water's gleaming gold
Without a single flaw.
A ship deep, resonant within,
Harmonious to the core,
That vibrates to her polished skin
The tune of wave and oar.

A racing eight and no man late,
And all hearts in the boat;
The men who work and never shirk,
Who long to be afloat.
The crew who burn from stem to stern
To win the foremost place,
The crew to row, the boat to go,
The eight to win the race.

The First Surveyor
His Widow Speaks

AB Paterson ('THE BANJO')

'The opening of the railway line! The Governor and all!
With flags and banners down the street, a banquet and a ball.
Hark to 'em at the station now! They're raising cheer on cheer!
'The man who brought the railway through – our friend the engineer!'

'They cheer *his* pluck and enterprise and engineering skill!
'Twas my old husband found the pass behind the big red hill.
Before the engineer was grown we settled with our stock
Behind that great big mountain chain, a line of range and rock –
A line that kept us starving there in weary weeks of drought,
With ne'er a track across the range to let the cattle out.

''Twas then, with horses starved and weak and scarcely fit to crawl,
My husband went to find a way across that rocky wall.
He vanished in the wilderness, God knows where he was gone,
He hunted till his food gave out, but still he battled on.
His horses strayed – 'twas well they did – they made towards the grass,
And down behind that big red hill they found an easy pass.

'He followed up and blazed the trees, to show the safest track,
Then drew his belt another hole and turned and started back.
His horses died – just one pulled through with nothing much to spare;
God bless the beast that brought him home, the old white Arab mare!
We drove the cattle through the hills, along the new-found way,
And this was our first camping ground – just where I live to-day.

'Then others came across the range and built the township here,
And then there came the railway line and this young engineer.
He drove about with tents and traps, a cook to cook his meals,
A bath to wash himself at night, a chain-man at his heels.
And that was all the pluck and skill for which he's cheered and praised,
For after all he took the track, the same my husband blazed!

'My poor old husband, dead and gone with never feast nor cheer;
He's buried by the railway line! – I wonder can he hear
When down the very track he marked, and close to where he's laid,
The cattle trains go roaring down the one-in-thirty grade.
I wonder does he hear them pass and can he see the sight,
When through the dark the fast express goes flaming by at night?

'I think 'twould comfort him to know there's someone left to care,
I'll take some things this very night and hold a banquet there!
The hard old fare we've often shared together, him and me,
Some damper and a bite of beef, a pannikin of tea:
We'll do without the bands and flags, the speeches and the fuss,
We know who *ought* to get the cheers and that's enough for us.

'What's that? They wish that I'd come down – the oldest settler here!
Present me to the Governor and that young engineer!
Well, just you tell his Excellence and put the thing polite,
I'm sorry, but I can't come down – I'm dining out tonight!'

Kingsford-Smith

Winifred Tennant

Ask the sun; it has watched him pass –
A shadow mirrored on seas of glass;
Ask the stars that he knew so well
If they beheld where a bird-man fell.
Ask the wind that has blown with him
Over the edge of the ocean's rim,
Far from the charted haunts of men,
To the utmost limits and back again.
Ask the clouds on the mountain height,
The echoes that followed him in his flight,
The thunder that prowls the midnight sky,
If a silvered 'plane went riding by.

If the birds could talk, would they tell the fall
Of a god who winged above them all?
Of an eagle man, by the world's decrees,
King of the blue immensities?

Harry Morant

Will Ogilvie

Harry Morant was a friend I had
    In the years long passed away,
A chivalrous, wild and reckless lad,
    A knight born out of his day.

Full of romance and void of fears,
    With a love of the world's applause,
He should have been one of the cavaliers
    Who fought in King Charles' cause.

114

He loved a girl, and he loved a horse,
    And he never let down a friend,
And reckless he was, but he rode his course
    With courage up to the end.

'Breaker Morant' was the name he earned,
    For no bucking horse could throw
This Englishman who had lived and learned
    As much as the bushmen know.

Many a mile have we crossed together,
    Out where the great plains lie,
To the clink of bit and the creak of leather –
    Harry Morant and I.

Time and again we would challenge Fate
    With some wild and reckless 'dare',
Shoving some green colt over a gate
    As though with a neck to spare.

At times in a wilder mood than most
    We would face them at naked wire,
Trusting the sight of a gidyea post
    Would lift them a half-foot higher.

And once we galloped a steeplechase
    For a bet – 'twas a short half-mile
While one jump only, the stiffest place
    In a fence of the old bush style.

A barrier built of blue-gum rails
    As thick as a big man's thigh,
And mortised into the posts – no nails –
    Unbreakable, four foot high.

Since both our horses were young and green
    And had never jumped or raced,
Were we men who had tired of this earthly scene
    We could scarce have been better placed.

'*Off!*' cried 'The Breaker', and off we went
   And he stole a length of lead.
Over the neck of the grey I bent
   And we charged the fence full speed.

The brown horse slowed and tried to swerve,
   But his rider with master hand
And flaming courage and iron nerve
   Made him lift and leap and land.

He rapped it hard with every foot
   And was nearly down on his nose;
Then I spurred the grey and followed suit
And, praise to the gods – he rose!

He carried a splinter with both his knees
   And a hind-leg left some skin,
But we caught them up at the wilga trees
   Sitting down for the short run-in.

The grey was game and he carried on
   But the brown had a bit to spare;
The post was passed, my pound was gone,
   And a laugh was all my share.

'The Breaker' is sleeping in some far place
   Where the Boer War heroes lie,
And we'll meet no more in a steeplechase –
   Harry Morant and I.

How McDougal Topped the Score

Thomas E Spencer

A peaceful spot is Piper's Flat. The folk that live around –
They keep themselves by keeping sheep and turning up the ground;
But the climate is erratic, and the consequences are
The struggle with the elements is everlasting war.
We plough, and sow, and harrow – then sit down and pray for rain;
And then we all get flooded out and have to start again.
But the folk are now rejoicing as they ne'er rejoiced before,
For we've played Molongo cricket, and McDougal topped the score!

Molongo had a head on it, and challenged us to play
A single-innings match for lunch – the losing team to pay.
We were not great guns at cricket, but we couldn't well say no,
So we all began to practise, and we let the reaping go.
We scoured the Flat for ten miles round to muster up our men,
But when the list was totalled we could only number ten.
Then up spoke big Tim Brady: he was always slow to speak,
And he said – 'What price McDougal who lives down at Cooper's Creek?'

So we sent for old McDougal, and he stated in reply
That he'd never played at cricket, but he'd half a mind to try.
He couldn't come to practise – he was getting in his hay,
But he guessed he'd show the beggars from Molongo how to play.
Now, McDougal was a Scotchman, and a canny one at that,
So he started in to practise with a paling for a bat.
He got Mrs Mac to bowl to him, but she couldn't run at all,
So he trained his sheep-dog, Pincher, how to scout and fetch the ball.

Now, Pincher was no puppy; he was old, and worn, and grey;
But he understood McDougal, and – accustomed to obey –
When McDougal cried out 'Fetch it!' he would fetch it in a trice,
But, until the word was 'Drop it!' he would grip it like a vice.
And each succeeding night they played until the light grew dim:
Sometimes McDougal struck the ball – sometimes the ball struck him.
Each time he struck, the ball would plough a furrow in the ground;
And when he missed, the impetus would turn him three times round.

The fatal day at last arrived – the day that was to see
Molongo bite the dust, or Piper's Flat knocked up a tree!
Molongo's captain won the toss, and sent his men to bat,
And they gave some leather-hunting to the men of Piper's Flat.
When the ball sped where McDougal stood, firm planted in his track,
He shut his eyes, and turned him round, and stopped it – with his back!
The highest score was twenty-two, the total sixty-six,
When Brady sent a yorker down that scattered Johnson's sticks.

Then Piper's Flat went in to bat, for glory and renown,
But, like the grass before the scythe, our wickets tumbled down.
'Nine wickets down, for seventeen, with fifty more to win!'
Our captain heaved a sigh, and sent McDougal in.
'Ten pounds to one you'll lose it!' cried a barracker from town;

But McDougal said, 'I'll tak' it, mon!' and plonked the money down.
Then he girded up his moleskins in a self-reliant style,
Threw off his hat and boots and faced the bowler with a smile.

He held the bat the wrong side out, and Johnson with a grin
Stepped lightly to the bowling crease, and sent a 'wobbler' in;
McDougal spooned it softly back, and Johnson waited there,
But McDougal, crying 'Fetch it!', started running like a hare.
Molongo shouted 'Victory! He's out as sure as eggs,'
When Pincher started through the crowd, and ran through Johnson's legs.
He seized the ball like lightning; then he ran behind a log.
And McDougal kept on running, while Molongo chased the dog!

They chased him up, they chased him down, they chased him round and then
He darted through the slip-rail as the scorer shouted 'Ten!'
McDougal puffed; Molongo swore; excitement was intense;
As the scorer marked down twenty, Pincher cleared a barbed-wire fence.
'Let us head him!' shrieked Molongo. 'Brain the mongrel with a bat!'
'Run it out! Good old McDougal!' yelled the men of Piper's Flat.
And McDougal kept on jogging, and then Pincher doubled back,
And the scorer counted 'Forty' as they raced across the track.

McDougal's legs were going fast, Molongo's breath was gone –
But still Molongo chased the dog – McDougal struggled on.
When the scorer shouted 'Fifty' then they knew the chase could cease;
And McDougal gasped out 'Drop it!' as he dropped within his crease.
Then Pincher dropped the ball, and as instinctively he knew
Discretion was the wiser plan, he disappeared from view;
And as Molongo's beaten men exhausted lay around
We raised McDougal shoulder-high, and bore him from the ground.

We bore him to McGinniss's where lunch was ready laid,
And filled him up with whisky-punch, for which Molongo paid.
We drank his health in bumpers and we cheered him three times three,
And when Molongo got its breath Molongo joined the spree.
And the critics say they never saw a cricket match like that,
When McDougal broke the record in the game at Piper's Flat;
And the folks were jubilating as they never did before;
For we played Molongo cricket – and McDougal topped the score!

The Tiger and The Don

Ted Egan

When I was a kid each summer meant long days at the MCG,
With my dear old dad and his Gladstone bag and a thermos of sweet black tea.
Sandwiches and fruit cake – sittin' up in the stand,
With my dad and his mates at the cricket, I tell you it was grand.

There'd be a big post mortem as every wicket fell,
They'd pick their 'greatest ever' teams – and they wove me in their spell.
They'd argue, but there was one point they all agreed upon,
There'd never be a pair to match The Tiger and The Don.

Dad said, 'Feast your eyes upon The Tiger and The Don,
You'll never see a pair like them again.
Don's the greatest bat of all, and when The Tiger's got the ball,
He puts the fear of God in all those Englishmen.'

They told me of The Tiger's skills and why there was no doubt,
Batsmen from around the world could never work him out.
Arms like pistons, charging in, murder in his eye,
I watched The Tiger's fearsome style and I understood just why.

He was a giant of a man, who bowled at medium pace,
But spinners mate, they went all ways and fizzed up in your face.
A 'wrong-un' that you'd never pick – and if that's not enough,
The type of killer instinct that would call the devil's bluff.

And oh the thrill, I feel it still, when The Don walked in to bat.
He'd look around and take his block and knock the bowlers flat,
Scorching drives and hooks and pulls – a cut, a daring glance,
Don's policy was, 'Never give the bowlers any chance.'

Down the pitch he'd dance to smash the spinners off their length,
He'd hook the quickies' bumpers and you marvelled at his strength,
An eye just like an eagle, his fame will linger on,
For there'll never be a batsman to match the mighty Don.

The greatest thing about them is a lesson for today,
No tantrums, no lairising – just play the proper way,
The Tiger and The Don were the greatest ever seen,
And they always played their cricket hard – but fair and clean.

Well my dad's declared – and it won't be long and I'll be trundled out,
But I love the game of cricket – of that there is no doubt,
And now I tell my grandkids of the times I look back on,
And my happy recollections of The Tiger and The Don.

Golden Dawn

Jim Haynes

A battling female larrikin, a tiger from Balmain,
Wait another hundred years you won't see her like again.
She'd hit the water and she'd go – Melbourne, Rome and Tokyo,
Gold and gold and gold – Dawn Fraser was her name.

She owned the 100 freestyle, smashed records by the score.
If she'd been appreciated she'd have smashed a whole lot more.
Many champs win medals though – records come and records go,
It's not records or medals that Australians love her for.

Dawn was always one of us – she never stood apart.
Though her courage and ability were with her from the start,
And if she turned to you and smiled – anyone, man, woman, child,
Could see the gold that matters – it's the gold that made her heart.

Ballad of Les Darcy

John Dengate

In Maitland town, long years ago, and so begins my song,
There toiled in a blacksmith's forge a sportsman young and strong;
He'd hands and arms like tempered steel; Les Darcy was his name,
He made the iron anvil peal and punched his way to fame.

High-ranking Yankee middleweights with reputations tall
Were fighting in Australian rings, defeating one and all;
But when they met the Maitland boy, with heads and hearts full sore,
Much sadder and much wiser men, they left Australia's shore.

'Now Darcy you must go to war!' the militarists raged
But Darcy's mother would not sign and he was underaged.
So midst a storm of foul abuse, Les Darcy sailed away
To earn his living with his fists in distant USA.

But death awaited Darcy in the land beyond the sea.
Of poison and a broken heart he died in Tennessee;
He's buried now near Maitland in the land where he was born,
And those who smeared Les Darcy's name; I sing their names to scorn.

Phar Lap

Anon

How you thrilled the racing public with your matchless strength and grace;
With your peerless staying power and your dazzling burst of pace.
You toyed with your opponents with a confidence so rare,
Flashing past the winning post with lengths and lengths to spare.
No distance ever proved too great, no horse or handicap,
Could stop you winning races like a champion – Phar Lap.

With a minimum of effort you would simply bowl along
With a stride so devastating and an action smooth and strong.
And you vied with the immortals when, on Flemington's green track,
You won the Melbourne Cup with nine-stone-twelve upon your back.
How the hearts of thousands quickened as you cantered back old chap,
With your grand head proudly nodding to the crowd that yelled, 'Phar Lap'.

Who that saw it could forget it – how you won the Craven Plate?
When a mighty son of Rosedale, whom we'd justly labelled 'great',
Clapped the pace on from the start in a middle-distance race,
Just to test you to the limit of endurance, grit and pace.
He was galloping so strongly that the stands began to clap,
For it seemed as though your lustre would be dimmed at last, Phar Lap.

But you trailed him like a bloodhound till your nostrils touched his rump
Then your jockey asked the question and, with one tremendous jump,
Something like a chestnut meteor hurtled past a blur of black
And, before the crowd stopped gasping, you were halfway down the track,
And, the further that you travelled, ever wider grew the gap,
And you broke another record – one you'd set yourself, Phar Lap.

The hopes of all Australians travelled with you overseas,
Wishing to inspire you to further victories.
And at Agua Caliente you proved you were the best,
Then your great heart stopped beating – so they brought it home to rest.
And Australians won't forget you while the roots of life hold sap;
For the greatest racehorse that was ever foaled was you, Phar Lap.

The Inside Story

Tall & Terrible Tales

We can't help ourselves, can we? Australians just have to exaggerate, add to, twist and colour every story they hear until, let's face it, it's fiction and we're telling lies! There's an old Aussie term for it that Harry Morant uses in a wonderful poem found elsewhere in this collection, 'We were standing by the fireside at the pub one wintry night, Drinking grog and "pitching fairies" . . .'

'Pitching fairies' and telling tales in the pub are old Aussie traditions. In more recent times the phrase 'Up to his neck in dead fairies' has been used to describe anyone caught in a web of lies (often as the result of the odd Royal Commission). This phrase, as those who have seen the pantomime *Peter Pan* will know, comes from the belief that, as Col Wilson puts it, 'Every time you tell a lie a little fairy has to die!'

My favourites in this section are the ones told in typical Aussie deadpan style. I've included 'That Day at Boiling Downs', complete with its century-old (and now politically incorrect and racist) attitudes, because I love the understated style and always laugh out loud when the narrator, who is talking about a rampaging mass murderer, tells us, 'Sammy he got overheated and dropped dead of apoplexy: I felt better when he did!' I've also included the true version of what the dog did in the tuckerbox near Gundagai, and the only poem in the book you can't recite, " 'Ough!' A Fonetic Fansy".

Australians love to tell stories against themselves and insult their mates. I've seen foreigners stand amazed at the insults Australians casually hurl at one another! In many places in the world such comments would lead to bloodshed or civil war – here it's a sign of affection! It's this ability to laugh at ourselves which, for me, defines our Aussie humour more than any other characteristic.

The Inside Story

Charlee Marshall

I was reading in a paper that was wrapped around the cheese
How the miracles of med'cine have become realities;
How women wanting babies can obtain them by the dozen
From the local Doctor's cold-room – all conveniently frozen.
And I must confess the notion left me feeling rather cold,
For I much preferred the method that we used in days of old.

But the skilful city surgeon and his art must surely pale
When you see the stockmen operate out in the post and rail;
Stitching up dog-ravaged wethers, and a mulga stick for breaks,
While the kids still have their ear lopped to survive the bite of snakes;
Shot-gun dentists, cures with castor oil, I guess I've seen the lot,
And the drastic use of stock-knives to control the Barcoo Rot.

I pointed out this very fact last Christmas on the phone
To a mate of mine, Ken Cooper, who was working down near Scone;
And he told me of an accident – the solemn truth, he swore –
(In the land of Cornstalk Promises, that matters any more?
But Ken had lived in Queensland, and that's good enough for me,
So I reckon he's the Barnard of the Outback Surgery.)

Ken was working on a fence-line with a bloke called Slogger Brown;
He was running out the wire while his mate was cutting down.
A mob of sheep stood waiting for the foliage to land –
When a crooked branch jumped back, and knocked
   the chain-saw from his hand!
Oh, God! It was a shocking sight to turn your limbs to jelly:
The whirring blade came down across the bushman's hairy belly!

Ken told me all the details, but my tears were soon in flood,
For the ear-piece of the telephone was slow-ly oozing blood –
But, before he grabbed the throttle, and could get the thing controlled,
His mate – his sole companion – was completely disembowelled;
And it wasn't just a matter of where this or that part fits –
His whole internal mechanism was chopped in little bits!

My friend had been a butcher when he worked the Queensland scene;
A sort of 'reverse surgeon' – if you follow what I mean –
He knew it would be seconds before Slogger breathed his last,
So he had to do some surgery, and do it bloody fast!
He grabbed a ewe around the throat and slit its nether hide ...
He hauled the steaming entrails out, and pushed them all inside.

Though he lacked finesse and finish, he was long on commonsense,
For he drew the gash together with some staples from the fence;
And joining veins and sinews is quite simple when you know
A bit of gum-tree gumption ... and a twitch from Cobb and Co.
What's it matter in a stomach – upside down or front to back?
Guts are guts – they gain no glamour from the neatness of the pack.

Anyhow, he did some plumbing, so the inlet soon aligned;
The outlet quickly took its place with stiches unrefined.
He used a roll of tie-wire, but he must have hit the mark,
'Cos Old Slogger picked a crow-bar up and went to strip the bark;
So – Ken retrieved the chain-saw, and wiped the blood away;
And they stood another twenty posts before the close of day.

Well, for weeks I've sat and wondered if his tale was really true –
I've heard a lot of stories of what lonely bushmen do –
So I rang Ken up the other day, and I mentioned, on the side,
'I suppose you miss Old Slogger – I presume the poor cow died.'
'Oh, you'll never kill Old Slogger,' Ken said. 'He's as tough as teak –
He's out fencing on Urella – and he had a lamb last week!'

Scotty's Wild Stuff Stew

Francis Humphris-Brown

The cause of all the trouble
Was McCabe, the jackaroo,
Who had ordered what, facetiously,
He'd christened 'Wild Stuff Stoo'.
He had shot a brace of pigeons
And had brought them home unplucked;
It was not the first occasion,
And no wonder Scotty bucked
As aside he threw the pigeons
And addressed the jackaroo:

'Ye'll pluck those blinded pigeons,
Or ye'll get no blinded stoo.'
But the jackeroo objected,
And objected strongly, too.
Said he, 'I'm not a slushy;
You can keep your blinded stoo.'
But Scotty didn't argue much,
He winked across at Blue
And, turning to the slushy, said,
'I'll give him "Wild Stuff Stoo".'
The next day it was Sunday, and,
Not having much to do,
We all assisted Scotty
In the making of a stoo.

We raked along the wool-sheds,
In the pens and round about –
It was marvellous, all the wild things
That us rousies fossicked out;
There was Ginger found a lizard,
Which they reckoned was a Jew –
It was rather rough to handle,
But it softened in the stew;
Then Snowy found some hairy things
Inside a musterer's tent;
And Splinter found a lady frog –
And in the lady went.
From McGregor, who'd been foxing,
We obtained a skin or two,
It should have gone to bootlace
But it went into the stoo.
Then someone found a 'Kelly'
That the boundary-rider shot –
It was more or less fermented,
Still, it went inside the pot;
And Scotty found some insects
With an overpowering scent,
And the slushy trapped a mother mouse –
And in poor mother went.

There was some hesitation
'Bout a spider in a tin:
We didn't like the small red spot,
But Scotty dumped it in.
There were a host of other things –
I can't recall the lot –
That were cast into eternity
Per medium of the pot.
And when the jackaroo arrived
A happy man was he
To find that Scotty, after all,
Had cooked a stoo for tea.
He rolled his eyes, and snuffed the fumes,
'Twas dinkum stuff he swore;
He complimented Scotty, and
He passed his plate for more.
And when we'd let him have his fill,
We took him round to view
A list of what had left this world
To enter Scotty's stew.

I grant you there were wild things
Connected with that stoo,
But there was nothing wilder
Than McCabe the jackaroo.
He got the dries and then the shakes,
And we felt shaky too;
We were thinking of the spider
With the red spot in the stoo.
We rushed him to the homestead,
They told him there 'twas flu,
But us rousies, we knew better –
It was Scotty's 'Wild Stuff Stoo'.
But Scotty isn't cooking now,
For Scotty long is dead;
They say he turned it in through booze
At Thurlagoona shed;
And away across the border
There's a certain jackaroo,
Who for years has never tasted
What he christened 'Wild Stuff Stoo'.

Dipso and the Twins

Jim Haynes

Dipso Dan has made us suffer
For his alcoholic sins,
But strike me pink he made us laugh
The day he met the twins!

They were college mates of Dougie's son
Stayin' over for some function,
The B and S Ball perhaps it was,
Or the game against Cooper's Junction.

And struth were they identical,
Talk about Bib and Bub –
So we thought we'd have a bit of fun
With Dipso down the pub.

The twins of course were in on it.
We made 'em dress the same
And practise identical movements,
And answering to one name.

All the regulars were in on it.
We waited till late in the night –
The plan was we'd ignore the twins
And give Dipso Dan a real fright.

And when we gave the nod to Doug
He says, 'Dipso you've had enough,
You'll be bloody seeing double
If you drink any more of the stuff.'

This is the cue for the twins to enter,
Perfectly synchronised,
They walked right up beside Dan and stopped
And you should have seen his eyes.

And when they ordered a beer in unison
His hair began to stand,
And when they lifted their glasses
And drained 'em as one,
His glass slipped from his hand.

129

'Thanks,' said the twins together,
And then they left the bar.
Dipso Dan was white as a ghost,
We thought we'd gone too far.

'Are you alright Dan?' asked Nugget,
'DDD ... Did you see that?' says Dan,
'It's enough to make me quit the grog,
It's enough to reform a man!'

Well, Doug can't stand it any more,
He wants no damage done.
'Calm down Dan – it was just a joke,
They're identical mates of me son.'

We were having you on – c'mom relax,
You won't see any more of 'em.'
'Well ya had me fooled,' said Dipso Dan,
'Identical eh, all bloody four of 'em!'

Clancy of the Underflow

Anon

Mister Clancy was a debtor, and I'd written him a letter
Bluntly asking for the fiver that I'd lent him long ago.
He was loafing when I lent it and was drinking when he spent it
And he painted things vermilion round about the Underflow.

And an answer quite expected came in ciphers disconnected
And I think the same was written with his pipestem dipped in beer,
It was Clancy's self that penned it, and he said, 'Old chap, I'll send it
When the Lachlan sheds have cut out in the twilight of the year.'

Often in my frenzied fancy curses hurl themselves at Clancy
Gone a-roving down the Cooper where the Western slopers go.
As the sun is slowly setting, Clancy rides along forgetting
All those little obligations due to men he used to know.

For the bush has friends to meet him, and they chuckle as they greet him,
As they join the reckless skiting in the humble shanty bar,
For the view's of beer extended, and the two ales nicely blended
130   And at night the amber radiance of Hennessy's Three Star.

And I somehow rather fancy that I'd like to damage Clancy,
Like to bash that burly figure till he couldn't come or go.
But then I think my turn'll never come while I am vernal,
For he knows the art of boxing, Clancy of the Underflow.

The Swagman at the Golden Gate

Anon

Saint Peter put his quart-pot down and rubbed his saintly eyes,
As through the clouds came a figure bowed pursued by swarms of flies;
Came tramping up to Heaven's Gate and stood there in amaze.
He dropped his swag and tuckerbag and said, 'Well, spare me days!

'I've humped this old Matilda since the age of seventeen.
There's not a track in the great outback that we two haven't seen;
So when I rolled me final swag I thought I'd cleaned the slate –
But stone the crows! Before me nose I see another gate!

'In fifty years of tramping and covering all the while
Twelve miles a day, at least to say with two gates to the mile –
I'm not much good at figures but the way I calculate
In my career I've opened near on fifty thousand gates.

'There was gates that fairly haunt me, there was gates of every sort,
Sagging gates and dragging gates; high, low, long and short.
Gates that seemed to challenge you and gates that seemed to grin –
Lazy gates and crazy gates that hung by half a hinge;

'Gates tied up with fencing wire and gates with fancy scrolls,
With patent catch and homemade latch, and gates made out of poles.
Wide gates and narrow gates, bit barriers and small,
Rusted gates and busted gates – I've wrestled with them all;

'Now, I've opened them and shut 'em till the sight of all I hate,
And I'd sooner miss yer Heavenly Bliss than open that there gate!
What's that? You say you'll open it! Well, that's what I call nice!
And close it too when I've got through? This MUST be Paradise.'

131

The Geebung Polo Club

AB Paterson ('THE BANJO')

It was somewhere up the country, in a land of rock and scrub,
That they formed an institution called the Geebung Polo Club.
They were long and wiry natives from the rugged mountainside,
And the horse was never saddled that the Geebungs couldn't ride;
But their style of playing polo was irregular and rash –
They had mighty little science, but a mighty lot of dash:
And they played on mountain ponies that were muscular and strong,
Though their coats were quite unpolished, and their manes and tails were long.
And they used to train those ponies wheeling cattle in the scrub:
They were demons, were the members of the Geebung Polo Club.

It was somewhere down the country, in a city's smoke and steam,
That a polo club existed, called the Cuff and Collar Team.
As a social institution 'twas a marvellous success,
For the members were distinguished by exclusiveness and dress.
They had natty little ponies that were nice, and smooth, and sleek,
For their cultivated owners only rode 'em once a week.
So they started up the country in pursuit of sport and fame,
For they meant to show the Geebungs how they ought to play the game;
And they took their valets with them – just to give their boots a rub
Ere they started operations on the Geebung Polo Club.

Now my readers can imagine how the contest ebbed and flowed,
When the Geebung boys got going it was time to clear the road;
And the game was so terrific that ere half the time was gone
A spectator's leg was broken – just from merely looking on.
For they waddied one another till the plain was strewn with dead,
While the score was kept so even that they neither got ahead.
And the Cuff and Collar captain, when he tumbled off to die,
Was the last surviving player – so the game was called a tie.

Then the captain of the Geebungs raised him slowly from the ground,
Though his wounds were mostly mortal, yet he fiercely gazed around;
There was no one to oppose him – all the rest were in a trance,
So he scrambled on his pony for his last expiring chance,
For he meant to make an effort to get victory to his side;
So he struck at goal – and missed it – then he tumbled off and died.

By the old Campaspe River, where the breezes shake the grass,
There's a row of little gravestones that the stockmen never pass,
For they bear a crude inscription saying, 'Stranger, drop a tear,
For the Cuff and Collar players and the Geebung boys lie here.'
And on misty moonlit evenings, while the dingoes howl around,
You can see their shadows flitting down that phantom polo ground;
You can hear the loud collisions as the flying players meet,
And the rattle of the mallets, and the rush of ponies' feet,
Till the terrified spectator rides like blazes to the pub –
He's been haunted by the spectres of the Geebung Polo Club.

The Greatest Kick of All

Denis Kevans

Some kicks shine like silver-foil, and some kicks shine like jewels!
But the greatest kickers in the world are playing Aussie Rules.
And the kick that shattered diamonds on a day in Melbourne Town,
Was Mulrooney's seven-pointer, and it clinched the footie crown.
Seven pointer? You are joking! Seven points, mate, every one.
So, zip the lip and listen, and I'll tell you how it's done.

There was Archie McNamara who could kick balls out of sight,
But Archiebald Mulrooney had a kick like dynamite.

He kicked the ball so hard one day, a Melbourne paper states,
St Peter marked it as it whistled past the pearly gates.

When saints were playing secretly to ascend to heaven's station,
They would telephone Mulrooney, he'd improve their levitation.
When the spacecrew in the rocket had no grog there 'not a drap'
He kicked 'em up a carton, with a message 'beer on tap'.
Could he kick? When he was little, he toed his bother's arse,
And he landed in a ski-lift up in Kosciusko Pass.

But he's bruised himself a little and his instep's out of joint,
From kicking up the broken lift at Sydney's Centrepoint.

It's the Melbourne Footie Final, his team is six points shy,
Till Archie, like a swallow, leaps up climbing in the sky,
And, like a Chinese juggler, fingertips the ball, and then
He wipes it on his guernsey, the famous number ten ...

The timer's eyes are tightening, his finger's on the hooter,
And the crowd commence their chanting: Archie boot'er! Archie boot'er!

Archie boot'er? Is that a mantra? (He was studying the Edda)
Archie boot'er! Archie boot'er! or a brand of local cheddar?

Archie boot'er! is that a mountain in Arabian Romance,
Where the prince of jewelled treasures led his harem in a dance?

Where the what ... Boot'er Archie Boot'er ... did they mean? he wonders,
As he gallops for the goalposts, 'n he dodges, dives and blunders,

Boot'er Archie boot'er! And the bell goes ding-a-ling,
And Archie punts that football with a paralyzing ping!

The ball explodes off Archie's boot, now don't none of youse laugh,
Archie kicks that ball so hard, he busts it clean in half!

The two halves keep on going, he has silenced every doubter,
The bladder whizzes through the goal, the cover through the outer.

The crowd is watching breathless ... s'impossible, is he gunna?
It's six points for the bladder, for the cover? just the oner!

This was the seven pointer, the first one ever scored,
Ten times ten thousand voices opened throttles up and roared.

The flagman, like a sailor on a carrier at sea,
Was waving all his flags at once, and then he yelled: Yippee!

The bell it stopped, the whistle blew, the scorer marked it up,
And that's how big Mulrooney won the Melbourne Footie Cup.

That Day at Boiling Downs

Jack Mathieu

He was driving Irish tandem, but perhaps I talk at random –
I'd forgotten for a moment you are not all mulga bred;
What I mean's he had his swag up through his having knocked his nag up;
He had come in off the Cooper – anyhow that's what he said.

And he looked as full of knowledge as a thirty-acre college
As he answered to the question – 'How's things look the way you come?'
'Well, they *were* a trifle willing for a bit. There's been some killing;
In fact, I'm the sole survivor of the district ... mine's a rum!'

Then we all got interested in the chap as he divested
Himself of a fat puppy that he carried in his shirt;
But he said no more until he had put down his swag and billy,
And had taken off his bluchers just to empty out the dirt.

Bits of cork were tied with laces round his hat in many places,
Out of which he gave the puppy some refreshment, and began –
'Sammy Suds was boundary-riding, quite content and law-abiding,
Till he bought some reading-matter one day off a hawker man.

'Then he started to go ratty, and began to fancy that he
Was an Injun on the warpath; so he plaited a lassoo,
Shaved and smeared his face with raddle, and knocked up a greenhide saddle,
After creeping on his belly through the grass a mile or two.

'Then he decked himself in feathers, and went out and scalped some wethers –
Just to give himself a lesson in the sanguinary art;
Sammy then dug up the hatchet, chased a snake but couldn't catch it,
Killed his dog, lassooed a turkey, scalped the cat and made a start.

'And he caused a great sensation when he landed at the station;
And the boss said, "Hullo! Sammy, what the devil's up with you?"
"I am Slimy Snake the Snorter! Wretched pale-face, crave not quarter!"
He replied, and with a shotgun nearly blew the boss in two.

'Next, the wood-and-water joey fell a victim to his bowie,
And the boss's weeping widow got a gash from ear to ear;
And you should have seen his guiver when he scalped the bullockdriver
And made openings for a horseboy, servantmaid, and overseer.

'Counting jackeroos and niggers, he had put up double figures,
When ensued his awful combat with a party of new-chums,
All agog to do their duty, with no thought of home or beauty –
But he rubbed them out as rapid as a schoolboy would his sums.

'Out across the silent river, with some duck-shot in his liver,
Went the storeman, and a lassooed lady left in the same boat.
Sam then solved the Chinese question – or at least made a suggestion –
For he dragged one from a barrel by the tail and cut his throat.

'But, with thus the job completed, Sammy he got overheated
And dropped dead of apoplexy: I felt better when he did!
For I'd got an awful singeing while I watched this mulga engine
Doing all that I've related – through a cracked brick oven lid.

'And when now I find men strangled, or I come across the mangled
Corpses of a crowd of people or depopulated towns,
Or even a blood-stained river, I can scarce repress a shiver,
For my nerves were much affected that day out on Boiling Downs.'

Believe it or Not

A 'Mac' Cormack

He was a gunshearer, a ringer of sheds who had come to the end of his run,
He let out a yell and threw down his blades when the last of his pen was done.
Then he went to the office and asked for his cheque, the Manager paid him in cash,
He rolled his blankets and started for home ere he gambled at cards and got rash.

He camped for the night in some trees by the road, away from the cold and the damp,
When a swagman came out of the evening dusk and started to make his camp.
'Come and join me, old-timer,' the shearer said, 'I've got enough tucker for two.'
'Well, me tuckerbag's light,' the old fellow said, 'Thanks, mate, I don't mind if I do.'

When the meal was over they started to talk the way that travellers do,
The old man said, 'You been travelling long? Your swag and your blankets look new.'
'No, I'm not on the track,' the shearer said, 'I'm a shearer just finished me run;
And I've five hundred dollars in this here purse to prove that me job's been done.'

'Oh? Five hundred dollars?' the old man said, 'That's a lot of money, me son,
'There's many a man been murdered for less and buried some place on the run.'
Then he went to his bag and took out a knife and also a sharpening stone,
As he sharpened the edge he looked up and said, 'You should never have travelled
    alone!'

The shearer thought what a fool he'd been to open his mouth so wide,
He was sure the old man would wait till he slept then bury the knife in his side.
So he laid in his blankets and waited to hear the sound that the swagman slept,
When he heard the first snore he slipped out of bed and into the darkness he crept.

He hadn't gone far when he thought he could hear footsteps not far at his back,
So he quickened his pace from a walk to a trot, but those feet kept pounding the track.
At last he was running flat out in the dark, with fear he was almost blind,
But the faster he went, the faster they came, those footsteps pounding behind.

Then he stumbled and fell with a terrible thud over a log on the track;
As he lay there gasping he fancied he felt the point of the knife in his back.
There he trembled with energy spent, he knew that his race had been run,
When the swagman fell over the log at his side and whispered, 'Who's after us, son?'

The shearer heaved a great sigh of relief and said, 'No one's after us, Dad!'
'Well, if no one's after us,' the swagman said, 'what the hell are we running for, lad?'

Poor Ol' Grandad

Grahame Watt

Poor Ol' Grandad's passed away, cut off in his prime.
He never had a day off crook – gone before his time.
We found him in the dunny, collapsed there on the seat,
A startled look upon his face, his trousers round his feet.
The doctor said his heart was good – fit as any trout.
The constable he had his say, 'foul play' was not ruled out.
There were theories at the inquest of snake bite without trace,
Of redbacks quietly creeping and death from outer space.
No one had a clue at all – the judge was in some doubt,
When Dad was called to have his say as to how it came about.
'I reckon I can clear it up,' said Dad with trembling breath,
'You see it's quite a story – but it could explain his death.
This here exploration mob had been looking at our soil,
And they reckoned that our farm was just the place for oil.
So they came and put a bore down and said they'd make some trials,
Drilled a hole as deep as Hell, they said about three miles!
Well, they never found a trace of oil and off they went, post haste,
And I couldn't see a hole like that go to flamin' waste!
So I moved the dunny over it – real smart move I thought,
I'd never have to dig again – I'd never be 'caught short'.
That day I moved the dunny it looked a proper sight,
But I didn't dream poor Grandad would pass away that night!
Now I reckon what has happened – poor Grandad didn't know,
The dunny was re-located when that night he had to go,
And you'll probably be wondering how poor Grandad did his dash . . .
Well, he always used to hold his breath – until he heard the splash!'

Ode to a Sneeze

George Wallace

I sneezed a sneeze into the air.
It fell to earth I know not where,
But hard and froze were the looks of those
In whose vicinity I snooze.

The Man from Kaomagma

Anon

There was movements on the station, for the wog had passed around,
Salmonella, I regret, had got away.
Makes you run like wild bush horses – Sorbent made a thousand pounds,
And everybody's crack began to fray.

All the tried and noted bush quacks from the stations near and far
Had mustered at the homestead overnight,
But their cures proved ineffective, from cement to Stockholm tar,
And it wasn't plugged by trusty Araldite.

There was Harrigan who strained his piles when a hard-'un got caught up,
The effort turned his hair as white as snow.
So he took to liquid paraffin and drank it by the cup;
But now he don't need that to make him go!

And Clancy, with his overflow, came down to get a hand,
His gripes had got him crippled with the pain,
There was not a dunny held him, not a pedestal could stand
A hundred cu-secs rushing down the drain.

But one was there, a stripling, with his backside tightly shut,
Against wogs that cut a mountain man to size.
He wouldn't go outside, boys, to that lonely little hut
No diarrhoea from him could be prized.

For he hailed from Kaomagma down by Sulphanilamide
Where the wogs are twice as big and twice as tough,
Where their guts are lined with leather (they're impregnable inside)
138   And a man that holds his own is good enough.

When the wog was at its zenith even he was seen to weaken
But surrender? No! He'll not sit on the can!
Till intestinal agony had got him, and he shrieked,
'Look out! I'm going, boys!' and off he ran.

He sent the flintstones flying with the patter of his feet,
He cleared his fallen comrades in his stride;
Then the man from Kaomagma safely gained the toilet seat,
It was grand to find the loo unoccupied!

And he strained there single-handed till his sides were white with foam,
Though he ne'er allowed his sphincter to go slack,
But it was a false alarm and so he turned his head for home
And alone and unassisted staggered back.

But this hardy little mountain man could hardly raise the trots
While Kaomagma settled his insides;
In intestinal panacea, and you may believe or not
But without it he'd have surely filled his strides.

Next morning we were sitting near the woodheap in the sun,
Not saying much, just resting there quite idle,
With one eye on the dunny just in case we had to run,
When the mountain man came out, and with his bridle.

He saddled up his pony and he slowly rode away
Till his figure was a speck against the sky.
And we watched in thoughtful silence; no one had a word to say
When he violently exploded by and by.

Now down by Kaomagma where the little houses raise
Their weather-silvered shingles to the sky,
Where the stockmen go from habit (you can strain for seven days
But you can't get water when the well goes dry);

And down beside the Overflow where the dust is blowing grey
They tell the tale, those men who won't be beat,
And the man from Kaomagma is a household word today,
How he exploded, not admitting he was beat.

A Bushman's Holiday

Colin Newsome

It was not only just by chance, I heard old bushmen say
To get blind drunk and pooh your pants was a Bushman's Holiday
A change from tucker in the scrub, he'd gorge on roasted fowls
And luscious meals cooked in the pub which loosened up his bowels.
Snoring in a hotel bed, he found that he had sinned,
And he had poohed the bed instead when he was passing wind.
Then he'd work for months again. Completely sobered up,
He'd leave to catch the bus or train to see the Melbourne Cup.
Soon he came back to the scrub and looked foolish when he said
'I got drunk at the local pub and poohed my pants instead!'
City folk would look askance, 'Bush' people all would say,
'Good on you mate! You poohed your pants! That's a Bushman's holiday!'

Hard work was done by men who'd shear the sheep and cut the logs.
The bushman helped to pioneer the land with horse and dogs.
He used to live on billy tea and damper and corn beef,
And passing wind both ends would be his best form of relief.
A careless pattern, this, which grew from living on hard tack;
He didn't go so often to the toilet out the back.
Leaning from his saddle seat he'd let the loud winds pass;
His horse would shy and stoop to eat a blade of Mitchell grass.
'You'd better steady up, old mate', companions used to say,
'You are a perfect candidate for a bushman's holiday!'
Sometimes in company he'd forget; or to amuse the boys,
He'd lift his leg up and he'd let some wind with roaring noise.

At Christmas Eve or Yearly Show he always came to town,
Where small town smarties had to go to try and take him down.
Soon everybody was his mate; he'd buy them all some beer,
Then to the toilet ran too late – confirming his worst fear!
He looked sheepish, though he grinned, and foolishly he said
'I thought that I was passing wind, and poohed my pants instead!'
He, wearing no pyjamas, sinned while in a hotel bed;
He went to pass a gust of wind and poohed the bed instead.
When a Bushman came to wed he had to change his ways;
No more to pooh a hotel bed on Bushman's Holidays!
'His new born son is like his dad!' his wife would often say,
'I'll change his nappy. Yes! He's had a Bushman's Holiday!'

I'm the Man

Frank Daniel

I'm the one they talk about, the 'Man from Snowy River'.
The one who did those daring deeds that made old Clancy shiver.
Its true, I had a skinny horse he wasn't all that hot,
In days gone by one had to do his best with what he'd got.
I came from Snowy River, up by Kosciusko's side.
As a lad I had no saddle and bareback learnt to ride.

I heard about the escapee, the 'colt from old Regret',
And always one for a bit of fun, I joined up for a bet.
I turned up at the Homestead with that wild and woolly lot,
And the old man said I'd never do, 'wouldn't keep up at a trot'.
But then my good friend Clancy stood up for me with a grin,
And the old man never argued, 'cause he knew he couldn't win.

We galloped off into the hills, my horse was pulling badly,
Whenever we had company, that horse would go so madly.
We found a mob of brumbies and the colt was with them too,
And the old man gave his orders as into the scrub they flew.
The stockmen rode to wheel them, Clancy raced along their wing,
And my young heart beat so rapidly as I heard his stockwhip ring.

When we reached the mountain's summit, even Clancy pulled his steed,
But the yang that I was riding had no mouth and would not heed.
They say I swung my stockwhip round, they say I gave a cheer,
But I was struggling with my nag, those cheers were yells of fear.
It was only fear that saved me, fear had glued me to my seat,
And I never ever dared deny my confidence in that feat.

When I finally reached the bottom of that terrible descent,
I saw a wisp of dust to tell which way the brumbies went.
I found them in a dead-ender, in a gully walled with stone,
That's how I came to turn 'em back, and how I did it on my own.
Now I know I haven't got the right to stake my claim to fame,
So, having set the story straight, I'll just leave out my name.

The Cross-Eyed Bull

Col Wilson ('BLUE THE SHEARER')

Did I ever tell you blokes about the cross-eyed bull I'd bought?
I couldn't put it in the shows, at least, that's what I thought.
And then I meet this bloke. He says: 'I'd like to take a look.
Those eyes aren't bad. Ring up the vet. His number's in the book.'

Although I don't have too much time, I ring him up that day.
I say: 'Me bull's got cross-eyes. Can you get out straight away?'
And out he comes. He looks. He thinks.
He takes this tube of glass, walks round to the bull's backside,
And puts it up – that hole just under the tail.

Then he draws a mighty breath. He blows. He puffs. He sucks.
The eyes rotate. They straighten up. The vet says 'Fifty bucks.'
'Fifty bloody bucks,' I think, 'Now, there's a tidy sum,
Just for half-a-minute's work,
Blowing up some piece of glass tubing.'

Still and all, I pay the vet, he'd straightened up the eyes.
I take me bull to Sydney Show, and win a major prize.
I cart him round the bush a bit, we're doing well, and then –
I've got to take him home, because his eyes are crossed again.

This time no vet. I know the drill. I'll save meself some dough.
I get me tube, and shove it in, and I begin to blow.
I blow and puff, and puff and blow, and still the eyes stay crossed.
I'm forced to ring the bloody vet, and mourn the dough I've lost.

And out he comes. A very knowing smile upon his face.
He knows I've tried to fix me bull – I've left the tube in place.
He grasps the tube. Reverse it. Gives one tremendous puff.
I see the eyes rotate again, and straighten, sure enough.

I pay the vet, and say to him. 'Look, just before you go,
Don't tell me the secret's knowing in which end to blow.
'No mate.' He says. 'You can blow from North East West or South.
But you didn't think I'd use the end, that you've had in YOUR mouth.'

Showtime

Greg Scott

Two city slickers wandered 'round an agricultural show;
The atmosphere intrigued them, there was much they didn't know.
They'd seen a shearing demo', an exciting woodchop trial;
The rodeo had stunned them, and the clowns had made them smile.

They walked down sideshow alley with the spruikers in pursuit,
And marvelled at pavilions full of vegetables and fruit.
They bought themselves an ice cream and, with showbags brimming full,
Stopped to watch an old bloke groom his giant Santa bull.

They struck up conversation as he squatted on his stool
And answered all their questions, he was clearly no man's fool.
And he soon warmed to his audience and didn't need much push
To regale them with his stories of a lifetime in the bush.

They chatted for a little while, then, as they moved away,
One stopped to ask the old bloke if he had the time of day.
'I left me watch at home', he said, 'I couldn't say for sure,'
Then he swung the bull's balls sideways and said, 'Twenty-five past four.'

They stared at one another then back to where he sat;
Said one slicker to the other, 'My God!! Did you see that?'
They scratched their heads and looked around and tried to work it out;
Some sort of scrotal sundial that they'd never heard about.

The old bloke saw them looking on in awe and admiration,
Then came up with the answer, quite a simple explanation.
He said 'I'm sorry gentlemen, I didn't mean to shock,
But when I swing the bull's balls sideways, I can see the Town Hall clock!'

How We Cashed the Pig

Jack Sorensen

We shore for a farmer at Wallaby Bend,
   Myself and my mate, Dan McLean;
And while we were toiling, an old bushman friend,
   Wrote saying the farmer was mean.

We finished his shearing (the flock was not big),
   And imagine our wrath and dismay,
When he went to a sty and returned with a pig,
   And said, 'This is all I can pay.'

We set off next morn down the long dusty track,
   In the blackest of humours I fear.
I carried our pig in a bag on my back,
   While McLean trudged along with our gear.

I talked as we journeyed – it lightened my load –
   And was pointing out how we'd been robbed,
When we came to a shanty that stood by the road,
   And I turned out my pockets and sobbed.

'Cheer up,' cried McLean, 'we will drink and forget
   That old blighter back at the Bend.'
I said in soft accents imbued with regret,
   'Alas! we have nothing to spend.'

My comrade replied, 'What a dullard you are,
   We'll drink and make merry in style.'
Then seizing our pig he walked into the bar,
   And ordered our drinks with a smile.

Our host filled 'em up and went off with the pig,
   As though the affair was not strange;
We scarcely had time our refreshments to swig,
   When he came back with ten piglets change.

We stayed at the shanty that night and next day
   (Good liquor was much cheaper then),
And gladly rejoicing we went on our way,
   With a basket of eggs and a hen.

The Trailer

Col Wilson ('BLUE THE SHEARER')

In my very early childhood, I learned to crawl and walk,
To use the potty on command, to gurgle, goo, and talk,
And in good time, I went to school, and learned to read and write,
To co-exist in playgrounds. To run and jump, and fight.

When I grew up, I got a job. A wife, and family too.
In short, I did the kind of things that most men get to do.
And whilst my life may not have gained the ultimate success,
I can say, with modesty, it's not a total mess.

That's why I find it difficult to contemplate my failure;
Despite my years of trying to, I still can't back a trailer.
All my friends who have one, seem to do it well,
So why do my attempts end up a journey into hell?

When I bought my trailer, six by four and painted green,
I thought it was the nicest trailer I had ever seen.
I hooked it up, and drove it home, determined to arrive
In a blaze of glory, by backing up the drive.

I knew the theory, left-hand down, to back it to the right,
Right-hand down to guide it left. As I said before, I'm bright.
But theory into practice, though it may sound commonsense,
For me, seemed quite impossible, and so, I hit the fence.

Quite a crowd soon gathered round. Advice was far from lacking,
With every new arrival saying: 'Having trouble backing?'
I finally unhooked it, and wheeled it through the gate,
Up the drive, and round the back, so I could concentrate

On learning how to back it, this trailer so perverse
Instead of getting better though, I kept on getting worse.
You can see where I've been learning, my area of practice,
The woodpile fence is broken, and all the shrubs are cactus.

The corner of the garage is gone, no trees are left alive,
And I've completely flattened both the downpipes in the drive.
The clothes hoist has a nasty bend. The sprinklers are no more,
And the imprint of the number plate is on the toilet door.

145

My backing reputation now, is legend in this town.
I'm down the street. Some smartarse says:
'Hey Blue it's lefthand down.'
But since I've bought my trailer, I have to persevere.
Accidents don't worry me. It's ridicule I fear.

So, when I take it to the dump, I pray no one's around,
But the news just spreads like wildfire. Spectators abound.
They hope I'm going to duplicate that trailer-backing sin.
And go too near the edge again, and drop the damn thing in.

But finally, I've solved it. The problem's not so hard.
I only drive it forward now, when I'm not in the yard.
In the matter of reversing, there's really nothing to it.
When I need to back it, I just get the wife to do it.

Nine Miles from Gundagai

Trad/Jack Moses

I'm used to punching bullock teams across the hills and plains.
I've teamed outback for forty years in blazing droughts and rains.
I've lived a heap of troubles down without a blooming lie,
But I can't forget what happened to me nine miles from Gundagai.

'Twas getting dark, the team got bogged, the axle snapped in two,
I lost me matches and me pipe, gawd, what was I to do?
The rain came on, 'twas bitter cold, and hungry too was I,
And the dog ... he shat in me tucker box, nine miles from Gundagai!

Some blokes I know has lots of luck, no matter how they fall,
But there was I, Lord love a duck, no bloody luck at all!
I couldn't make a pot of tea or get me trousers dry,
And the dog shat in me tucker box, nine miles from Gundagai!

I can forgive the blinking team, I can forgive the rain,
I can forgive the cold and dark and go through it all again,
I can forgive me rotten luck – but hang me till I die ...
146 I can't forgive that bloody dog – nine miles from Gundagai!

There's Only the Two of Us Here

Ted Harrington

I camped one night in an empty hut on the side of a lonely hill,
I didn't go much on empty huts, but the night was awful chill.
So I boiled me billy and had me tea, and seen that the door was shut,
Then I went to bed in an empty bunk by the side of the old slab hut.

It must have been about twelve o'clock – I was feeling cosy and warm –
When at the foot of me bunk I sees a horrible ghostly form.
It seemed in shape to be half an ape with a head like a chimpanzee,
But wot the hell was it doin' there, and wot did it want with me?

You may say if you please that I had DTs or call me a crimson liar,
But I wish you had seen it as plain as me, with its eyes like coals of fire.
Then it gave a moan and a horrible groan that curdled me blood with fear,
And, 'There's only the two of us here,' it ses. 'There's only the two of us here!'

I kept one eye on the old hut door and one on the awful brute;
I only wanted to dress meself and get to the door and scoot.
But I couldn't find where I'd left me boots so I hadn't a chance to clear
And, 'There's only the two of us here,' it moans. 'There's only the two of us here!'

I hadn't a thing to defend meself, not even a stick or a stone,
And 'There's only the two of us here!' it ses again with a horrible groan.
I thought I'd better make some reply, though I reckoned me end was near,
'By the Holy Smoke, when I find me boots, there'll be only one of us here!'

I gets me hands on me number tens and out through the door I scoots,
And I lit the whole of the ridges up with the sparks from me blucher boots.
So I've never slept in a hut since then, and I tremble and shake with fear
When I think of the horrible form wot moaned, 'There's only the two of us here!'

The Ghost of the Murderer's Hut

AB Paterson ('THE BANJO')

My horse had been lamed in the foot
  In the rocks at the back of the run,
So I camped at the Murderer's Hut,
  At the place where the murder was done.

The walls were all spattered with gore,
  A terrible symbol of guilt;
And the bloodstains were fresh on the floor
  Where the blood of the victim was spilt.

The wind hurried past with a shout,
  The thunderstorm doubled its din
As I shrank from the danger without,
  And recoiled from the horror within.

When lo! at the window a shape,
  A creature of infinite dread;
A thing with the face of an ape,
  And with eyes like the eyes of the dead.

With the horns of a fiend, and a skin
  That was hairy as satyr or elf,
And a long, pointed beard on its chin –
  My God! 'twas the Devil himself.

In anguish I sank on the floor,
  With terror my features were stiff,
Till *the thing* gave a kind of a roar,
  Ending up with a resonant 'Biff!'

Then a cheer burst aloud from my throat,
  For the thing that my spirit did vex
Was naught but an elderly goat –
  Just a goat of the masculine sex.

When his master was killed he had fled,
   And now, by the dingoes bereft,
The nannies were all of them dead,
   And only the billy was left.

So we had him brought in on a stage
To the house where, in style, he can strut,
And he lives to a fragrant old age
   As the Ghost of the Murderer's Hut.

Lay of the Motor Car

AB Paterson ('THE BANJO')

We're away! and the wind whistles shrewd
   In our whiskers and teeth;
And the granite-like grey of the road
   Seems to slide underneath.
As an eagle might sweep through the sky,
   So we sweep through the land;
And the pallid pedestrians fly
   When they hear us at hand.

We outpace, we outlast, we outstrip!
   Not the fast-fleeing hare,
Nor the racehorses under the whip,
   Nor the birds of the air
Can compete with our swiftness sublime,
   Our ease and our grace.
We annihilate chickens and time
   And policemen and space.

Do you mind that fat grocer who crossed?
   How he dropped down to pray
In the road when he saw he was lost;
   How he melted away
Underneath, and there rang through the fog
   His earsplitting squeal
As he went – Is that he or a dog,
   That stuff on the wheel?

The Saucepan Cupboard

Col Wilson ('BLUE THE SHEARER')

There's a corner in our kitchen, a dark and sombre place,
Where frying pans and saucepans disappear without a trace.
I'm sure that goblins live there, maybe gremlins, I don't know,
But that corner saucepan cupboard is a place I'm scared to go.

I used to think the cupboard underneath the sink was bad,
Trying to find a dishcloth can nearly send me mad,
But that corner saucepan cupboard, where the goblins dwell,
Is, to a sensitive new-age guy, a sure foretaste of Hell.

The frying pan I'm seeking's on the bottom of the pile,
And as for finding saucepan lids – It's OK for you to smile,
But I'll bet in YOUR house, that dreadful goblin clan
Is setting up an ambush for the unsuspecting man.

It doesn't seem to matter with what care I pack them in,
When the door is open, there's an avalanche of tin.
I watch with fear and horror, as I leap out of the way,
And think maybe Kentucky Fried should be the meal today.

That way, I wouldn't have to cook, use pot or frying pan.
Kentucky Fried, or Fish and Chips, that seems a decent plan.
But what about those pots and pans strewn around the floor?
I pick them up, and throw them in, and try to close the door.

My darling says I'm paranoid. It could be that she's right,
But I'll swear I hear those Goblins in the wee hours of the night,
Working with their gremlin mates at sabotage, so when
The cupboard door is open, they cascade out again.

I know there's something in there. The cat is terrified,
And won't go near the cupboard for fear of what's inside.
Cats understand the occult. I explain this to my wife,
She says she's never heard such stupid rubbish in her life.

If frying pans, and saucepans, and the other things in there,
Were only made disposable, I wouldn't have a care.
I'd do away with saucepan cupboards, make use of the space,
The goblins then, might go away, to haunt some other place.

Now I don't want to scare you, but keep the kids away,
From dark and sombre cupboards where the goblins like to play.
If frying pans can disappear, so can little kids,
To be held forever captive amongst those saucepan lids.

So for your own protection, and that of the family,
Take a few precautions, and some good advice from me.
Lock the cupboard, take the key, and throw it far away,
And tell your wife and family that: 'We're eating out today.'

Tryin' to Get a Quid

Richard R Davidson

The old man sat on the tractor seat,
There was dust in his hair and grease on his feet,
And he said, 'This job has got me beat,
Tryin' to get a quid.

'The pressure's low and the engine's hot,
The tracks are loose and the gears are shot,
But this old bitch is all I've got,
To try and get a quid.'

He turned down the bank with an awful roar,
And he made for the other side full bore,
And he opened the taps as he hit the floor,
Tryin' to get a quid.

But the scoop got snagged on a big white rock,
And he swore and cursed as he did his block,
Put the governor over the safety stop.
Tryin' to get a quid.

She blew right up when the con rod broke,
And the old man died in a cloud of smoke.
As he passed he said, 'It ain't no joke
This tryin' to make a quid!'

But ... he was insured for twenty grand,
Which the company paid on his wife's demand,
And she said as she took the cheque in hand ...
'At last he's got a quid!'

Chain-saw Massacre

Col Wilson ('BLUE THE SHEARER')

I'm not a proper greenie – I still burn wood for heat.
Wood that's dead and fallen down. Green trees I won't deplete.
I scour the paddocks round my town, amid the brush and fern,
To find some wood, and cut it up, and take it home to burn.

But Bushman's saws, and axes, have proven such a bore,
That I've gone and bought a chain-saw, from the local store.
'Now is the winter of my discontent.' That bloody saw of mine,
Must have been in Shakespeare's mind, when he penned that line.

I'm not a man of violence. I'm rarely known to curse.
(Now and then, I'll use one to illustrate a verse.)
I'm a quiet man. A gentle man. Forever seeking peace,
But lately, violence in my soul is fighting for release.

As an instrument of torture, the chain-saw's pretty good,
But it's pretty bloody useless when it comes to cutting wood.
There you go. I'm swearing. That's not like me at all.
My parents used to caution me that bad words mean a fall.

I recall my mother warning me, when I was just a lad,
That: 'Swearing's really wicked.' 'That's right,' said my Dad,
'Naughty little curse words, such as dash and blow,
Lead you on to worse words, and take you down below.'

In hindsight now, I understand why my folk rarely swore –
They never had to use a two-stroke motor-bloody-saw.
By non-operating chain-saws, they were not tormented.
The stinking, rotten, mongrel things, hadn't been invented.

They were not frustrated when the bastard wouldn't start.
Or wouldn't cut, or threw its chain. No. Swearing is an art
Perfected by the chain-saw user out there in the mulga,
Inventing brand new phrases, both profane and vulgar.

Oh! They won't start the chain-saw. On that point, I agree.
But they lift the art of swearing to the very 'nth' degree.
Bullockies and shearers, stevedores and boozers,
Are just ordinary swearers, compared to chain-saw users.

I've developed such a hatred, for everyone connected,
With chain-saw manufacture, and even those suspected
Of adding to the torture of chain-saw using folk,
Who suffer from their failure. I tell you. It's no joke.

But I am going to be revenged. My demonic plan
Is to become a chain-saw massacrer. To dismember every man,
From the one who first invented it, whoever that may be,
And finish with that mongrel bastard who sold mine to me.

What joy! What retribution! All that blood and gore.
Armless, legless, headless corpses, strewn around the floor.
But that lovely vision in my mind is rudely blown apart –
I can't be a chain-saw massacrer,
THE BLOODY THING WON'T START!!!

The Dogs' Meeting

Anon

The dogs once held a meeting, they came from near and far.
Some came by aeroplane and others came by car,
But before they were allowed inside the meeting hall,
Each had to take his arsehole off and hang it on the wall.

And hardly were they seated, each mother, son and sire,
When a dirty little yeller dog began to holler, 'Fire!'
Then out they ran in panic, they didn't stop to look,
Each dog just grabbed an arsehole from off the nearest hook.

Because they got them all mixed up it makes them very sore,
To have to wear an arsehole that they've never worn before!
Sometimes it's unbearable and, if you look around,
You'll see dogs try to make it fit by rubbing on the ground.

And that's the reason why you see, when walking down the street,
All dogs will stop and swap a smell with every dog they meet.
And that is why a dog will leave a nice, big, juicy bone,
To sniff another arsehole – he hopes to find his own!

A Snake Yarn

WT Goodge ('THE COLONEL')

'You talk of snakes,' said Jack the Rat,
'But, blow me, one hot summer,
I seen a thing that knocked me flat –
Fourteen foot long, or more than that,
It was a reg'lar hummer!
Lay right along a sort of bog,
  Just like a log!

'The ugly thing was lyin' there
And not a sign o' movin',
Give any man a nasty scare;
Seen nothin' like it anywhere
Since I first started drovin'.
And yet it didn't scare my dog.
  Looked like a log!

'I had to cross that bog, yer see,
And bluey I was humpin';
But wonderin' what that thing could be
A-layin' there in front o' me
I didn't feel like jumpin'.
Yet, though I shivered like a frog,
  It *seemed* a log!

'I takes a leap and lands right on
The back of that there whopper!'
He stopped. We waited. Then Big Mac
Remarked, 'Well, then, what happened, Jack?'
'Not much, said Jack, and drained his grog.
  'It *was* a log!'

Piddling Pete

Anon

A farmer's dog came into town,
His christian name was Pete.
A noble pedigree he had,

To see him was a treat.
And as he trotted down the street
'Twas beautiful to see
His work on every corner,
His work on every tree.

He watered every gateway, too,
And never missed a post,
For piddling was his speciality
And piddling was his boast.
The city curs looked on, amazed,
With deep and jealous rage
To see a simple country dog
The piddler of the age!

Then all the dogs from everywhere
Were summoned with a yell
To sniff the country stranger o'er
And judge him by the smell.
Some thought that he a king might be,
Beneath his tail, a rose.
So every dog drew near to him
And sniffed him by the nose.

They smelled him over one by one,
They smelled him two by two;
But noble Pete, in high disdain,
Stood still till they were through.
Then, just to show the whole shebang
He didn't give a damn
He trotted in a grocer's shop
And piddled on a ham.

He piddled in a mackerel keg,
He piddled on the floor,
And when the grocer kicked him out
He piddled through the door.
Behind him all the city dogs
Lined up with instinct true
To start a piddling carnival
And see the stranger through.

They showed him every piddling post
They had in all the town,
And started in, with many a wink,
To pee the stranger down.
They sent for champion piddlers
Who were always on the go
And who sometimes gave a piddling stunt
Or gave a piddling show.

They sprung these on him suddenly
When midway through the town.
Pete only smiled, and piddled off
The ablest, white or brown.
For he was with them, every trick,
With vigour and with vim.
A thousand piddles, more or less,
Were all the same to him.

So he was wetting merrily
With hind leg kicking high
When most were hoisting legs in bluff
And piddling mighty dry.
On and on, Pete sought new grounds
By piles of scrap and rust
Till every city dog ran dry
And only piddled dust.

Still on and on went noble Pete
As wet as any rill
When all the champion city dogs
Had come to a standstill.
Then Pete did free-hand piddling
With fancy flirts and flips
Like the 'double dip' and 'gimlet twist'
And all the latest hits.

And all the time the country dog
Did never wink or grin
But blithely piddled out of town
As he had piddled in.

The city dogs a meeting held
To ask, 'What did defeat us?'
But no one ever put them wise
That Pete had diabetes!

Directions

Janine Haig

He was in some far-off paddock doing something to a fence
When he called up on the 2-way in a voice all tight and tense:
'I've got a punctured tyre and the spare is flat as well.
It's hot, I'm out of water and my day has gone to Hell.
I need another tyre – there's a couple in the shed,
So look at them real careful; bring the one with the thickest tread.
Could you throw it in an old ute and bring it out to me?
I know it's quite a bother – there's no other choice, you see.

'If you go along the road across the creek heading east
And follow it until you reach the carcass of a beast,
Then chuck a left along the track – it's rough but pretty straight –
So take it easy as you go until you reach the gate.
The gate's an old wire mongrel so undo it with great care
(When I get the time it's on my list to be repaired).
Head west along the fence-line till the big dam comes in sight,
Then when you reach the pig trap, spin the wheel and chuck a right.

'Take care across the gully – it's better if you creep,
Put the ute in low range cos it's slippery and it's steep.
When you reach the bore drain you will see it's pretty clogged,
Find second gear and give it some – or else you might get bogged.
There's a stony ridge ahead then, where the road is hard to pick,
But if you keep on heading northish where the mulga's pretty thick
You'll come out on a grassy plain – where all the grass is dead,
Then you'll see some tangled wire and old fence posts up ahead.
And over to your left you'll see a big old gidyea tree,
And underneath it, red with rage,
A bloke in shorts – that's me!'

Someone Pinched Our Firewood

Jim Haynes

Someone pinched our firewood, what a mongrel act!
It's about as low as you can go – but it's a bloody fact!
We spent a whole day cutting it – bashing round the scrub,
I bet the bloke who pinched it spent the whole day in the pub.

We nearly got the trailer bogged – flat tyre on the ute,
So when we finally got it home we thought, 'You bloody beaut!
No more cutting firewood at least until the Spring.'
We unloaded it and split it up to size and everything.

Stacked it really neatly, a ute and trailer load,
Trouble was we stacked it too close to the road!
And some miserable mongrel started sneaking 'cross the park,
Every couple of nights or so to pinch some – after dark.

Now, as luck would have it, we had gunpowder in the shed,
We took the middle out of one log and we packed that in instead.
Then back upon the pile it went ... next night he took the bait,
We'd soon know who the bugger was, we settled back to wait.

He was a contract shearer, only new in town,
I never got to meet him 'cos he didn't stick around.
The house was only rented, the whole town heard the pop,
They reckon the Aga Cooker split right across the top.

Justice is its own reward but I wish I'd heard that cove,
Explaining to the landlord the condition of his stove.
The folk in our town mostly are a warm and friendly lot,
Until you pinch our firewood – and then we're bloody not!

The Day I Shot the Telly

Bob Magor

I prepared to shoot a rabbit
Which on weekends was my habit
In the sixties, back when I was just a lad.
And I grabbed my gun and bolted
With the rifle breech unbolted.
I'd been taught this safety practice by my dad.

From the garden Mum was pleading
Could I help her with some weeding?
Thought the rifle now was loaded, it could wait.
For I'd only be a minute
So I left the bullet in it
And I stood the loaded gun against the gate.

Well the daylight was receding
By the time I finished weeding
So I grabbed the gun and wandered back indoors.
Where the TV still was going
It was 'Bandstand' that was showing
So I settled back to see what was in store.

Little Pattie looking pretty
And the Delltones sang a ditty
With the legend JO'K all systems go.
All the music highly rated
But the chap I really hated
Was that Brian Henderson, who ran the show.

He was talking when I got him
For I drew a bead and shot him.
I said 'Bang bang' but no corpse there could I see.
So I lined up with a snigger,
Cocked the gun and pulled the trigger
And the world as I then knew it ceased to be.

Cripes, I forgot the gun was loaded
And the TV screen exploded.
As I sat in fright cemented to the chair.
Shattered picture tube suspended
And the goldfish tank upended
As the smell of smoke and gunfire filled the air.

There were valves and things exploding.
My composure was eroding.
As a burst of sparks drew patterns on the wall.
And I got a sinking feeling
Watching shrapnel peel the ceiling
And a smoking cat ran howling through the hall.

I had hit the man dead centre.
Yes, I'd fixed that damn presenter
Though he haunted me with no time to rejoice.
From a crackling left hand speaker
Somewhat dry and slightly weaker
Out this hole that once was picture, came his voice.

It was a nasty shock he gave me
Just as Mum rushed in to save me
But the sight of so much carnage made her stare.
As she viewed the lounge room blasted
I dribbled out, 'I got the bastard'
And I heard Mum say, 'I'm pleased, but who and where?'

I'd acute smoke inhalation,
Shock and TV screen abrasion
And I will admit, I'd messed myself as well.
Quite relieved it all had ended,
Then a chilling thought descended . . .
When he came home I'd the old man still to tell.

I was shaking like a jelly
And there wasn't much on telly,
So I went to bed, quite early I recall.
'Cause I didn't feel like eating,
I was bracing for a beating.
When Dad came home I heard him through the wall.

From outside Dad yelled and stuttered
'Someone singed the cat,' he muttered.
He was not a happy pappy, I could tell.
I'd contractions in my belly
When Mum choked 'Bob shot the telly.' –
And the old man had a door to fix as well.

Well I had a nasty time then
Child abuse was not a crime then.
Father fixed the box and had the lounge re-done.
Though for weeks he weighed the option
Of my name up for adoption . . .
But he kept me 'cause I was his only son.

Skinnydipping

Murray Hartin

The temperature was soaring, the sun was beating down,
Matt walked by the river on the other side of town.
He had a look about and there was no-one there but him,
So he ripped off all his clothes and jumped in for a swim.

The water cooled his sweaty hide, he swam and splashed about,
He felt a whole lot better and started to get out.
He headed for his clothes and was reaching for his jocks,
When two young girls came walking from behind a pile of rocks.

Matty quickly grabbed his hat and covered up his front,
The girls just stood and giggled, so Matt became quite blunt.
'If you two girls were ladies, you'd turn around,' said Matt.
'And if you, sir, were a gentleman, you'd bow and raise your hat!'

The Addict

Col Wilson ('BLUE THE SHEARER')

This bloke in the surgery, says: 'Doctor. I'm in pain.
I broke me whosiwhatsis. Can you straighten it again?'
'Let's take a look.' The Doctor says: 'My God, that does look sore.
I've never seen a fellow with a broken one before.
You can tell me how you did it, while I fix this plaster cast.'
'OK Doc. I'll tell you. Just straighten out me mast.'

'It's all because this wife of mine, is one-armed bandit mad.
She plays the pokies day and night. She's really got it bad.
In the early hours, this morning, I woke, and thought – "Ullo" –
She's got me by the gearshift, and she's moving to and fro.
But she's dreaming. Playing pokies. Gripping hard enough to choke it.
For half an hour she kept it up. And in the end, she broke it.'

'Half an hour?' the Doctor says. 'It must have hurt like hell.
She might have thought to let you go, if you'd have thought to yell.'
'I couldn't,' says the bloke. 'The pain was murder in me loins.
And anyway. Me mouth was filled with fifty ten-cent coins.'

161

'Ough!' A Fonetic Fansy

WT Goodge ('THE COLONEL')

The baker-man was kneading dough
  And whistling softly, sweet and lough.
Yet ever and anon he'd cough
  As though his head was coming ough!
'My word!' said he, 'but this is rough;
  This flour is simply awful stough!'
He punched and thumped it through and through
  As all good bakers always dough!
'I'd sooner drive,' said he, 'a plough,
  Than be a baker anyhough!'
Thus spake the baker kneading dough;
  But don't let on I told you sough!

A Grave Situation

Claude Morris

When I staggered away from my favourite pub,
The night was dark and still,
And I thought I'd take a short cut home,
That led over Cemetery Hill.
Now I'm not a hero as everyone knows,
And I have no reckless trends,
But ghosts and the like leave me cold, as it were,
And spirits and I are old friends.

I wobbled along through the cemetery gates,
Begging my legs to behave,
And everything went pretty well, so I thought,
Till I fell down a newly-dug grave.
For a moment I thought I had landed in hell,
And ended my earthly career.
I sniffed like a hound for the sulphurous fumes,
Expecting Old Nick to appear.

But reason returned and I staggered erect,
My prison so dark, to survey,
And tested my bones for a fracture or two,

But everything functioned OK.
I made a feeble attempt to get out,
But it needed no more than a glance
To tell me that in my condition,
I hadn't the ghost of a chance.

I reckoned I'd have a lay-off for awhile,
And when I woke sober and fit,
I'd surely come up with a first-class idea,
That would get me up out of the pit.
Just then I could hear fast oncoming steps,
That seemed too good to be true,
But ere I could 'Coo-ee' or offer advice,
In the grave there were suddenly two!

It happened he fell in the grave's other end,
With no one to cushion his fall;
But he rose like a shot with a high-pitched yelp,
And attempted to scale up the wall.
This chap was at pains to be up and away,
As the capers he cut, plainly told;
He jumped and he scrambled and jumped again,
But his fingers and toes wouldn't hold.

I hadn't yet spoken – I'd hardly a chance,
The way he cavorted about,
And I had to admire the way that he fought
To sever all ties and get out.
Of course, he believed there was nobody near –
He thought he was there all alone,
And I got the idea it had entered his head
That the grave was becoming his own.

I felt a bit sad for the poor little guy,
Now acting a little distraught,
And I thought he'd relax if I gave him the drum,
That he wasn't alone, as he thought.
So I walked up behind him and tapped on his back
As he paused for another wild bid;
'You CAN'T make it mate,' I breathed in his ear –
But by the Lord Harry, he DID!

The Will

Bob Miller

All the tears have long ceased falling from our in-laws and our kin
Since the day my English aunty cashed her chips and chucked it in.
Do not think us heartless scoundrels if we mock this solemn show
But our family's seen recession and we're rather short on dough.
We just viewed her timely passing like some wilting daffodil,
'Till a letter from her lawyers said we're mentioned in the will.
Well, Eureka, what a beauty. Just imagine how we felt.
No more we'd live in poverty, no more we'd strain the belt.

This dear old duck was loaded, couldn't count the dough she's got.
We could sell this cockroach castle, build a mansion, buy a yacht.
We'd be livin' soon in luxury. God bless her now-failed health –
And me, her only favourite nephew, surely I would cop this wealth.
So I rang the council foreman, said 'It's me, you ugly slob.
You can keep the pay you owe me and just stick your flamin' job.
No I won't be back tomorrow and I won't be back next year.
See I'm off to merry England. You'll just have to persevere.'

Then I hurried to the banker, said 'You slimy crawlin' louse,
You can shove that loan I begged for, for that stinkin' little house.
I'll have more than Kerry Packer, and me aunty you can thank.
Not one word, you silly jackass, or I might buy your little bank.'
This newfound strength I revelled in, I was feeling strong and hearty,
But I had to sell the Kingswood for some dough to chuck a party.
As I clambered up the gangplank I then told the watching pack,
'Yeah, the richest thing you'll ever see, is me when I get back.'

When they read my dear old aunty's will they started from the ground.
The butler copped the silverware, the maid ... a thousand pound.
She left Aunt Doris one Rolls-Royce, old Joe one block of flats,
Then the room was stunned to silence as the lawyer mentioned ... cats,
To those mongrel, moggy mousers she'd bequeathed a million quid –
Well, I very nearly fainted and I'm sure Aunt Martha did.
But I knew my turn was coming as the lawyers carried on:
'I now leave my greatest treasure to my sister's darling son.'

'I leave to him my family ring to carry through the years.'
'A stupid ring!' I said. 'That's all?' I near burst into tears.
I grabbed the lawyer by the throat and I almost run amok.
Saying, 'Give the cat the bloody ring, I'll take the million bucks.'
The hand of fate plays cruel tricks, as I learned on my way home;
For days I leaned across the rail and watched the briny foam.
In a fit of mad depression just for what she'd done to me,
I took old aunty's cursed ring and hurled it, in the sea.

Then I settled back into a chair with a smile upon my face,
But while reading through the papers I collapsed in sheer disgrace.
See, the ring that was still sinking now a thousand fathoms down
Had belonged to Mary, Queen of Scots ... worth forty million pound!
I'm back home now, I'm on the dole and living in a tent.
I ponder on my fortune – how it came and sort of went.
I sit each night upon this rock, just toying, with a notion:
Yeah, I wonder just how hard it is to drain that cursed ocean.

The Liars

Henry E Horne

Ten boys sat in a ring and played at telling lies,
An outback pastime, with a strayed young dog for prize.
The Parson they informed, who strolled to see their fun,
The pup was for the cove who told the biggest one.

The good old man looked upon that ring of boys and sighed.
'I'm sorry to hear such a thing as this,' he cried.
'I never dared to tell a lie, nor ever knew,
Such sinful sport, my lads, when I was young like you.'

Ten faces fell, not from shame, but sheer defeat;
Ten little liars dropped the game, for they were beat.
Ten boys arose – a sullen band – quite broken up;
And Jim, the judge, said, 'Billy, hand the bloke the pup.'

And Yet Sometimes ...

Recollections & Reflections

*A*h, whatever happened to nostalgia? How the human spirit yearns for what is gone! Australian writers of verse share, with all those who ever wrote verse, the desire to recollect and reflect on past pleasures, sorrows and mistakes. Because our heritage is defined by a pioneering past we tend to feel the passing of that era more than writers from other countries feel their longer histories weighing down on them.

Memories of childhood feature quite prominently in this section, as do memories of days gone by, especially in the bush, when we had more time to spare and more time to spend with other people. There's the constant longing, in poems like 'Bees' and 'My Hat', for things that are gone and for times now past.

Some of my favourites are the poems recalling camaraderie or poignant moments of friendship and recognition, like 'The Austral Light' and 'Ned's Delicate Way'. Perhaps most powerful of all are the poems of lost opportunity like 'Song of Childhood' and 'When the Ladies Come to the Shearing Shed'. Nostalgia, like fine wine, improves with age and the realisation that the time available for us to enjoy our nostalgic thoughts (or our best reds) is ever decreasing – a very nostalgic thought in itself! So . . .

> Put the good wine down to rest,
> But please don't save it up for 'best'
> Let me taste yours, and you taste mine,
> For life's too short to drink bad wine!

And Yet Sometimes ...

Bruce Simpson ('LANCEWOOD')

Now the droving is done and no more from the scrub,
Come the drovers to camp by the Newcastle pub,
They are gone from the routes with their horses and packs
And the tall grasses grow o'er their deep trodden tracks.
Now there's never a campfire the stockroute along,
For the transports have silenced the night-watcher's song.
And yet sometimes on nights filled with thunder and rain,
In my dreams I am back on the stockroutes again
With a wild restless mob ever ready to rush,
On a camp mid the antbeds and dry underbrush.

'Twas a grim hundred miles down the Murranjii track
Where the night camps were bad and the scrublands were black,
A vast wasteland unwanted that seemed without end
From the scrub covered jump-up to Bucket Creek bend.
Then we prayed for fine weather – a clear Autumn sky
When we entered the scrubs of the grim Murranjii.
And we doubled the watches and cursed long and plain
When the Murranjii met us with thunder and rain,
For when big mobs rushed there, there was little recourse,
Save to trust to your luck and to trust to your horse,
And there, many a drover when things went amiss
In the Murranjii scrublands faced grim Nemesis.

And the big bullocks knew for they gave no rest
As they grudgingly walked from their runs in the West,
For they sulked and they pined for their far distant hills
And they scorned the long troughs at the Murranjii mills.
They would moan soft and low for their pandanus springs
And they watched us like hawks from the lead and the wings.
But they'd ring in rebellion and baulk in dismay
When the Mitchell grass plains stretched ahead and away.
Now there's never a campfire the stockroutes along
For the transports have silenced the night-watcher's song.

There is bitumen now where the big diesels roll
And the dead men grow lonely by Murranjii hole.
Now the shy curlews wail and their sad chorus swells
As though missing the music of Condamine bells.
For the droving is done and the drovers no more
String their mobs to the lake by the Newcastle store,
They have hung up their whips and like me settled down
In a job that's secure mid the comforts of town,
And yet sometimes on nights filled with thunder and rain
In my dreams I am back on the stockroutes again,
With a good horse beneath – with the timber a-crack
'Round a mob of wild stores on the Murranjii track.

Song of Childhood

John Dengate

Where have the days of my childhood gone –
Time has plundered the years.
Stolen my gift of golden days;
Left me with ashes and tears.
I've wandered along the lonely roads;
Over the paddocks I've run . . .
Drugged with the summer cicadas' song;
Drunk with freedom and sun.

Take me back to a fibro house
In a suburb carved from the bush.
Give me an acre of grass to cut
And a rusty mower to push.
Give me a summery Saturday
Just after the war was won,
With Dad and my uncles drinking beer,
Sprawled on the grass in the sun.

They spoke with a curious, proud elan;
Their laughter was careless and free.
Fresh from the battles against Japan
They seemed immortal to me.
But how can an innocent boy discern
What's fallible, false or true?
Their mortal footsteps are faltering now
And mine are faltering too.

Bring out the bat and the worn cork ball
And we'll bowl at an old wooden case.
She'll jump and turn on the asphalt road . . .
She'll come at a lively pace!
But barefoot, careless and undismayed
We'll drive and hammer and glance . . .
Now the ball is lost in the tangled years –
My hands couldn't hold the chance.

When Bertha Comes to Tea

Henry Lawson

When Bertha comes to tea
(The kettle sings in glee)
The cups and saucers clatter
As they hear her chatter, chatter.
And you wonder what's the matter
When Bertha comes to tea.

When Bertha comes to tea
(Her age, I think, is three)
She keeps you in a flutter,
Cutting cake and bread and butter.
'Where *does* it go?' you mutter,
When Bertha comes to tea.

When Bertha comes to tea
(She isn't shy, not she)
The house cat sees, clearly,
She loves him very dearly,
But – he's suffocated, nearly,
When Bertha comes to tea.

When Bertha comes to tea
(Along with you and me)
She's sure to bring her dolly;
Then away with melancholy,
And let us all be jolly
When Bertha comes to tea.

The Song of the Cicadas

Roderic Quinn

Yesterday there came to me
From a green and graceful tree,
As I loitered listlessly
Nothing doing, nothing caring,
Light and warmth and fragrance sharing
With the butterfly and bee,
While the sapling-tops a-glisten
Danced and trembled, wild and willing,
Such a sudden sylvan shrilling
That I could not choose but listen.

Green cicadas, black cicadas,
Happy in the gracious weather,
Floury-baker, double-drummer,
All as one and all together,
How they voiced the golden summer!

Stealing back there came to me
As I loitered listlessly
'Neath the green and graceful tree,
Nothing doing, nothing caring,
Boyhood moments spent in sharing
With the butterfly and bee
Youth and freedom, warmth and glamour,
While cicadas round me shrilling,
Set the sleepy noontide thrilling
With their keen insistent clamour.

Green cicadas, black cicadas,
Happy in the gracious weather,
Floury-bakers, double-drummers
All as one and all together –
How they voiced the bygone summers!

The Biggest Disappointment

Joy McKean

They had my future wrapped up in a parcel
And no one even thought of asking me.
The day I turned fifteen I caught the mail train
To find what else might be in life for me.
I rode on trucks and trains and lived on nothin';
Served me right for wanting to be free –
Ah, well that's the way society looked at it,
But it didn't seem to be that way to me.
A lot more dinner times than there were dinners,
I learned a lot that hurt me at the time;
Then this quiet country boy went home a diff'rent man,
With a memory of distance on my mind.
But I always spoke too loud and laughed too often,
Maybe drank too many glasses down;
And perhaps my clothes were older than I realised,
A relief to all concerned when I left town.
And the biggest disappointment in the family was me;
The only twisted branch upon our good old fam'ly tree,
I just couldn't be the person they expected me to be
And the biggest disappointment in the world was me.

Along by Merry Christmas Time

Henry Lawson

Along by merry Christmas time they buy the aged goose,
And boil the dread plum pudding, because of ancient use.
But to sneer at old time customs would be nothing but a crime,
For the memory of the Past is aye bound up in Christmas time.

Then Jim comes home from shearing, and he gets a little gay,
With Dad, perhaps, or Uncle, but they're right on Christmas Day:
For be it on the Never, or 'neath the church bells' chime,
The family gets together, if they can, at Christmas time.

And, after tea at Christmas, they clear the things away
And play the dear old silly games our grand-folk used to play
And Dad gives a recitation that used to be the joy
Of all the Western countryside, when Father was a boy.

Along by merry Christmas time, and ere the week is o'er
We meet and fix up quarrels that each was sorry for.
Our hearts are filled with kindness and forgiveness sublime,
For no one knows where one may be next merry Christmas time.

The Christmas Chook

Charlee Marshall

'Tis Christmas Eve on Eularoo,
The West is full of cheer;
The children dream of Santa Claus,
The stockmen dream of beer.
I stand out by the chopping block,
The axe I hold in check;
I grip our rooster by the legs
And focus on his neck,

'No more you'll break my morning snooze,
You would-be Country Crier!
No more you'll scratch my seedlings out
Beneath the rusty wire.'
Delicious thoughts of breast and sage
Begin to fill my brain;
I grip the handle lower down
And raise it up again.

But then I think about the drought –
The cattle lying dead;
The hungry sheep, too weak to stand,
Beside the shearing shed;
The kangaroos are dying out
Around the salty bore.
With death so rife, what right have I
To seek to foster more?

174

I have a family to support,
The girls are home from school,
And chicken on the Christmas plate
Has always been our rule.
No need to blink your shining eye,
I shall not be remiss,
Your father and your grandfather
Were drumsticks, just like this.

I know you thought your life was hard
With twenty nagging hens;
I know you mostly hid away
Behind the docking pens.
But we're a pair, cock, you and me –
I *dare* not spare your life;
How could I face with empty hands
My daughters and my wife?

Remember all those orphan lambs –
You let them share your grain –
Remember how you watched the skies
And helped me call the rain?
We've done it hard, cock, all our lives
We've taken many a knock;
I wish you wouldn't turn your head –
Just keep it on the block.

The sun has lit the Western sky,
It's time to go inside –
There's Christmas pudding to be stirred,
And presents to divide.
'And is the rooster plucked and clean?'
I know my wife has said:
Ar-r, I'm sick of poultry all the time;
Let's have lamb chops instead!

When Grandad Sang

Jim Haynes and Marion Fitzgerald

When Grandad sang 'The Road to Gundagai',
'Twas often after harvesting was done.
We'd hear him whistle as he came inside,
And he'd call our Grandma 'Flo' instead of 'Mum',
And us kids'd go all giggly and shy,
When Grandad sang 'The Road to Gundagai'.

When Grandad sang 'The Road to Gundagai',
He'd twirl our Grandma round the kitchen floor.
'Stop it you old fool!' our Gran would cry.
'Put me down – you'll hurt yourself for sure!'
But there be a certain softness in her eye,
When Grandad sang 'The Road to Gundagai',

When Grandad sang 'The Road to Gundagai',
We'd catch a glimpse of quite a younger man,
A girl there too, before the years slipped by,
And they became our Grandad and our Gran,
For we'd sense the love their hearts could not deny,
When Grandad sang 'The Road to Gundagai'.

The Days When We Went Swimming

Henry Lawson

The breezes waved the silver grass,
    Waist-high along the siding,
And to the creek we ne'er could pass
    Three boys on bare-back riding;
Beneath the sheoaks in the bend
    The waterhole was brimming –
Do you remember yet, old friend,
    The times we 'went in swimming'?

The days we 'played the wag' from school –
  Joys shared – and paid for singly –
The air was hot, the water cool –
  And naked boys are kingly!
With mud for soap the sun to dry –
  A well planned lie to stay us,
And dust well rubbed on neck and face
  Lest cleanliness betray us.

And you'll remember farmer Kutz –
  Though scarcely for his bounty –
He leased a forty-acre block,
  And thought he owned the county;
A farmer of the old world school,
  That men grew hard and grim in,
He drew his water from the pool
  That we preferred to swim in.

And do you mind when down the creek
  His angry way he wended,
A green-hide cartwhip in his hand
  For our young backs intended?
Three naked boys upon the sand –
  Half buried and half sunning –
Three startled boys without their clothes
  Across the paddocks running.

We've had some scares, but we looked blank
  When, resting there and chumming,
One glanced by chance along the bank
  And saw the farmer coming!
And home impressions linger yet
  Of cups of sorrow brimming;
I hardly think that we'll forget
  The last day we went swimming.

Slight Autobiography

Rex Ingamells

When I was ten at Burra I would speak
with waterhen beside the reedy creek.
I was a Copper Miner after school,
taking it easy down there in the cool.

At lunch-time I would wander on the flat
beside the School, some notion in my hat
that Gordon's dying stockman went that way;
and there he goes for me until this day.

Down Murray reaches in a frail canoe –
though all the world should doubt me, this is true –
went Captain Sturt eleven years ago.
I tell you I was there and ought to know.

And any day in our King William Street,
if you would come with me, perhaps you'd meet
Deakin and Cook, just dropped along to see
if anyone has them in memory.

Lawson steps round a corner now and then,
flipping a wisp of rhyme from off his pen,
and that goes singing through my head as though
it holds a truth which everyone should know.

Candle in the Dark

Frank Daniel

When I was just a youngster I'd lie in bed so quiet,
Listening to crickets and night owls – dogs barking in the night.
The leaves against the window, wind hissing through the pines,
The choofing of the Cooma Mail, south bound on frosted lines.

And when the clouds came over that brought torrential storms,
My room would dance a pantomime of darkened, ghostly forms.
Then I'd call out loud for Mother as I lay there, stiff and stark,
And she'd hurry in to comfort me, a candle in the dark.

In my teens, as wisdom came and truth was prone to hurt,
When learning was experience and toil and sweat and dirt,
Some moments of my childhood still lived in silent form,
The terror of the lightning and the thunder in the storm.

As I grew older through the years sometimes in my dreams
My mind would fill with memories, near bursting at the seams.
Or sometimes just a passing phrase, perhaps a chance remark,
Would rekindle thoughts of Mother, with her candle in the dark.

We all know life's swift passing has its comfort and its pain.
So my years were filled with sunshine and at times a little rain.
The grandeur of fulfilment, the pride of doing well,
The loss of cherished loved ones and the tears that often fell.

Now my time is nearly done I know my prayers are not in vain.
At the end of that long tunnel the light is clear and plain;
For way off in the distance, midst a soft and hallowed arc,
Stands the form of my dear Mother – with her candle in the dark!

On Looking through an Old Punishment Book

Henry Lawson

At Eurunderee School: A Dirge

I took the book of punishment,
　　And ran its columns down;
I started with an open brow
　　And ended with a frown;
I noted long-forgotten names –
　　They took me unaware;
I noted old familiar names,
　　But my name wasn't there!

I thought of what I might have been,
　　And Oh! my heart was pained
To find, of all the scholars there,
　　That I was never caned!
I thought of wasted childhood hours,
　　And a tear rolled down my cheek –
I must have been a model boy,
　　Which means a little sneak!

'Oh! give me back my youth again!'
  Doc Faustus used to say –
I only wish the Powers could give
  My boyhood for a day.
A model boy! Beloved of girls!
  Despised by boys and men!
But it comforts me to think that I've
  Made up for it since then.

The Day th' Inspector Comes

PJ Hartigan (JOHN O'BRIEN)

It doesn't seem like school at all
The day th' Inspector comes;
You'd think the youngsters, big and small
Were shined up for a fancy ball –
Such fal-de-dal-de-dums;
There's shoes and frocks and stockings white,
And frizzy hair in ribbons bright
What's been tied up in rags all night,
And curly-wurly-ums.
We're all wound up and sitting tight,
The day th' Inspector comes.

We're not supposed to know what day
It is th' Inspector comes;
But Sister gets a ring to say,
'Brown paper parcel's on the way.'
Then us and her is chums –
She hunts us round to try to make
Things decent for th' Inspector's sake;
You wouldn't believe what pains we take,
Nor how excitement hums;
We work with broom and mop and rake
Before th' Inspector comes.

The spiders gets it in the chest
The day th' Inspector comes;
The stupid boys they graft the best,
And down comes every hornet's nest

In smither-rither-rums;
And Sister says, 'Boys, burn that mess.'
There's filled-up exers, numberless,
And broken slates and canes, I guess,
What all your fingers numbs –
We jams the lot behind the press
Before th' Inspector comes.

We have the blackboards cleaned real hard
The day th' Inspector comes;
The fireplace is freshly tarred,
There's not a paper round the yard,
Nor crust of bread nor crumbs.
Inside's a table neat whereat
Is sticks of chalk and pencils pat,
A comfy chair, a bonzer mat,
And real geran-i-ums.
We only put on dog like that
The day th' Inspector comes.

He'd like to nip you in the stew
The very day he comes;
He thinks he's pretty cute, he do;
But Sister knows a thing or two
Outside kirriculums.
To ketch you on the hop's his whim,
But she has everything in trim;
So when he sneaks up sour and prim
To start his tantarums,
We're sitting up expecting him,
The day th' Inspector comes.

She sticks in front the kids that fag,
The day th' Inspector comes;
But coves like me that loaf and lag,
And other coves that play the wag,
Or has thick craniums,
We sit along the wall all day,
And get swelled heads to hear her say,
'That lot back there would turn you grey
Just mixem-gatherums.'

The best ones always are away,
The day th' Inspector comes.

But still we grin at all the jokes
The day th' Inspector comes;
It's great to hear him give some pokes,
Especially at the 'clever' blokes
What gets mixed in their sums.
At all them little jokes we roar
And then he starts to crack some more –
He's cracked them fifty times before –
And them kinunderums.
We take him off behind the door,
The day th' Inspector comes.

The Sister looks a bit knocked out
The day th' Inspector comes;
She has a headache and a pout,
But sticks to us without a doubt,
And in his ear she drums,
That we could really do the lot
Except the little bit we got;
But, golly, don't we get it hot,
Next day about the sums.
You'd think we didn't do a jot,
The day th' Inspector comes.

But this is where she does him brown,
The day th' Inspector comes.
Which makes a smile replace a frown –
He holds the sewing upside down,
And haws and hems and hums;
She knows she has him beaten quite,
And crowds it on him left and right,
He handles it as if 'twould bite,
And don't we just enjoy the sight
The day th' Inspector comes.

Yes, school is not too bad at all
The day th' Inspector comes;
You sit up along the wall,

And don't let on you hear him call,
Keep playing hidey-hums;
But when he's gone with all he knows,
You feel like when the circus goes,
You come to school in shabby clothes,
No fril-de-dill-de-dums.
And you can thank for all your woes
The day th' Inspector comes.

An Advertisement

WT Goodge ('THE COLONEL')

I saw it in
THE BULLETIN.
    And thought it took the bun!
That excellent
Advertisement
    Of Buckley and of Nunn!
The letterpress is not prolix,
A simple label they affix:
'This style at Twenty-Nine-and-Six!'
    WHY CAN'T I ORDER ONE!

Oh, dark or fair,
Or plump or spare,
    There's none unhandsome, none!
And, large or small,
And short or tall,
    They charm me, every one!
Although I'm conscious, in advance,
With winsome grace and elegance
I have not even Buckley's chance!
    No chance whatever! Nunn!

The Old Black Billy an' Me

Louis Esson

The sheep are yarded, an' I sit
Beside the fire an' poke at it.
Far from the booze, an' clash o' men,
Glad, I'm glad I'm back again
On the station, wi' me traps
An' fencin' wire, an' tanks an' taps,
Back to salt-bush plains, an' flocks,
An' old bark hut be th' apple-box.
I turn the slipjack, make the tea,
All's as still as still can be –
An' the old black billy winks at me.

Clancy of the Overflow

AB Paterson ('THE BANJO')

I had written him a letter which I had, for want of better
Knowledge, sent to where I met him down the Lachlan, years ago;
He was shearing when I knew him, so I sent the letter to him,
Just on spec, addressed as follows, 'Clancy of the Overflow'.

And an answer came directed in a writing unexpected
(And I think the same was written with a thumb-nail dipped in tar);
'Twas his shearing mate who wrote it, and verbatim I will quote it;
'Clancy's gone to Queensland droving, and we don't know where he are.'

In my wild erratic fancy visions come to me of Clancy
Gone a-droving 'down the Cooper' where the Western drovers go;
As the stock are slowly stringing, Clancy rides behind them singing,
For the drover's life has pleasures that the townsfolk never know.

And the bush has friends to meet him, and their kindly voices greet him
In the murmur of the breezes and the river on its bars,
And he sees the vision splendid of the sunlit plains extended,
And at night the wondrous glory of the everlasting stars.

I am sitting in my dingy little office, where a stingy
Ray of sunlight struggles feebly down between the houses tall,
And the foetid air and gritty of the dusty, dirty city
Through the open window floating, spreads its foulness over all.

And in place of lowing cattle, I can hear the fiendish rattle
Of the tramways and the buses making hurry down the street;
And the language uninviting of the gutter children fighting
Comes fitfully and faintly through the ceaseless tramp of feet.

And the hurrying people daunt me, and their pallid faces haunt me
As they shoulder one another in their rush and nervous haste,
With their eager eyes and greedy, and their stunted forms and weedy,
For townsfolk have no time to grow, they have no time to waste.

And I somehow rather fancy that I'd like to change with Clancy,
Like to take a turn at droving where the seasons come and go,
While he faced the round eternal of the cash-book and the journal –
But I doubt he'd suit the office, Clancy of the Overflow.

Ned's Delicate Way

Henry Lawson

Ned knew I was short of tobacco one day,
And that I was too proud to ask for it;
He hated such pride, but his delicate way
Forbade him to take me to task for it.

I loathed to be cadging tobacco from Ned,
But, when I was just on the brink of it:
'I've got a new brand of tobacco,' he said –
'Try a smoke, and let's know what you think of it.'

The Austral 'Light'

Harry Morant ('THE BREAKER')

We were standing by the fireside at the pub one wintry night
Drinking grog and 'pitching fairies' while the lengthening hours took flight,
And a stranger there was present, one who seemed quite city-bred –
There was little showed about him to denote him 'mulga-fed'.

For he wore a four-inch collar, tucked-up pants, and boots of tan –
You might take him for a new-chum, or a Sydney city man –
But in spite of cuff or collar, Lord! he gave himself away
When he cut and rubbed a pipeful and had filled his coloured clay.

For he never asked for matches – although in that boozing band
There was more than one man standing with a matchbox in his hand;
And I knew him for a bushman 'spite his tailor-made attire.
As I saw him stoop and fossick for a fire-stick from the fire.

And that mode of weed-ignition to my memory brought back
Long nights when nags were hobbled on a far North-western track;
Recalled campfires in the timber, when the stars shone big and bright,
And we learned the matchless virtues of a glowing gidgee light.

And I thought of piney sand-ridges – and somehow I could swear
That this tailor-made young johnny had at one time been 'out there'.
And as he blew the white ash from the tapering, glowing coal,
Faith! my heart went out towards him for a kindred country soul.

185

My Hat!

Will Ogilvie

The hats of a man may be many
  In the course of a varied career,
And some have been worth not a penny
  And some have been devilish dear;
But there's one that I always remember
  When sitting alone by the fire.
In the depth of a Northern November,
  Because it fulfilled my desire.

It was old, it was ragged and rotten
  And many years out of the mode,
Like a thing that a tramp had forgotten
  And left at the side of the road.
The boughs of the mulga had torn it,
  Its ribbon was nought but a lace,
An old swaggie would not have worn it
  Without a sad smile on his face.

When I took off that hat to the ladies
  It was rather with sorrow than swank,
And often I wished it in Hades
  When the gesture drew only a blank;
But for swatting a fly on the tucker
  Or lifting a quart from the fire
Or belting the ribs of a bucker
  It was all that a man could desire.

When it ought to have gone to the cleaner's
  (And stayed there, as somebody said!)
It was handy for flogging the weaners
  From the drafting-yard into the shed.
And oft it has served as a dish for
  A kelpie in need of a drink;
It was all that a fellow could wish for
  In many more ways than you'd think.

It was spotted and stained by the weather,
  There was more than one hole in the crown,
And it made little difference whether
  The rim was turned up or turned down.
It kept out the rain (in a fashion)
  And kept off the sun (more or less),
But it merely commanded compassion
  Considered as part of one's dress.

Though it wasn't a hat you would bolt with
  Or be anxious to borrow or hire,
It was useful to blindfold a colt with
  Or handle a bit of barbed wire.
Though the world may have thought it improper
  To wear such old rubbish as that,
I'd have scorned the best London-made topper
  In exchange for my battered old hat.

Harry Pearce

David Campbell

I sat beside the red stock route
And chewed a blade of bitter grass
And saw in mirage on the plain
A bullock wagon pass.
Old Harry Pearce was with his team.
'The flies are bad,' I said to him.

The leaders felt his whip. It did
Me good to hear old Harry swear,
And in the heat of noon it seemed
His bullocks walked on air.
Suspended in the amber sky
They hauled the wool to Gundagai.

He walked in Time across the plain,
An old man walking in the air,
For years he wandered in my brain;
And now he lodges there.
And he may drive his cattle still
When Time with us has had his will.

When the Ladies Come to the Shearing Shed

Henry Lawson

'The ladies are coming,' the super says
To the shearers sweltering there,
And 'the ladies' means in the shearing-shed:
'Don't cut 'em too bad. Don't swear.'
The ghost of a pause in the shed's rough heart,
And lower is bowed each head;
And nothing is heard, save a whispered word,
And the roar of the shearing-shed.

The tall, shy rouser has lost his wits,
And his limbs are all astray;
He leaves a fleece on the shearing-board,
And his broom in the shearer's way.
There's a curse in store for that jackaroo
As down by the wall he slants –
And the ringer bends with his legs askew
And wishes he'd 'patched them pants'.

They are girls from the city. (Our hearts rebel
As we squint at their dainty feet.)
And they gush and say in a girly way
That 'the dear little lambs' are 'sweet'.
And Bill, the ringer, who'd scorn the use
Of a childish word like 'damn',
Would give a pound that his tongue was loose
As he tackles a lively lamb.

Swift thoughts of homes in the coastal towns –
Or rivers and waving grass –
And a weight on our hearts that we cannot define
That comes as the ladies pass.
But the rouser ventures a nervous dig
In the ribs of the next to him:
And Barcoo says to his pen-mate: 'Twig
The style of the last un, Jim.'

Jim Moonlight gives her a careless glance –
Then he catches his breath with pain –
His strong hand shakes and the sunlights dance
As he bends to his work again.
But he's well disguised in a bristling beard,
Bronzed skin, and his shearer's dress;
And whatever Jim Moonlight hoped or feared
Were hard for his mates to guess.

Jim Moonlight, wiping his broad, white brow,
Explains, with a doleful smile:
'A stitch in the side,' and 'he's all right now' –
But he leans on the beam awhile,
And gazes out in the blazing noon
On the clearing, brown and bare –
She has come and gone, like a breath of June,
In December's heat and glare.

The bushmen are big rough boys at the best,
With hearts of a larger growth;
But they hide those hearts with a brutal jest,
And the pain with a reckless oath.
Though the Bills and Jims of the bush-bard sing
Of their life loves, lost or dead.
The love of a girl is a sacred thing
Not voiced in a shearing-shed.

The Bonny Port of Sydney

Henry Lawson

The lovely Port of Sydney
  Lies laughing to the sky,
The bonny Port of Sydney,
  Where the ships of nations lie.
You shall never see such beauty,
  Though you sail the wide world o'er,
As the sunny Port of Sydney,
  As we see it from the Shore.

The shades of night are falling
On many ports of call,
But the harbour lights of Sydney
Are the grandest of them all;
Such a city set in jewels
Has ne'er been seen before
As the harbour lights of Sydney
As we see them from the Shore.

I must sail for gloomy London,
Where there are no harbour lights,
Where no sun is seen in winter,
And there are no starry nights;
And the bonny Port of Sydney –
I may never see it more,
But I'll always dream about it
As we view it from North Shore.

The Good Old Concertina

Henry Lawson

'Twas merry when the hut was full of jolly girls and fellows.
We danced and sang until we burst the concertina's bellows.
From distant Darling to the sea, from the Downs to Riverina,
Has e'er a gum in all the west not heard the concertina?

'Twas peaceful round the campfire blaze, the long white branches o'er us;
We'd play the tunes of bygone days, to some good old bush chorus.
Old Erin's harp may sweeter be, the Scottish pipes blow keener;
But sing an old bush song for me to the good old concertina.

'Twas cosy by the hut-fire bright when the pint pot passed between us;
We drowned the voice of the stormy night with the good old concertina's.
Though trouble drifts along the years, and the pangs of care grow keener,
My heart is gladdened when it hears the good old concertina.

Paddy Magee

Harry Morant ('THE BREAKER')

What are you doing now, Paddy Magee?
Grafting, or spelling now, Paddy Magee?
Breaking, or branding? Or overlanding,
Out on the sand-ridges, Paddy Magee?
Is your mouth parched, from an all-night spree?
Taking a pick-me-up, Paddy Magee?
Cocktail – or simple soda and b.? –
Which is the 'antidote', Paddy Magee?

Still 'shook' on some beautiful, blushing she?
Girl on the Bogan side, Paddy Magee?
A hack providing for moonlight riding,
Side-saddle foolery, Paddy Magee?
Up on the station – or in the town –
Or on the Warrego, droving down,
Whatever you're doing – wherever you be –
Here's lashin's o' luck to ye! Paddy Magee!

In the Droving Days

AB Paterson ('THE BANJO')

'Only a pound,' said the auctioneer,
'Only a pound; and I'm standing here
Selling this animal, gain or loss.
Only a pound for the drover's horse;
One of the sort that was ne'er afraid,
One of the boys of the Old Brigade;
Thoroughly honest and game, I'll swear,
Only a little the worse for wear;
Plenty as bad to be seen in town,
Give me a bid and I'll knock him down;
Sold as he stands, and without recourse,
Give me a bid for the drover's horse.'

Loitering there in an aimless way
Somehow I noticed the poor old grey,
Weary and battered and screwed, of course,
Yet when I noticed the old grey horse,
The rough bush saddle, and single rein
Of the bridle laid on his tangled mane,
Straightway the crowd and the auctioneer
Seemed on a sudden to disappear,
Melted away in a kind of haze,
For my heart went back to the droving days.

Back to the road, and I crossed again
Over the miles of the saltbush plain –
The shining plain that is said to be
The dried-up bed of an inland sea,
Where the air so dry and so clear and bright
Refracts the sun with a wondrous light,
And out in the dim horizon makes
The deep blue gleam of the phantom lakes.

At dawn of day we would feel the breeze
That stirred the boughs of the sleeping trees,
And brought a breath of the fragrance rare
That comes and goes in that scented air;
For the trees and grass and the shrubs contain
A dry sweet scent on the saltbush plain.
For those that love it and understand,
The saltbush plain is a wonderland.
A wondrous country, where nature's ways
Were revealed to me in the droving days.

We saw the fleet wild horses pass,
And the kangaroos through the Mitchell grass,
The emu ran with her frightened brood
All unmolested and unpursued.
But there rose a shout and a wild hubbub
When the dingo raced for his native shrub,
And he paid right dear for his stolen meals
With the drovers' dogs at his wretched heels.
For we ran him down at a rattling pace,
While the pack horse joined in the stirring chase.

And a wild halloo at the kill we'd raise –
We were light of heart in the droving days.

'Twas a drover's horse, and my hand again
Made a move to close on a fancied rein.
For I felt the swing and the easy stride
Of the grand old horse that I used to ride
In drought or plenty, in good or ill,
That same old steed was my comrade still;
The old grey horse with his honest ways
Was a mate to me in the droving days.

When we kept our watch in the cold and damp,
If the cattle broke from the sleeping camp,
Over the flats and across the plain,
With my head bent down on his waving mane,
Through the boughs above and the stumps below
On the darkest night I would let him go
At a racing speed; he would choose his course,
And my life was safe with the old grey horse.
But man and horse had a favourite job,
When an outlaw broke from a station mob,
With a right good will was the stockwhip plied,
As the old horse raced at the straggler's side,
And the greenhide whip such a weal would raise,
We could use the whip in the droving days.

'Only a pound!' and this was the end –
Only a pound for the drover's friend.
The drover's friend that had seen his day,
And now was worthless, and cast away
With a broken knee and a broken heart
To be flogged and starved in a hawker's cart.
Well, I made a bid for a sense of shame
And the memories dear of the good old game.

'Thank you? Guinea! and cheap at that!
Against you there in the curly hat!
Only a guinea, and one more chance,
Down he goes if there's no advance,
Third, and the last time, one! two! three!'

And the old grey horse was knocked down to me.
And now he's wandering, fat and sleek,
On the lucerne flats by the Homestead Creek;
I dare not ride him for fear he'd fall,
But he does a journey to beat them all,
For though he scarcely a trot can raise,
He can take me back to the droving days.

Bees

Roland Robinson

(Related by Percy Mumbilla)

From the hollow trees in their native home
    them old fellows cut the honeycomb.
On honey and little white grubs they fed,
'cause them young bees was blackfellers' bread.
That's why they was so mighty and strong
    in their native home in Currarong.
An' them old fellers' drink was honey-bul:
    honey and water, a coolamon full.
Naked through the bush they went,
    an' never knew what sickness meant.
Them native bees could do you no harm,
they'd crawl all over your honey-smeared arm.
But them Eyetalian bees, they'd bung
    your eyes right up. When we was young
    we used to rob their honey-trees.
Savage! They'd fetch your blood. Them bees
    would zoom an' zing an' chase a feller
        from Bombaderry to Bodalla.
Well, old Uncle Ninah, old Billy Bulloo,
    old Jacky Mumbulla, King Merriman too,
them fierce old fellers, they're all gone now.
An' the wild honey's still in the gumtree bough.

Betting & Beer

Turf & Turps

Why do betting and beer, or 'turf and turps', get a section all their own? I imagine I hear this cry from some of you dear readers, but mostly those of you who didn't grow up in twentieth century Australia! Those of you who did may not agree with my decision – but you will know why I placed such a topic alongside patriotism, philosophy and love!

The Australian obsession with booze is a well-documented aspect of our history, so the joys and sorrows of our love affair with alcohol certainly deserve a place here. I know historians and Queenslanders will take issue with me but I include 'rum' under the heading of 'beer' for the poetic purposes of this volume. That's poetic licence (or liquor licence, if you like, in this case).

True, I could have teamed grog with football, cricket or sport in general. But the truth is that racing has all the best verse! This is mainly due to Paterson being a keen racing man and amateur rider (he rode frequently at Randwick and elsewhere). His pen name 'The Banjo' was taken from a station racehorse on the family property. CJ Dennis and many recent bush bards have followed his lead and made racing one of the most popular subjects of 'bush' verse.

As well as that, the racing game, more than any other sport I know, is a microcosm of our society which attracts and involves all types of people from the city and the bush. On a racetrack you'll find the rich and the poor, the privileged and the battler, the dreamers and the crooks. Racing has all the best yarns and tall stories – so 'Betting and Beer', or 'Turf and Turps', it is!

After all, this is a nation that once used grog as currency – and declares a public holiday and comes to a standstill for a horse race!

Betting and Beer

JG Medley

Put three or four quid on the horses,
    And a couple of pounds on the trots;
Ten bob for the dogs in their courses,
    And something or other for spots –
And if there is anything over
    That hasn't been got by the cats,
What ho! for a future in clover
    By way of a ticket in Tatts.

Oh! Betting and Beer are the basis
    Of the only respectable life.
Much better to go to the races
    Than moulder at home with the wife.
I'd much sooner go to the races
    Than take all the kids to the sea.
My family knows what their place is,
    And that is at home – without me.

Sydney Cup Day

Anon

It was on a Sydney Cup Day,
While strolling round the course,
Joe Thompson he comes up to me
And says, 'Do ya wanna back me horse?
Now if you want to back it
The odds are three to one,
Just give me thirty smackers
And I'll give you back a ton.'

Oh he may be very tricky,
And he may be very sly,
He can always find his match
He only has to try;
And what he does is clever,
On that we all agree,
He may have got at one or two,
But he won't get at me.

Now Joe acts the injured party,
And bitterly complains.
Says he's offerin' me a certainty
If I only had the brains,
But if I didn't want it,
Well, he'd find some other bloke.
But in the meantime, while I'm thinkin'
Could I spare a chap a smoke?

Well I looked at Joe before me
And I lit his cigarette,
And gave him one for later on
And a fiver for a bet,
And he sauntered off towards the ring
His hat pushed on the side,
A man of means once again,
With a fiver's worth of pride.

Oh he may be very tricky,
And he may be very sly,
He can always find his match,
He only has to try,
And what he does is clever,
On that we all agree,
But an old tout who's down and out
Can always count on me!

Hard Luck

AB Paterson ('THE BANJO')

I left the course, and by my side
    There walked a ruined tout –
A hungry creature evil-eyed,
    Who poured this story out.

'You see,' he said, 'there came a swell
    To Kensington today,
And if I picked the winners well,
    A crown at least he'd pay.

'I picked three winners straight, I did,
 I filled his purse with pelf,
And then he gave me half a quid,
 To back one for myself.

'A half a quid to me he cast,
 I wanted it indeed.
So help me Bob, for two days past
 I haven't had a feed.

'But still I thought my luck was in,
 I couldn't go astray,
I put it all on Little Min,
 And lost it straightaway.

'I haven't got a bite or bed,
 I'm absolutely stuck,
So keep this lesson in your head:
 Don't over-trust your luck!'

The folks went homeward, near and far,
 The tout, Oh! where was he?
Ask where the empty boilers are,
 Beside the Circular Quay.

Lifespan

Anon

Horse and mule live thirty years and nothing know of wines and beers.
Goats and sheep at twenty die, never tasting Scotch or rye.
The cow drinks water by the ton, and at eighteen is mostly done.
The dog at sixteen cashes in without the aid of rum or gin.
The cat in milk and water soaks and then, in twelve short years, it croaks.
The sober, modest, bone-dry hen lays eggs for nogs, then dies at ten.
The animals are strictly dry, they sinless live and swiftly die.
While sinful, gin-full, rum-soaked men survive for three score years and ten.
And some of us, though mighty few, stay pickled till we're ninety-two.

The Amateur Rider

AB Paterson ('THE BANJO')

Him going to ride for us! *Him* – with the pants and the eyeglass and all.
Amateur! don't he just look it – it's twenty to one on a fall.
Boss must be gone off his head to be sending our steeplechase crack
Out over fences like these with an object like that on his back.

Ride! Don't tell *me* he can ride. With his pants just as loose as balloons,
How can he sit on his horse? And his spurs like a pair of harpoons;
Ought to be under the Dog Act, he ought, and be kept off the course.
Fall! why, he'd fall off a cart, let alone off a steeplechase horse.

Yessir! the 'orse is all ready – I wish you'd have rode him before;
Nothing like knowing your 'orse, sir, and this chap's a terror to bore;
Battleaxe always could pull, and he rushes his fences like fun –
Stands off his jump twenty feet, and then springs like a shot from a gun.

Oh, he can jump 'em all right, sir, you make no mistake, 'e's a toff;
Clouts 'em in earnest, too, sometimes, you mind that he don't clout you off –
Don't seem to mind how he hits 'em, his shins is as hard as a nail,
Sometimes you'll see the fence shake and the splinters fly up from the rail.

All you can do is to hold him and just let him jump as he likes,
Give him his head at the fences, and hang on like death if he strikes;
Don't let him run himself out – you can lie third or fourth in the race –
Until you clear the stone wall, and from that you can put on the pace.

Fell at that wall once, he did, and it gave him a regular spread,
Ever since that time he flies it – he'll stop if you pull at his head,
Just let him race – you can trust him – he'll take first-class care he don't fall,
And I think that's the lot – but remember, *he must have his head at the wall.*

Well, he's down safe as far as the start, and he seems to sit on pretty neat,
Only his baggified breeches would ruinate anyone's seat –
They're away – here they come – the first fence, and he's head over heels for a crown!
Good for the new chum, he's over, and two of the others are down!

Now for the treble, my hearty – By Jove, he can ride, after all;
Whoop, that's your sort – let him fly them! He hasn't much fear of a fall.
Who in the world would have thought it? And aren't they just going a pace?
Little Recruit in the lead there will make it a stoutly run race.

Lord! But they're racing in earnest – and down goes Recruit on his head,
Rolling clean over his boy – it's a miracle if he ain't dead.
Battleaxe, Battleaxe yet! By the Lord, he's got most of 'em beat –
Ho! did you see how he struck, and the swell never moved in his seat?

Second time round, and, by Jingo! he's holding his lead of 'em well;
Hark to him clouting the timber! It don't seem to trouble the swell.
Now for the wall – let him rush it. A thirty-foot leap, I declare –
Never a shift in his seat, and he's racing for home like a hare.

What's that that's chasing him – Rataplan – regular demon to stay!
Sit down and ride for your life now! Oh, good, that's the style – come away!
Rataplan's certain to beat you, unless you can give him the slip;
Sit down and rub in the whalebone now – give him the spurs and the whip!

Battleaxe, Battleaxe, yet – and it's Battleaxe wins for a crown;
Look at him rushing the fences, he wants to bring t'other chap down.
Rataplan never will catch him if only he keeps on his pins;
Now! the last fence! and he's over it! Battleaxe, Battleaxe wins!

Well, sir, you rode him just perfect – I knew from the first you could ride.
Some of the chaps said you couldn't, an' I says just like this a' one side:
Mark me, I says, that's a tradesman – the saddle is where he was bred.
Weight! you're all right, sir, and thank you; and them was the words that I said.

Decisive

Denis Kevans

Drinking makes me more decisive,
More decisive, year by year,
Much more decisive, I decide
I'll go and have another beer.

Wait Till Chewsdy

CJ Dennis

Wait till after Chewsdy, wife.
　'Taint far ahead to look,
A change is comin' in your life,
　Or else I'm much mistook,
I'll buy you rugs an' furs an' things
　An' di'monds by the ton.
We're 'ome at last when Chewsdy's past
　An' Melbun Cup is run.

Wait till after Chewsdy, Bill.
　You're silly if you frets;
I'll pay that quid; you know I will;
　An' settle all me debts.
The tip's a cert; the 'orse can spurt
　An' last the distance too.
I'm 'ome all right by Chewsdy night
　When all me dreams come true.

I knows, I knows; too well I knows
　I've said it all before;
But blokes 'as got to learn I s'pose;
　I'll never switch no more.
Me mind's made up. This Melbun Cup
　You'll 'ave no chance to scoff.
I mean to stick to my first pick
　An' never git put off.

So wait till after Chewsdy, mate.
　Till after Chewsdy, wife.
A man can't be the fool of fate
　For all 'is nach'ril life.
An' yet, an' yet, I can't forget
　Past years, an' nags I backs.
In pichers grim I visions 'im,
　That coot wot dogs me tracks –

Never the same bloke year by year,
   'E waits there on the course
To pour 'is poison in my ear –
   That 'ound wot knows a 'orse.
'E knows a man wot knows a man
   Wot knows the stable well.
'E knows, 'e knows – Lord! Wot 'e knows
   'Ud take a book to tell.

An' must I meet 'im once again –
   My Jonah, still disguised?
An' must I 'ark to that dead nark
   An' stand there, 'ipnertised?
Keep 'im away! Keep me, I pray,
   From speakin', still bewitched,
The bitterest word a man e'er 'eard:
   'I 'ad it; but I switched.'

A Post-Cup Tale

CJ Dennis

I 'ad the money in me 'and!
Fair dinkum! Right there, by the stand.
   I tole me wife at breakfus' time,
   Straight out: 'Trivalve,' I sez 'is prime.
Trivalve,' I sez. An', all the week,
I swear ther's no one 'eard me speak
   Another 'orse's name. Why, look,
   I 'ad the oil straight from a Book
On Sund'y at me cousin's place
When we was torkin' of the race.
   'Trivalve,' 'e sez. ''Is chance is grand.'
I 'ad the money in me 'and!

Fair in me 'and I 'ad the dough!
An' then a man 'as got to go –
   Wot? Tough? Look, if I 'adn't met
   Jim Smith (I ain't forgave 'im yet)
'E takes an' grabs me be the coat.
'Trivalve!' 'e sez. 'That 'airy goat!'
(I 'ad the money in me 'and
Just makin' for the bookie's stand)
'Trivalve?' 'e sez. 'Ar, turn it up!
'Ow could 'e win a flamin' Cup?'
   Of course, I thort 'e muster knoo.
'Im livin' near a trainer, too.

Right 'ere, like that, fair in me fist
I 'ad the notes! An' then I missed –
   Missed like a mug fair on the knock
Becos 'is maggin' done me block.
'That airy goat?' 'e sez. ''E's crook!'
Fair knocked me back, 'e did. An' look,
   I 'ad the money in me 'and!
   Fair in me paw! An', un'erstand,
Sixes at least I coulder got –
Thirty to five, an' made me pot.
Today I mighter been real rich –
   Rollin' in dough! Instid o' which,
'Ere's me – Aw! Don't it beat the band?
I 'AD THE MONEY IN ME 'AND!
   Put me clean off, that's wot 'e did ...
   Say, could yeh len' us 'arf a quid?

How the Favourite Beat Us

AB Paterson ('THE BANJO')

'Aye,' said the boozer, 'I tell you it's true, sir,
   I once was a punter with plenty of pelf,
But gone is my glory, I'll tell you the story
   How I stiffened my horse and got stiffened myself.

''Twas a mare called the Cracker, I came down to back her,
   But found she was favourite all of a rush,
The folk just did pour on to lay six to four on,
   And several bookies were killed in the crush.

'It seems old Tomato was stiff, though a starter;
   They reckoned him fit for the Caulfield to keep.
The Bloke and the Donah were scratched by their owner,
   He only was offered three-fourths of the sweep.

'We knew Salamander was slow as a gander,
   The mare could have beat him the length of the straight,
And old Manumission was out of condition,
   And most of the others were running off weight.

'No doubt someone "blew it", for everyone knew it,
   The bets were all gone, and I muttered in spite,
"If I can't get a copper, by Jingo, I'll stop her,
   Let the public fall in, it will serve the brutes right."

'I said to the jockey, "Now, listen, my cocky,
   You watch as you're cantering down by the stand,
I'll wait where that toff is and give you the office,
   You're only to win if I lift up my hand."

'I then tried to back her – "What price is the Cracker?"
   "Our books are all full, sir," each bookie did swear;
My mind, then, I made up, my fortune I played up
   I bet every shilling against my own mare.

'I strolled to the gateway, the mare in the straight way
   Was shifting and dancing, and pawing the ground,
The boy saw me enter and wheeled for his canter,
   When a darned great mosquito came buzzing around.

'They breed 'em et Hexham, it's risky to vex 'em,
   They suck a man dry at a sitting, no doubt,
But just as the mare passed, he fluttered my hair past,
   I lifted my hand, and I flattened him out.

'I was stunned when they started, the mare simply darted
   Away to the front when the flag was let fall,
For none there could match her, and none tried to catch her –
   She finished a furlong in front of them all.

205

'You bet that I went for the boy, whom I sent for
　　The moment he weighed and came out of the stand –
"Who paid you to win it? Come, own up this minute."
　　"Lord love yer," said he, "why, you lifted your hand."

"Twas true, by St Peter, that cursed "muskeeter"
　　Had broke me so broke that I hadn't a brown,
And you'll find the best course is when dealing with horses
　　To win when you're able, and *keep your hands down.*'

Flying Kate

Anon

It makes us old hands sick and tired to hear
　　Them talk of their champions of today,
Eurythmics and Davids, yes, I'll have a beer,
　　Are only fair hacks in their way.

Now this happened out West before records were took,
　　And 'tis not to be found in the guide,
But it's honest – Gor' struth, and can't be mistook,
　　For it happened that I had the ride.

'Twas the Hummer's Creek cup, and our mare, Flying Kate,
　　Was allotted eleven stone two;
The race was two miles, you'll agree with me mate,
　　It was asking her something to do.

She was heavy in foal, but the owner and me
　　Decided to give her a spin,
We were right on the rocks, 'twas the end of a spree,
　　So we needed a bit of a win.

I saddled her up and went down with the rest,
　　Her movements were clumsy and slow,
The starter to get us in line did his best,
　　Then swishing his flag he said, 'Go!'

The field jumped away but the mare seemed asleep,
    And I thought to myself, 'We've been sold,'
Then I heard something queer, and I felt I could weep,
    For strike me if Kate hadn't foaled.

The field by this time had gone half-a-mile,
    But I knew what the old mare could do,
So I gave her a cut with the whip – you can smile,
    But the game little beast simply flew.

'Twas then she showed them her wonderful speed,
    For we moved down the field one by one,
With a furlong to go we were out in the lead,
    And prepared for a last final run.

Then something came at us right on the outside,
    And we only just scratched past the pole,
When I had a good look I thought I'd have died,
    For I'm blowed if it wasn't the foal.

Casey's Luck

Joy McKean

Now Casey was a racing man, he dealt in thoroughbreds,
Wherever there's a meeting on, that's where Casey heads.
With Little Joe his travelling mate and a horse called 'Holy Dan',
He'll dine on lobster one week and the next on bread and scran.

I met him in the pub today, I said, 'Casey, how's ya luck?'
With tears in his eyes he looked into mine and said, 'I'm a dying duck!
Been down to Hall's Creek meeting, I thought I'd scoop the pool.
I should have made a fortune, but instead I'm made a fool!'

As we stood in the crowded bar room, midst the laughter and the cheer,
I brightened up old Casey with a round or two of beer.
We found a quiet corner and Casey he got bold,
He grabbed his beer in beefy hands and here's the tale he told.

''Twas a sore disgrace I can tell ya. It shoulda been in the bag,
But the Ladies' Bracelet and the cash were won by a station nag.
I was broke and getting desperate, I'd been bragging round the place
And the last event on the programme was a native stockman's race.'

'So I hauled Little Joe to the creek bed and to the ashes of a fire,
In a second flat I stripped him of his pants and fancy attire.
I blackened him all over with ashes and bacon fat,
And said, 'Now Joe, you must ride this race in twenty seconds flat.'

'Well Joe and Holy Dan romped home, beat the others by a mile,
And I front up for the winnings with a grin right across my dial.
Said the judge, "I've never seen a stockman ride a horse like that."
But Joe, the stupid so-and-so, stood around to cop the rap!'

'I frown and I give him the office that he'd better shoot straight through.
Then the judge says, "Just a moment, that native's eyes are blue!"
Well they didn't tar and feather us, but it caused me lots of strife,
And now I'm barred from the Kimberleys for the rest of my racing life!'

The Exacta

Denis Kevans

One day Donny went to the races,
And, after the last, he reckoned,
'You Beauty!' always came first,
'You Bastard!' always came second.

TAB Punter's Song

John Dengate

Each Saturday morning I crawl out of bed
Hung-over from Friday's excess,
Feeling crook in the 'comics' and crook in the head
With a mountain of sins to confess,
But then I remember it's race day again
And I collect up my clothes from the floor;
I tune into Mahony's selections at ten –
The adrenalin's pumping once more.

I have a quick piss, I give breakfast a miss,
Wallet and form guide I grab,
Then I suddenly bolt like a two-year-old colt
Away down the road to the TAB.
It's number of units and number of race,
The numbers spin round in my brain,
And I stand there blaspheming and cursing the place,
The biro is broken again.

Oh, the long shots are rough and the favourites are short
And I never know what's running dead
So I ring up my mate, but he got home so late
His mother won't rouse him from bed.
Ron Quinton could win on a horse made of tin
So I back everything that he rides
And the big Melbourne grey is a good thing each way,
And a couple of others besides.

And fellas, quinellas are always a chance
And doubles are sometimes a go
So when I walk out I feel light in the pants
For the TAB has got most of my dough.
At Warwick Farm, Randwick or Rosehill they race,
It's a sign of our moral decay,
But wipe that superior look off your face,
I expect a trifecta today.

A short break for grub, then I'm into the pub
And I stand there and weep in my booze
For the horses I back veer all over the track
And they lose and they lose and they lose.
Oh! seek not escape in the gambling my friend
Though life may be hum-drum and drab;
Seek solace in psalms or in fair ladies' arms
But never go into a TAB.

When Monkeys Rode the Greyhounds Round the Track at Harold Park

Denis Kevans

When monkeys rode the greyhounds round the track at Harold Park,
The race was through the hurdles, and it was a lovely lark,
The jockeys? little monkeys, fully grown, who stuck like glue,
With their silks a lovely colour, and their numbers printed, too.

'Hold him, up, don't go too early, keep his nose down on the rail,
If you fall off going outward, grab him homeward by the tail,'
And the monkeys nodded wisely as they trotted to the boxes,
Some whips were cackyhanded while the rest were orthodoxes.

'The Ashton Circus monkeys are the best,' said Paddy West,
But Charlie, down from Koolewong, said 'Sorley's rode with zest,'
'The jockeys are not monkeys,' countered Tess from Terrigal,
'They're undersized apprentices in hairy overalls.'

'The greatest hurdle jockey that this country ever knew.
Was a little spider monkey who had wandered from the zoo,
With a style like Darby Munro, in a finish he was grand,
He could pull the leaders backward with a tug of either hand.'

So Sal from Saratoga threw her tuppence in the hat,
But Wallie from Wallacia was not satisfied with that –
'A little cappucino off a ship from Singapore
Had the poker-face of Thompson, and the sit of Georgie Moore.

'You can spiel your spider monkeys, you can prattle all you like,
But the little cappucino was as good as Jimmy Pike.'
'There's been a plunge,' said Tommy, 'Hey, there's been a plonk,' said Ron.
'The monkeys came in regiments, they've place their bets and gone ...'

The inter-com was sounding, and the lights came on the track,
And a drunk I knew kept yelling – 'Hey, what did the monkeys back?'
'I didn't see their numbers, they just pointed at the boards,
The bookies scribbled tickets and they poked 'em in their cords'.

They were legging up the monkeys, and their style had to be seen,
They were straight as Malcolm Johnston when he rode for Theo Green,
And the trainers gave instructions emphasizing points precisely,
And they pointed with their fingers, and the monkeys nodded wisely.

Away the doggies scampered for the bunny on the rail,
Some monks were sitting backwards, some were clinging to a tail,
Some were riding it like cossacks holding on with nails and teeth,
While two were on the favourite with a third slung underneath.

They came to the first hurdle and the monkeys started vaulting
From one dog to the other with some brilliant somersaulting,
One produced a lariat, lassooed the leading dog,
Who fell down with a broken leg, and lay there like a log.

At the third it was amazing they were falling off like fruit,
And around the rail in ragged ranks the dogs in hot pursuit,
One monkey took a pickaback on the electric hare,
And was singing Annie Laurie like a real fair dinkum lair.

There were monkeys in the flower-beds, and monkeys up the pole,
One dived into a bookie's bag and grabbed himself a roll,
They seemed to scatter everywhere, before you'd time to shout,
One dived into the sentry-box, and pulled the switches out.

This caused a pandemonium, the night was black as tar,
But the monkeys who were punting gave a loud and long hurrah,
The little beggars seem to sense the action on the track,
And the drunk I knew kept burbling: 'What did the monkeys back?'

In five or several minutes then the lights came flashing on,
'Have a Captain Cook,' said Tommy – 'Oh, gawd save us all,' said Ron,
Monkey two was riding eight, and five was riding three,
And four were on the favourite who was wobbling at the knee.

Three was riding seven, and five was riding four,
And as they cleared the final jump, the monkeys gave a roar,
But the monkeys in the flower-bed they thought they'd do a jig,
They looked like The Bushwhackers in the middle of a gig.

Two monkeys, with their legs tied, and a grin upon their face,
Were limping to the finish in a triple-legged race,
And a monkey, and another, with a little bit of twine,
Pulled a dog who died from laughing, by the tail, across the line.

There were many protests entered, 4328,
And three other monkeys pulled a dog across the line too late,
And the drunk he came towards me, and he gave my ribs a prod,
'What did you have your money on, the monkey or the dog?'

The Tote was re-assembled, and they flashed the number 2,
And all the monkeys backed it, well, you should've seen the queue,
With scornful shouts of merriment, they queued along the rails,
The girls like Susan Peacock, and the boys in hats and tails.

I was staring at my tickets, and I went to get a shot,
You guessed it, all the pies were cold, and all the beer was hot,
But I couldn't believe the numbers, not as long as I will live,
My two monkey, dog trifecta paid a million dollar div.

Do They Know?

AB Paterson ('THE BANJO')

Do they know? At the turn to the straight
   Where the favourites fail,
And every atom of weight
   Is telling its tale;
As some grim old stayer hard-pressed
   Runs true to his breed,
And with head just in front of the rest
   Fights on in the lead;
When the jockeys are out with the whips,
   With a furlong to go;
And the backers grow white to the lips –
   Do you think *they* don't know?

Do they know? As they come back to weigh
   In a whirlwind of cheers,

Though the spurs have left marks of the fray,
 Though the sweat on the ears
Gathers cold, and they sob with distress
 As they roll up the track,
They know just as well their success
 As the man on their back.
As they walk through a dense human lane,
 That sways to and fro,
And cheers them again and again,
 Do you think *they* don't know?

Lunch for Dipso Dan

Jim Haynes

Dipso Dan is a man who can strike any time,
You rarely get any warning,
He's thrown out of the pub as the minister passes
Late one Saturday morning.

'G'day there Reverend,' says Dipso Dan,
'Got any good tips today?'
'Well Dan,' says His Reverence, '**Lunch** might be
A good thing for you I'd say.'

'Thanks for that Reverend, Good on ya,' says Dan,
'I never forget what I'm told.'
And to himself he mutters, 'Never heard of **Lunch**,
It must be a two-year-old.'

Back into the pub goes Dipso Dan,
The drinking day is still young.
And the first thing he sees is a sign that says,
'**Lunch** is 12 to 1'.

'Strewth, look at the odds!' says Dipso Dan,
'That's gotta be worth a chance!'
But a firm hand grips his collar
And another the seat of his pants.

He's back on the street, but now he's obsessed,
'That **Lunch** might be a goer.

I'll go down the Royal and back it,' says Dan,
'Before the odds get any lower'.

So Dan staggers off to the other pub,
At the other end of the shops.
Halfway down there's the Chinese restaurant –
That's exactly where Dan stops.

And he stares at the sign in the window.
It says, '**Lunch** is 11 to 2'.
'They're backing the thing for a fortune,' says Dan,
'That minister musta knew!'

'Fancy missin' out on 12s,
That's just the thing to spoil
Me afternoon, I'll hurry up,
I'll back it at the Royal.'

Dan staggers on and he's almost there
When he stops with a strangled yell.
'**Lunch** 1 to 2', says the blackboard sign
At the door of the Royal Hotel.

'Bloody odds-on, I've missed it,' says Dan,
'Me chance of a fortune is wrecked!'
Then he slides down the wall of the Royal Hotel,
Booze and exercise take their effect.

He sleeps through the paddy-wagon ride
But he wakes when they lock the cell.
He hears them walking away with the keys
And he knows he'll have to yell.

'I wanna know about **Lunch**,' yells Dan,
'And I've got a terrible thirst.'
'Bad luck about **lunch**,' the sergeant yells back,
'Cos I'm telling ya, sober up first.'

'**Sober Up** first eh,' says Dipso Dan,
'So much for the minister's hunch.'
He lies down on the bed, '**Sober Up** first, eh,
Thank gawd I didn't back **Lunch**!'

The Morning After

Col Wilson ('BLUE THE SHEARER')

To-day's the first day of the rest of my life,
And I wish I were dead, but I won't tell the wife.
When I woke up this morning she looked in my eye,
And said: 'How do you feel?' I said: 'Marvellous. Why?'
She told me: 'Last night, my wife's intuition,
Felt some concern for your general condition.'
And then it came back. Last night we had guests,
And I'd entertained with considerable zest.

Still. I wouldn't let on that I wasn't too good,
And I went to the bathroom, as all poets should.
I looked in the mirror, and what did I see?
I was shaving a stranger. That couldn't be me.
I knew I felt crook, but that bloke looked like death,
About to expire on his terminal breath.
But reason prevailed. I accepted my fate,
But how did I get in this terrible state.

It wasn't the sherry. I only had two,
And of whisky and vodka – not more than a few.
Three or four cans of convivial beer.
That can't be the reason I'm feeling so queer.
During dinner, the wines, the white and the red,
But never so much as to go to my head.
Maybe the brandy. But I only had one,
And that wasn't enough to have brought me undone.

Now, let's take it slowly. I've just had a thought.
With the coffee and chocolates, I did have some port.
In fact in that company, the port flowed quite well.
So it's due to the port, that I'm feeling like hell.
I know I'll recover. The question is 'when?'
And IF I recover, will it happen again?
In the meantime, I'll try to pretend I'm OK
And hope to survive 'til the end of the day.

And my darling persists with that 'serve you right' smirk.
Whistling away as she does the housework.
I'm damn sure she knows how it cuts like a knife,
'Please God. Can't I swap for a taciturn wife?
I promise I'll never drink port while I live,'
And that is a promise I'll cheerfully give.
I'll just stick to sherry, and whisky and beer,
And white and red wine, and a brandy to clear
All the cobwebs away from my suffering brain,
And Port shall not touch my gullet again.

But, I've just thought of something. I think I should wait.
It may NOT be the drink, but something I ate.
I DID have the dips, cheeses, entrees, main meal,
Dessert and some chocolates. No wonder I feel
As though forces of evil are loose in my head,
And my stomach is asking to be put to bed.
And I'm blaming the port, that innocent wine,
Maybe I will have the odd sip again.
In the meantime, my body's in terrible strife –
Today's the worst day in the rest of my life.

A Rum Complaint

Claude Morris

The old fellow held out his hands that shook
Like the leaves of a wind-blown tree,
And begged the doctor for relief
From his ghastly malady.

The doctor gave him a thorough check,
With sure and competent touch.
'There's nothing much wrong with you,' he said,
'Except that you drink too much.'

'That's all very well,' the old fellow, said –
'You can blame the grog if you will,
But it's not what I drink that's gettin' me down –
It's the bloody amount that I spill.'

Bundaberg Rum

Bill Scott

God made sugar cane grow where it's hot
and teetotal abstainers to grow where it's not.
Let the sin-bosun warn of perdition to come,
we'll drink it and chance it, so bring on the rum.

Bundaberg rum, overproof rum,
will tan your insides and grow hair on your bum.
Let the blue ribbon beat on his empty old drum
or his waterlogged belly, we'll stick to our rum.

These are men who drink it, men indeed,
of the bushranging oldtime hairynecked breed.
They shave with their axes, they dress in old rags,
they feed on old boots, they sleep on old bags.
Dull care flies away when their voices resound
and the grass shrivels up when they spit on the ground.

When they finally die and are sunk in the clay
their bodies are pickled and never decay.
On the morning of Judgment, when the skies are rolled back,
they'll stroll from their graves up the long golden track
and their voices will echo throughout Kingdom Come
as they toast the archangels in overproof rum.

Choice Booze

Anon

Now Louis likes his native wine and Otto likes his beer,
The Pommy goes for 'half and half' because it gives him cheer.
Angus likes his whisky neat and Paddy likes his tot,
The Aussie has no drink at all – he likes the bloody lot!

Drink

Anon

There he is, the dirty skunk,
In the bar-room, stinking drunk.
A bloke should be fined just for knowing him –
He was drinking here when I came in!

The Overflow

Anon

Sure, the beer I love to taste it, but it breaks me heart to waste it,
As the careless barman spills it and the bubbles rise like snow.
And I somehow rather fancy that the barman's name is Clancy,
And the waste upon the counter is just Clancy's overflow!

The Publican's Toast

Anon

It's nice to take a glass each night before you toddle home.
It's nice to take a glass with friends, or take a glass alone.
I must explain my meaning though, before I let it pass . . .
I mean just take the contents – and not the bloody glass!

A Song of Light

John Barr

There have plenty songs been written of the moonlight on the hill,
Of the starlight on the ocean and the sun-flecks on the rill,
But one glorious song has never fallen yet upon my ear,
'Tis a royal song of gladness of the gaslight on the beer.

I have watched an amber sunset creep across a black-faced bay;
I have seen the blood-flushed sunrise paint the snow one winter day,
But the gleam I will remember best, in lingering days to come,
Was a shaft of autumn radiance lying on a pint of rum.

I have seen the love stars shining through bronze hair across my face,
I have seen white bosoms heaving 'neath a wisp of open lace,
But resplendent yet in memory, and it seemeth brighter far,
Was a guttered candle's flicker on a tankard in a bar . . .

Wonderful Love

Anon

The wonderful love of a beautiful maid, the love of a staunch, true man,
The love of a baby unafraid – have existed since life began.
But the greatest love, the love of loves, even greater than that of a mother,
Is the passionate, tender and infinite love of one drunken bum for another.

Sweeney

Henry Lawson

It was somewhere in September, and the sun was going down,
When I came, in search of 'copy', to a Darling-River town;
'Come-and-have-a-drink' we'll call it – 'tis a fitting name, I think –
And 'twas raining, for a wonder, up at Come-and-have-a-drink.

'Neath the public-house verandah I was resting on a bunk
When a stranger rose before me, and he said that he was drunk;
He apologised for speaking; there was no offence, he swore;
But he somehow seemed to fancy that he'd seen my face before.

'No erfence,' he said. I told him that he needn't mention it,
For I might have met him somewhere; I had travelled round a bit,
And I knew a lot of fellows in the bush and in the streets –
But a fellow can't remember all the fellows that he meets.

Very old and thin and dirty were the garments that he wore,
Just a shirt and pair of trousers, and a boot, and nothing more;
He was wringing-wet, and really in a sad and sinful plight,
And his hat was in his left hand, and a bottle in his right.

His brow was broad and roomy, but its lines were somewhat harsh,
And a sensual mouth was hidden by a drooping, fair moustache;
(His hairy chest was open to what poets call the 'wined',
And I would have bet a thousand that his pants were gone behind).

219

He agreed: 'Yer can't remember all the chaps yer chance to meet,'
And he said his name was Sweeney – people lived in Sussex-street.
He was campin' in a stable, but he swore that he was right,
'Only for the blanky horses walkin' over him all night.'

He'd apparently been fighting, for his face was black-and-blue,
And he looked as though the horses had been treading on him, too;
But an honest, genial twinkle in the eye that wasn't hurt
Seemed to hint of something better, spite of drink and rags and dirt.

It appeared that he mistook me for a long-lost mate of his –
One of whom I was the image, both in figure and in phiz –
(He'd have had a letter from him if the chap were living still,
For they'd carried swags together from the Gulf to Broken Hill).

Sweeney yarned awhile and hinted that his folks were doing well,
And he told me that his father kept the Southern Cross Hotel;
And I wondered if his absence was regarded as a loss
When he left the elder Sweeney – landlord of the Southern Cross.

He was born in Parramatta, and he said, with humour grim,
That he'd like to see the city 'ere the liquor finished him,
But he couldn't raise the money. He was damned if he could think
What the Government was doing. Here he offered me a drink.

I declined – *'twas* self-denial – and I lectured him on booze,
Using all the hackneyed arguments that preachers mostly use;
Things I'd heard in temperance lectures (I was young and rather green),
And I ended by referring to the man he might have been.

Then a wise expression struggled with the bruises on his face,
Though his argument had scarcely any bearing on the case:
'What's the good o' keepin' sober? Fellers rise and fellers fall;
What I might have been and wasn't doesn't trouble me at all.'

But he couldn't stay to argue, for his beer was nearly gone.
He was glad, he said, to meet me, and he'd see me later on;
He guessed he'd have to go and get his bottle filled again,
And he gave a lurch and vanished in the darkness and the rain.

And of afternoons in cities, when the rain is on the land,
Visions come to me of Sweeney with his bottle in his hand,
With the stormy night behind him, and the pub verandah-post –
And I wonder why he haunts me more than any other ghost.

Still I see the shearers drinking at the township in the scrub,
And the Army praying nightly at the door of every pub,
And the girls who flirt and giggle with the bushmen from the West –
But the memory of Sweeney overshadows all the rest.

Well, perhaps it isn't funny; there were links between us two –
He had memories of cities, he had been a jackaroo;
And, perhaps, his face forewarned me of a face that I might see
From a bitter cup reflected in the wretched days to be.

I suppose he's tramping somewhere where the bushmen carry swags,
Cadging round the wretched stations with his empty tucker-bags:
And I fancy that of evenings, when the track is growing dim.
What he 'might have been and wasn't' comes along and troubles him.

Trouble Brewing

Claude Morris

He came walking through the forest in the summer's glaring sun.
In his left hand was a bottle – in the other was a gun.
His beard was wild and bushy and his hair was shaggy too,
His old straw hat was full of holes, where tufts of hair came through.

I stood and waited for him as he came with steady stride,
And I studied his appearance till he soon was by my side.
He wasn't old, nor was he young, but somewhere in between,
And his heavy eyebrows almost hid his eyes of greyish green.

Then he handed me the bottle – 'You must have a drink.' he said.
And I heard him cock the rifle, and he aimed it at my head.
'Yes, take a swig of my home-brew, and you may be the first
To have a chance of trying out my recipe for thirst.'

And the rifle never wavered as it pointed straight at me,
And that close-up gaping barrel was a nasty thing to see.
I lifted up the bottle with a very shaky hand,
And a silent prayer to Heaven, as I followed his command.

I swallowed twice, and God above; that brew had come from Hell,
And I know my head exploded, and it drowned my dying yell.
I fell upon the dusty ground and grovelled there in pain,
Vowing he could shoot me, but I wouldn't drink again.

When the pain and shock receded, and I staggered to my feet,
'It was AWFUL – it was AWFUL,' I could hear my voice repeat.
Then I heard the brewer speaking, and he said, 'Yes, I agree –
Now give me back that bottle – and you hold the gun on me.'

An Alphabetical Australian Anecdote

GH Gibson ('IRONBARK')

A was an ant of the sojer sort
    What sat on a sun-baked plain;
B was the bite that he bit me with,
    And C was a cry of pain.

D was the damn that I damned him with,
    E was its echoing roll;
F was the fear that I'd sat too 'ard
    On the top of a red-'ot coal.

G was the grease-stained moleskin pants
    Which I had to get up and rub,
And H was my haste as I humped myself
    To the bar of the nearest pub.

I was the inn where the snake-juice flows,
    An' yer drought-struck throat gets sluiced;
J was a jag of the good old sort,
    An' the 'jumps' that jag produced.

K was the kind of a time I 'ad;
   L was a large-sized 'ead;
M was a mouth like a quick-lime pit,
   Or a mug full of melted lead.

N was the nasty things I saw
   As I lay on my back all day,
Which goggled their eyes as they grinned at me
   In the reg'lar jim-jam way.

O was an owl of the 'ard-boiled kind,
   Which I certainly seemed to be;
P was the pledge which I took before
   A remarkably fat JP.

Q was the quill which would not keep still
   As I signed my name, dead slow;
And R the respectable life I thought
   I'd lead for a month or so.

S was the swag which I 'umped next day,
   When the boss gave me the sack;
T was the terrible time I 'ad
   With the station cooks out back.

U is the unkind way they 'as
   With a cove when 'is luck is down;
And V's my vow to get square some day
   When I meet them cooks in town.

W the well-cooked feeds you want
   When the wallaby track you roam,
Which you never will get from a station cook
   If you tramp till the cows come home.

And now this alphabetical yarn
   Must stop, for I may allege
That XYZ are a bit too stiff
   For a cove wot's took the pledge.

The Brew

Mark Kleinschmidt

Old Bill and mate Blue came in from the bush,
They were sick of the dust and the flies.
And they landed a job at Eagle Farm,
Refuelling a giant of the skies.

Now the Concorde is special as aeroplanes go,
The brew for its engine is tops.
Some splashed on Bill's face, he licked his lips
And pronounced it much better than hops.

So they drained off a drop, had a wee dram,
And toasted, then went shout for shout.
How they ever got home at the end of the day,
Was something to wonder about.

Bill woke with the dawn to the telephone's ring,
His head held a jet engine's whine,
His proboscis had grown like a Concorde cockpit,
And there was his mate on the line.

'Hey, Bluey,' Bill said, 'have you looked in the glass?
I look like a bloody aeroplane.
I swear to you, son, it's a right lively drop,
But never, no never again.'

'Now listen up close,' came the crackling reply.
'May the Lord stike me down, cross my heart.
I'm calling you now from a phonebox in France;
Whatever you do, mate, don't fart!'

The Convicts' Rum Song

Anon

Cut yer name across me backbone,
Stretch me skin across a drum,
Iron me up on Pinchgut Island
From to-day till Kingdom Come!

I will eat yer Norfolk dumpling
Like a juicy Spanish plum,
Even dance the Newgate Hornpipe
If ye'll only gimme RUM!

The Glass on the Bar

Henry Lawson

Three bushmen one morning rode up to an inn,
And one of them called for drinks with a grin;
They'd only returned from a trip to the North,
And, eager to greet them, the landlord came forth,
He absently poured out a glass of Three Star,
And set down that drink with the rest on the bar.

'There, that is for Harry,' he said, 'and it's queer,
'Tis the very same glass that he drank from last year;
His name's on the glass, you can read it like print,
He scratched it himself with an old piece of flint;
I remember his drink – it was always Three Star' –
And the landlord looked out through the door of the bar.

He looked at the horses, and counted but three:
'You were always together – where's Harry?' cried he.
Oh, sadly they looked at the glass as they said,
'You may put it away, for our old mate is dead;'
But one, gazing out o'er the ridges afar,
Said, 'We owe him a shout – leave the glass on the bar.'

They thought of the far-away grave on the plain,
They thought of the comrade who came not again,
They lifted their glasses, and sadly they said:
'We drink to the name of the mate who is dead.'
And the sunlight streamed in, and a light like a star
Seemed to glow in the depth of the glass on the bar.

And still in that shanty a tumbler is seen,
It stands by the clock, ever polished and clean;
And often the strangers will read as they pass
The name of a bushman engraved on the glass;
And though on the shelf but a dozen there are,
That glass never stands with the rest on the bar.

On the Boundary

Love & Marriage

I suppose I have been a little loose with the term 'love' here. A couple of poems about what you would probably call 'lust' have managed to sneak in. They're quite inoffensive by today's standards so I suppose I can say they're about 'attraction' and leave it at that! I'm sure many readers will be surprised to find good old respectable 'Banjo' Paterson writing about the world's oldest profession. (I'm sure it was from second-hand knowledge!)

'On the Boundary' is the perfect title piece for this section. Whenever a man and a woman are forced together, by love, lust, marriage or convenience, they are both operating 'on the boundary' of their own gender-specific personalities in attempting to understand the emotional territory beyond the fence! Some of these verses are about looking over that fence and making visits to that territory. Other poems are about boundary disagreements, border skirmishes and retreats!

It is interesting to note that the great Aussie tradition of verse expression rubbed off on US President Herbert Hoover who, as a young man, lived in Kalgoorlie. His love poem to an Aussie girl is included here.

Incidentally, those who subscribe to the theory that Aussies are not much good at expressing their emotions and feelings about the opposite sex might like to read some of the more serious of these poems and think again.

On the Boundary

Barcroft Boake

I love the ancient boundary-fence –
That mouldering chock-and-log:
When I go ride the boundary
I let the old horse jog,
And take his pleasure in and out
Where sandalwood grows dense,
And tender pines clasp hands across
The log that tops the fence.

'Tis pleasant on the boundary-fence
  These sultry summer days;
A mile away, outside the scrub,
  The plain is all ablaze.
The sheep are panting on the camps –
  The heat is so intense;
But here the shade is cool and sweet
  Along the boundary-fence.

I love to loaf along the fence:
  So does my collie dog:
He often finds a spotted cat
  Hid in a hollow log.
He's very near as old as I
  And ought to have more sense –
I've hammered him so many times
  Along the boundary-fence.

My mother says that boundary-fence
  Must surely be bewitched;
The old man says that through that fence
  The neighbours are enriched;
It's always down, and through the gaps
  Our stock all get them hence –
It takes me half my time to watch
  The doings of that fence.

But should you seek the reason
  You won't travel very far:
'Tis hid a mile away among
  The murmuring belar:
The Jones's block joins on to ours,
  And so, in consequence,
It's part of Polly's work to ride
  Their side the boundary-fence.

Under the Wattle

'The Kangaroo'

'Why should not wattle do for mistletoe?'
Asked one – they were but two – where wattles grow.
He was her lover too, who urged her so;
'Why should not wattle do for mistletoe?'
A rose cheek rosier grew, rose lips breathed low,
'Since it is here, and you, I hardly know,
Why wattle should not do for mistletoe.'

Boomerang Cafe

John Williamson

At the Boomerang Cafe, where I first met you,
With lipstick on your lips, and vinegar on your chips
At the Boomerang Cafe, where I sat down beside you
Do you remember, m'darling?

You thought I was a fool as I rolled a cigarette
You thought I was too old, but I bet you don't forget
The Boomerang Cafe where I first met you
Do you remember, m'darling?

Was it long ago, or just the other day
You played with the sugar; and I didn't know what to say
Or was it just a daydream they'll never run again
Memories with you

At the Boomerang Cafe all I could see
Was your brown eyes that would change the world for me
And the Boomerang Cafe changed the world for you
Do you remember, m'darling?

I recall it was raining, the heavens tore apart
Or was it just the lightning and thunder in my heart?
At the Boomerang Cafe, where I first met you
Do you remember, m'darling?

Much – A Little While

Harry Morant ('THE BREAKER')

'Love me little – love me long' – laggard lover penned such song.
Rather Nell – in other style – love me much a little while!
If that minstrel ever knew maid so kissable as you –
(Like you? – there was never such!) he'd have written, 'Love me much!'
Other loves have passed away (springtimes never last alway!)
'Twill be better – will it not – to think that we once loved 'a lot'!

They Met in the Hall at a Charity Ball

AB Paterson ('THE BANJO')

They met in the hall, at a Charity Ball,
   Patronised by the pink of Society,
They were both in a state, I grieve to relate,
   That the Clergyman calls insobriety.

He wanted to know was she *comme il faut*,
   Or whether her manner was shadylike,
And he wondered in doubt, as she lowered a stout,
   In a style more proficient than ladylike.

He asked might he call, the night after the Ball,
   If she'd pardon his impetuosity,
She embraced him and said, 'You must come home to bed,
   Just to show there is no animosity.'

She sang him a song, as they rattled along,
   There were verses a little bit blue in it,
And a story she told of adventures of old,
   With a queer situation or two in it.

When they went to repose, and he threw off his clothes,
   In his anxious excitement to doss it, he
Was knocked when she bid him fork out two quid,
   Just to show there was no animosity.

'Twas a little bit rough, but he forked out the stuff,
   Though he thought it was very absurd of her,
Then she went down below, for a moment or so,
   And that was the last that he heard of her.

For a big-shouldered lout came and lumbered him out,
    And used him with awful ferocity,
He was very much hurt, but they chucked him his shirt,
    Just to show there was no animosity.

Do They Think that I Do Not Know?

Henry Lawson

They say that I never have written of love,
    As a writer of songs should do;
They say that I never could touch the strings
    With a touch that is firm and true;
They say I know nothing of women and men
    In the fields where Love's roses grow,
And they say I must write with a halting pen –
    Do you think that I do not know?

When the love-burst came, like an English Spring,
    In the days when our hair was brown,
And the hem of her skirt was a sacred thing
    And her hair was an angel's crown.
The shock when another man touched her arm,
    Where the dancers sat round in a row;
The hope and despair, and the false alarm –
    Do you think that I do not know?

By the arbour lights on the western farms,
    You remember the question put,
While you held her warm in your quivering arms
    And you trembled from head to foot.
The electric shock from her finger tips,
    And the murmuring answer low,
The soft, shy yielding of warm red lips –
    Do you think that I do not know?

She was buried at Brighton, where Gordon sleeps,
    When I was a world away;
And the sad old garden its secret keeps,
    For nobody knows to-day.

She left a message for me to read,
   Where the wild wide oceans flow;
Do you know how the heart of a man can bleed –
   Do you think that I do not know?

I stood by the grave where the dead girl lies,
   When the sunlit scenes were fair,
And the white clouds high in the autumn skies,
   And I answered the message there.
But the haunting words of the dead to me
   Shall go wherever I go.
She lives in the Marriage that Might Have Been –
   Do you think that I do not know?

They sneer or scoff, and they pray or groan,
   And the false friend plays his part.
Do you think that the blackguard who drinks alone
   Knows aught of a pure girl's heart?
Knows aught of the first pure love of a boy
   With his warm young blood aglow,
Knows aught of the thrill of the world-old joy –
   Do you think that I do not know?

They say that I never have written of love,
   They say that my heart is such
That finer feelings are far above;
   But a writer may know too much.
There are darkest depths in the brightest nights,
   When the clustering stars hang low;
There are things it would break his strong heart to write –
   Do you think that I do not know?

Mary Called Him 'Mister'

Henry Lawson

They'd parted but a year before – she never thought he'd come,
She stammer'd, blushed, held out her hand, and called him '*Mister* Gum'.
How could he know that all the while she longed to murmur 'John'.
He called her 'Miss le Brook', and asked how she was getting on.

They'd parted but a year before; they'd loved each other well,
But he'd been to the city, and he came back *such* a swell.
They longed to meet in fond embrace, they hungered for a kiss –
But Mary called him 'Mister', and the idiot called her 'Miss'.

He stood and lean'd against the door – a stupid chap was he –
And, when she asked if he'd come in and have a cup of tea,
He looked to left, he looked to right, and then he glanced behind,
And slowly doffed his cabbage-tree, and said he 'didn't mind'.

She made a shy apology because the meat was tough,
And then she asked him if he was sure his tea was sweet enough;
He stirred the tea and stipped it twice, and answer'd 'plenty, quite';
And cut the smallest piece of beef and said that it was 'right'.

She glanced at him at times and cough'd an awkward little cough;
He stared at anything but her and said, 'I must be off.'
That evening he went riding north – a sad and lonely ride –
She locked herself inside her room, and there sat down and cried.

They'd parted but a year before, they loved each other well –
But she was such a country girl and he was such a swell;
They longed to meet in fond embrace, they hungered for a kiss –
But Mary called him 'Mister' and the idiot called her 'Miss'.

As Long as Your Eyes are Blue

AB Paterson ('THE BANJO')

Wilt thou love me, sweet, when my hair is grey,
    And my cheeks shall have lost their hue?
When the charms of youth shall have passed away,
    Will your love as of old prove true?
For the looks may change, and the heart may range,
    And the love be no longer fond;
Wilt thou love with truth in the years of youth
    And away to the years beyond?

Oh, I love you, sweet, for your locks of brown
   And the blush on your cheek that lies –
But I love you most for the kindly heart
   That I see in your sweet blue eyes –
For the eyes are signs of the soul within,
   Of the heart that is leal and true,
And mine own sweetheart, I shall love you still,
   Just as long as your eyes are blue.

For the locks may bleach, and the cheeks of peach
   May be reft of their golden hue;
But mine own sweetheart, I shall love you still,
   Just as long as your eyes are blue.

Kitty's Broom

Harry Morant ('THE BREAKER')

When Kitty glides into the room – there I contrive to stay,
And watch her while she, with her broom, sweeps all the dust away.
For bright-faced slender Kitty's such a comely sight to see,
She grasps that broom with magic touch and waves it witchingly.
And with her white and shapely arms, where dimples love to play,
She wields that magic wand and charms dull care – and dust – away.
All life's care and sad concerns no longer darkly loom,
All shadow into sunlight turns – when Kitty 'does' the room.
Along life's thorny path of gloom I'd wend a cheerful way –
Did heaven send Kitty, with her broom, to brush the briars away!

Herbert Hoover's Love Song

Herbert Hoover

Do you ever dream, my sweetheart, of a twilight long ago,
Of a park in old Kalgoorlie, where the bougainvilleas grow,
Where the moonbeams on the pathways trace a shimmering brocade,
And the overhanging peppers form a lovers' promenade?

Where in soft cascades of cadence from a garden close at hand,
Came the murmerous, mellow music of a sweet, orchestral band.
Years have flown since then, my sweetheart, fleet as orchard blooms in May,
But the hour that fills my dreaming, was it only yesterday?

Stood we two a space in silence, while the summer sun slipped down,
And the grey dove dusk, with drooping pinions, wrapt the mining town,
Then you raised your tender glances darkly, dreamily to mine,
And my pulses clashed like symbols in a rhapsody divine.

And the pent-up fires of longing loosed their prison's weak control,
And in wild, hot words came rushing from my burning soul.
Wild hot words that spoke of passion, hitherto but half expressed,
And I clasped you close, my sweetheart, kissed you, strained you to my breast.

While the starlight-spangled heavens rolled around us where we stood,
And a tide of bliss kept surging through the current of our blood.
And I spent my soul in kisses, crushed upon your scarlet mouth,
Oh! My red-lipped, sunbrowned sweetheart, dark-eyed daughter of the south.

It was well that fate should part us, it was well my path should lead,
Back to slopes of high endeavour, aye, and was it well, indeed.
You have wed some southern squatter, learned long since his every whim,
Soothed his sorrows, borne his troubles, sung your sweetest songs for him.

I have fought my fight and triumphed, on the map I've writ my name,
But I prize one hour of loving, more than fifty years of fame.
It was but a summer madness that possessed us, men will hold,
And the yellow moon bewitched me with its wizardry of gold.

Let them say it, dear, but oft-times in the dusk I close my eyes
And in dreams drift back to where the stars rain splendour from the skies,
To a park in far Kalgoorlie, where the golden wattles grow,
Where you kissed me in the twilight of a summer long ago.

And I clasp you close, my sweetheart, while each throbbing pulse is thrilled,
By a low and mournful music that shall never more be stilled.

Where the Brumbies Come to Water

Will Ogilvie

There's a lonely grave half-hidden where the blue-grass droops above,
And the slab is rough that marks it, but we planted it for love;
There's a well-worn saddle hanging in the harness-room at home,
And a good old stock-horse waiting for the steps that never come;
There's mourning rank of riders closing in on either hand
O'er the vacant place he left us – he, the best of all the band,
Who is lying cold and silent with his hoarded hopes unwon
Where the brumbies come to water at the setting of the sun.

Some other mate with rougher touch will twist our greenhide thongs,
And round the fire some harsher voice will sing his lilting songs;
His dog will lick some other hand, and when the wild mob swings
We'll get some slower rider to replace him in the wings;
His horse will find a master new ere twice the sun goes down,
But who will kiss his light-o'-love a-weeping in the town? –
His light-o'-love, who kneels at night beyond the long lagoon
Where the brumbies come to water at the rising of the moon.

We've called her hard and bitter names who chose – another's wife –
To chain our comrade in her thrall and wreck his strong young life;
We've cursed her for her cruel love that seared like hate – and yet
We know when all is over there is one will not forget.
As she piles the white bush blossoms where her poor lost lover lies
With the death-dew on his forehead and the grave dark in his eyes,
Where the shadow-line is broken by the moonbeams' silver bars,
And the brumbies come to water at the lightning of the stars.

The Mini Skirt

Neil Carroll ('HIPSHOT')

The mini skirt is neat and trim,
But something else I've found.
Although they make a girl look slim,
They make a bloke look round.

Wife Swap

Frank Daniel

George was walking down the street
When a good old friend he chanced to meet.
Said George to Tom, 'G'day there mate!
I haven't seen you much of late!'
Said Tom to George, 'I've had some strife,
And I got this greyhound for my wife.'
'Well, half your luck,' George doffed his hat,
'Wish I could make a swap like that!'

Solace

Frank Daniel

Martha Mary Regan held her dying husband's hand.
Some forty years her senior, a proud and modest man.
For twenty years in wedded bliss he loved his Mary so –
This union saw a family – four sons were seen to grow.

The first three boys were big and strong, tall, solid and stout.
The fourth and youngest was a wimp, in looks he had missed out.
The old man cast a trusting eye towards his loving wife
And feebly whispered thanks to her for the good times in his life.

'But tell me – darlin' Mary, – please lay it on the line.
That skinny little bloke of ours – is he really mine?'
Mary squeezed his trembling hands then whispered in his ear.
'Yes my love, he is your son, rest assured and have no fear.'

Old Regan closed his dimming eyes – life faded from his face,
Mary took a long deep breath and sighed, 'Oh Saving Grace.
Thank God! He's gone with peace of mind, still with faith in me
Gone – and thank the Lord he didn't ask about the other three!'

Hitched

CJ Dennis

'An' – WILT – YEH – take – this – woman – fer – to – be –
  Yer – weddid – wife?' . . . O, strike me! Will I wot?
Take 'er? Doreen? 'E stan's there *arstin'* me!
  As if 'e thort per'aps I'd rather not!
  Take 'er? 'E seemed to think 'er kind was got
Like cigarette-cards, fer the arstin'. Still,
  I does me stunt in this 'ere hitchin' rot.
An' speaks me piece: 'Righto!' I sez, 'I will.'

'I will,' I sez. An' tho' a joyful shout
  Come from me bustin' 'eart – I know it did –
Me voice got sorter mangled comin' out.
  An' makes me whisper like a frightened kid.
  'I will,' I squeaks. An' I'd 'a' give a quid
To 'ad it on the quiet, wivout this fuss,
  An' orl the starin' crowd that Mar 'ad bid
To see this solim hitchin' up of us.

'Fer – rich-er – er – fer – por-er.' So 'e bleats.
  'In – sick-ness – an' – in –'ealth.' . . . An' there I stands,
  An' dunno 'arf the chatter I repeats,
  Nor wot the 'ell to do wiv my two 'ands.
  But 'e don't 'urry puttin' on our brands –
This white-'aired pilot-bloke – but gives it lip,
  Dressed in 'is little shirt, wiv frills an' bands.
'In sick-ness – an' – in –' Ar! I got the pip!

An' once I missed me turn; an' Ginger Mick,
  'Oo's my best-man, 'e ups an' beefs it out.
'I will!' 'e 'owls; an' fetches me a kick.
  'Your turn to chin!' 'e tips wiv a shout.
  An' there I'm standin' like a gawky lout.
(Aw, spare me! But I seemed to be all 'ands!)
  An' wonders wot 'e's goin' crook about,
Wiv 'arf a mind to crack 'im where 'e stands.

O, lumme! But ole Ginger was a trick!
  Got up regardless fer the solim rite
('E 'awks the bunnies when 'e toils, does Mick)
  An' twice I saw 'im feelin' fer a light
  To start a fag; an' trembles lest 'e might,
Thro' force o' habit like. 'E's nervis too;
  That's plain, fer orl 'is air o' bluff an' skite;
An' jist as keen as me to see it thro'.

But, 'struth, the wimmin! 'Ow they love this frill!
  Fer Auntie Liz, an' Mar, o' course, wus there;
An' Mar's two uncles' wives, an' Cousin Lil,
  An' 'arf a dozen more to grin and stare.
  I couldn't make me 'ands fit anywhere!
I felt like I wus up afore the Beak!
  But my Doreen she never turns a 'air,
Nor misses once when it's 'er turn to speak.

Ar, strike! No more swell marridges fer me!
  It seems a blinded year afore 'e's done.
We could 'a' fixed it in the registree
  Twice over 'fore this cove 'ad 'arf begun.
  I s'pose the wimmin git some sorter fun
Wiv all this guyver, an' 'is nibs's shirt.
  But, seems to me, it takes the bloomin' bun,
This stylish splicin' uv a bloke an' skirt.

'To – be – yer – weddid – wife –' Aw, take a pull!
  Wot in the 'ell's 'e think I come there for?
An' so 'e drawls an' drones until I'm full,
  An' wants to do a duck clean out the door.
  An' yet, fer orl 'is 'igh-falutin' jor,
Ole Snowy wus a reel good-meanin' bloke;
  If 'twasn't fer the 'oly look 'e wore
Yeh'd think 'e piled it on jist fer a joke.

An', when at last 'e shuts 'is little book,
   I 'eaves a sigh that nearly bust me vest.
But, 'Eavens! Now 'ere's muvver goin' crook!
   An' sobbin' awful on me manly chest!
   (I wish she'd give them water-works a rest.)
'My little girl!' she 'owls. 'O, treat 'er well!
   She's young – too young to leave 'er muvver's nest!'
'Orright, ole chook,' I nearly sez. O. 'ell!

An' then we 'as a beano up at Mar's –
   A slap-up feed, wiv wine an' two big geese.
Doreen sits next ter me, 'er eyes like stars.
   O, 'ow I wished their blessed yap would cease!
   The Parson-bloke 'e speaks a little piece,
That makes me blush an' 'ang me silly 'ead.
   'E sez 'e 'opes our lovin' will increase –
I *likes* that pilot fer the things 'e said.

'E sez Doreen an' me is in a boat,
   An' sailin' on the matrimonial sea;
'E sez as 'ow 'e 'opes we'll allus float
   In peace an' joy, from storm an' danger free.
   Then muvver gits to weepin' in 'er tea;
An' Auntie Liz sobs like a winded colt;
   An' Cousin Lil comes 'round an' kisses me;
Until I feel I'll 'ave to do a bolt.

Then Ginger gits end-up an' makes a speech –
   ('E'd 'ad a couple, but 'e wasn't shick.)
'My cobber 'ere,' 'e sez, ''as copped a peach!
   Of orl the barrer-load she is the pick!
   I 'opes 'e won't fergit 'is pals too quick
As wus 'is frien's in olden days, becors,
   I'm trustin', later on,' sez Ginger Mick,
'To celebrate the chris'nin'.' . . . 'Oly wars!

At last Doreen an' me we gits away,
   An' leaves 'em doin' nothin' to the scran.
(We're honey-moonin' down beside the Bay.)
   I gives a 'arf a dollar to the man
   Wot drives the cab; an' like two kids we ran
To ketch the train – Ah, strike! I could 'a' flown!
   We gets the carridge right agen the van.
She whistles, jolts, an' starts ... An' we're alone!

Doreen an' me! My precious bit o' fluff!
   Me own true weddid wife! ... An' we're alone!
She seems so frail, an' me so big an' rough –
   I dunno wot this feelin' is that's grown
   Inside me 'ere that makes me feel I own
A thing so tender like I fear to squeeze
   Too 'ard fer fear she'll break ... Then, wiv a groan
I starts to 'ear a coot call, 'Tickets, please!'

You could 'a' outed me right on the spot!
   I wus so rattled when that porter spoke.
Fer, 'struth! them tickets I 'ad fair forgot!
   But 'e jist laughs, an' takes it fer a joke.
   'We must ixcuse,' 'e sez, 'new-married folk.'
An' I pays up, an' grins, an' blushes red ...
   It shows 'ow married life improves a bloke:
If I'd bin single I'd 'a' punched 'is 'ead!

Who'll Give the Bride Away?

Bob Magor

Groom and groomsmen stared like brolgas
Standing stiffly in a line.
With the priest devoutly smiling –
Two young hearts he would entwine.

'Course the bride was late as usual
And they'd had a lengthy wait.
Then His Reverence got the signal –
They were coming through the gate.

As the wedding party entered
Bridesmaids straightened out the train.
While the organ geriatric
Thumped the 'Wedding March' refrain.

And the bride appeared resplendent
With the veil across her face.
Out of step her dad paced with her
Looking sadly out of place.

Like a bloated emperor penguin
He propelled her down the aisle.
And he wished he'd worn his work clothes –
Bib and brace were more his style.

But the aged priest beamed outwards
From his lofty pious perch
At the biggest mob of heathens
That he'd ever seen in church.

From his usual flock of twenty
It had swelled to overflow.
With two-thirds the town invited
While the rest gatecrashed the show.

The bride stood before the altar
With her father puffed with pride.
A deep sun-tanned Mallee cocky
Standing stiffly by her side.

Though his breath began to labour
For his cummerbund was tight
And like a hangman's noose, the collar,
Round his bull neck gave a bite.

Said the reverend, 'Dear beloved,
We have gathered here today ...'
And shortly after stopped proceedings
With, 'Who gives the bride away?'

The old cocky looked up sharply, saying,
'Is that some sort of joke?
Who gives? You think I'm giving ...
I've got news for you, old bloke!

'See that groom that stands before you
In his poncy velvet suit?
He's been hanging round for three years –
Useless hungry-gutted coot.

'Always seemed to come at meal times
And he'd skin my fridge of booze.
You wouldn't need to ask 'who gives her'
If you'd been there in my shoes.

'Then the mongrel got her pregnant
(Though I 'spose they're both to blame).
And he doesn't have a razoo
But she loves him just the same.

'So the wedding's in a hurry
With the baby on the way.
And I shouted her this white dress;
Though I thought it should be grey!

'Expensive wedding invitations
For the mob they have in tow.
And you ask a man "who gives her" . . .
Do you really want to know?

'Then the missus wants a new dress
And a handbag and some shoes.
And she didn't shop at Target
When the old girl went to choose.

'And she said my suit was shabby.
I should buy one like a swell.
And the groom, he'd only blue jeans,
So we bought him one as well.

'When I thought the worst was over
Then the daughter turned on tears.
Could I shout 'em a honeymoon? – Strewth,
They've been having one for years!

'You want to hear about receptions
Catered by the CWA?
It'll cost me bloody woolcheck . . .
And "who will give her" do you say.

'Take a look about you, reverend,
It's enough to make me scream.
Hordes of senile aunts and uncles
And the blasted football team.

'They've invited half the district
And I think it's rather rude
They come armed with ten buck presents
And eat sixty bucks of food.

'See that bloke there with the camera?
Steven Spielberg would be cheaper!
And you ask a man "Who gives her?"
It'd cost me less to keep her!

'And flowers! Are they expensive?
Take a look at this receipt.
Think I'll grow a heap next season
P'raps instead of planting wheat.

'And even you, Your Reverence;
Now you want a handout too.
And you ask me who will give her . . .
Boy, have I got news for you!

'Cause it's been a lousy year, Rev,
With the mouse plague and the drought.
And the mortgage says this wedding
I could really do without.

'But you've asked out loud, "who gives her?"
Well that's me, I'll have to say.
Cause after what this wedding's cost
She's all I've left to give away.'

Marri'd

Mary Gilmore

It's singing in and out,
　And feeling full of grace;
Here and there, up and down,
　And round about the place.

It's rolling up your sleeves,
　And whitening up the hearth,
And scrubbing out the floors,
　And sweeping down the path;

It's baking tarts and pies.
　And shining up the knives;
And feeling like some days
　Was worth a thousand lives.

It's watching out the door,
　And watching by the gate;
And watching down the road,
　And wondering why he's late;

And feeling anxious-like.
　For fear there's something wrong;
And wondering why he's kept,
　And why he takes so long.

It's coming back inside
　And sitting down a spell,
To sort o' make believe
　You're thinking things is well.

It's getting up again
　And wandering in and out;
And feeling wistful-like,
　Not knowing what about;

And flushing all at once
    And smiling just so sweet,
And feeling real proud
    The place is fresh and neat.

And feeling awful glad,
    Like them that watched Siloam;
And everything because –
    A man is coming Home!

The Bachelor's Return

Bob Miller

I've got some real fantastic news, though I say with tongue in cheek,
Yes, the wife has gone off visiting, to her mother's for a week.
I remembered many years ago, with a wretched little smile,
The lifestyle of a bachelor, I could handle for a while.
With subtle joy I took her in to catch the Greyhound bus,
A week to test my manhood, should be good for both of us.
I would again be master, no more pick up this and that,
My dog could come inside again, while outside goes her cat.

So I stopped to get some shopping, cause I probably needed some,
Just a dozen crates of fourex and a cask of bundy rum.
I could sit and watch the footy, with no whingin' anymore,
Discarding empty tinnies all around the loungeroom floor.
I could eat meat pies and pizzas, no more vegies would I need
And I'd use my grimy fingers, when I stopped to take a feed.
Yes, this week would be like heaven, everything would go to plan
'Cause a woman's not essential, for survival of a man.

I rang around some mates I knew, who were all single blokes.
Said, 'Come and watch the footy, have a beer and tell some jokes.
I'm batchin' mate,' I told them, 'everything'll be alright
If ya' get too flamin' sozzled, ya' can camp the flamin' night.'
So Jim and Blue and Murray, settled round the loungeroom floor,
Like a mob of naughty school boys, we all drank and smoked and swore.
But the booze was acting swiftly as I strained to stay erect
And it seemed to go unnoticed, that my home was being wrecked.

See Blue had burnt the carpet, with his bumpers all around
Murray chundered in the fishtank, now they floated upside down.
And Jim had fallen badly, from the table as he danced
In a tangled mess he flattened all her lovely indoor plants.
So I thanked the boys for coming as they staggered home next day.
The loungeroom was demolished and the beds in disarray.
But it's easy doing housework, as I hunted out the cat.
I can vacuum up the evidence in fifteen minutes flat.

So I dragged the vacuum floorward, from it's perch upon the shelf,
Yet I found it simpler watching, than to use the thing yourself,
And I instantly decided, that I'd have to clean it out.
First a 'doily, then some ornaments, swiftly vanished up the spout
So I took the hose and handle off and pulled the thing apart
But I must have dumped the switch on, cause I heard the motor start.
It was programmed for re-cycle, or some such mode I think
Cause it blasted soot and rubbish from the front door to the sink.

Now it took all night and one more day, to renovate that room
And now I know why Granny only used a flamin' broom.
Then I thought I'd do some washing as my socks were on the nose.
Our machine is automatic, should be simple, I suppose.
But I wasn't sure on cycles or on levels, rinse or spin
So I got me socks and threw a box of washing powder in.
A half an hour later, when I checked, me eyes were reeling
I'm sure she will be grateful that I've shampoo'd half the ceiling.

Now my health is slowly fading, it could be the booze; I fear
Cause me staple diet lately, has been toast and cans of beer.
Every morning when I wake up with this headache I deplore
I conclude it's dehydration, so I have to start once more.
I'm just a broken hollow shell of what I was last week.
If she says do this and that again, well I won't be givin' cheek.
I'll remember long the misery, the hunger and the pain
And I hope it's twenty, bloody years, before she goes again.

The Supermarket Syndrome

Col Wilson ('BLUE THE SHEARER')

I said I'd do the shopping at the supermarket store,
'That's lovely' sighed my darling, 'But don't get any more
Than I've written on this list. We must economise.'
And since I never disobey (in case I get chastised),
I set off for the supermarket, got myself a trolley.
I'd show my wife that I could shop as good as her, by golly.

Two small tins of salmon, the first thing on the list.
I think I know just where they are. Look! Sardines. I can't resist
Purchasing a can or two. It's ages since we had
Sardines on toast with melted cheese. One slip. That's not too bad.
Tea and coffee. Got them. And 'Wow! Tomato juice!'
And it says: 'No added sugar.' That's a healthy thing to choose.

What about a fruit knife? Ours are getting lost,
I think I'll get a couple at a reasonable cost.
Let's consult that shopping list. She says she needs some bread,
Better not lash out again. Otherwise I'm dead.
Those wholemeal rolls look tasty, though. I'll just get the six,
She wanted something else down here. Ah yes, the pudding mix.

Next she wants some frozen peas. Those meat pies look OK.
I'll get myself a couple for a cold and rainy day.
Light cheese slices, got them, but the tasty stuff looks nice,
And I'll get six frozen chickens while they're at a bargain price.
Continental frankfurts, Ooh! I love their special taste,
Half a dozen frankfurts, they wouldn't go to waste.

Now let's just check the trolley. Is there anything I've missed?
I think I'm in a bit of strife. I've lost the shopping list.
I think she said she wanted some tomato sauce and jelly,
Have you ever had that kind of sinking feeling in your belly?
I don't know why I'm terrified about my wife's aggression.
I'm a grown-up person now, I'll use my own discretion.

One thing that I'm certain of, we're short of wine and beer,
I know she won't be too upset if I get them here.
That checkout chick is sporting such a knowing sort of grin,
She likes to see the husbands, without their wives, come in.
Apparently, they're all like me, without the wives' constraint,
And driving up my driveway I admit, I'm feeling faint.

'You didn't get the salmon, or the cat food, or the bread.
You know how much I hate sardines. You've forgotten all I said.
Where's the milk and honey? And the tub of margarine?
The vegetables to make the soup? There's not a sign of greens.
Six cans of tomato juice? A card of plastic hooks?
And there's no room in the freezer for half a dozen chooks.
Fruit knives, meat pies, frankfurts. And look at all this grog,
And you've got twelve tins of dog food, and we haven't got a dog.
Where's the list I gave you? You lost it in the aisle?
You'll have to go back down again, and wipe that silly smile.'

I must say, she's ungrateful. The one thing on my mind,
Was trying to be helpful, trying to be kind.
And this is how she treats me. I'm wounded, insecure.
I don't think I want to do the shopping anymore.
And anyway, I can't go back to get the milk and honey.
With all those extra purchases, I've run right out of money.

Love Song

Helen Avery

I look at the hands on the table before me,
gnarled at the knuckles, and rough at the edge,
tanned to a leather, deep seamed and weathered,
strong in the fingers, as tough as the sedge.

These are the hands that handle rough fence posts,
dismantle an engine in black oil and grease,
wrestle with stock in hot sweat and bull dust,
fondle the work dog, and part the deep fleece.

Firm is their hold on the things they believe in,
they shade the eyes from the distance and sun,
shaped by the soil, and the earth that they work with,
they tilt back the hat when the day's work is done.

These are the hands that love me at night time,
gentle my fears, and tender my soul,
bring me to joy, and the sweet depths of passion,
walk by my side, and keep my life whole.

When Stock Go By

Harry Morant ('THE BREAKER')

Ah me! How clearly they come back –
Those golden days of long ago,
When down the droughty Bogan track
Tom came with stock from Ivanhoe.
The cattle passed our homestead gate,
Beside our well I watched them pass,
While Dad was in a fearful state
About his water and his grass.
Tom rode a bonny dark bay nag;
He wore a battered cabbage-tree;
And as I filled our water-bag,
He came and asked a drink from me.
Tom said that drink was just like wine;
He said my eyes were soft and brown;
He said there were no eyes like mine
From Dandaloo to Sydney Town.
I watched him with a trembling lip,
Yet little thought I then that he
Who asked a drink from me that trip,
Would next trip ask my Dad for me!
Tom's droving days long since are done;
The wet tear oft has dimmed my eye;
For days when I was wooed and won
Come back to me – when stock go by.

My Wife's Second Husband

Henry Lawson

The world goes round, old fellow,
  And still I'm in the swim,
While my wife's second husband
  Is growing old and grim.
I meet him in the city –
  It all seems very tame –
He glances at me sometimes
  As if I were to blame.

Oh, my wife's second husband
  Was handsome, young and true;
He had his boyish visions
  (I had my visions too).
He made a model lover –
  The greenest in the game –
They say, when I was married
  That I was just the same.

Though I am ten years older
  My hair is dark to-day,
While my wife's second husband
  Is quickly growing grey.
I drank when first he knew me,
  And he drank not at all;
I see that he, through drinking,
  Is going to the wall.

A sweet ill-treated woman,
  A drunken brute (Good Lord!) –
Ah, well, she got her freedom,
  And he got his reward.
He'll fight it out a season,
  For Fate will not be forced,
But my wife's second husband
  Shall surely be divorced.

I sympathize, and wonder
  What mutual friends would think
If my wife's second husband
  And I should have a drink.
And I a mere bystander –
  It almost seems absurd –
Might lay prophetically
  My hand on my wife's third.

But my wife's second husband
  His sorrows shall forget,
We'll clasp warm hands in friendship
  And clink our glasses yet.
We'll smoke cigars together,
  In pure philosophy,
While calmly contemplating
  The fate of number three.

The House Husband

Bob Miller

Now I'm really a touch old-fashioned,
Maybe five or ten years out of date,
But I like the way it used to be,
Back then, when things were straight.
I disagree with this new-age stuff,
All this swapping around of roles,
Like us blokes at home doin' the washing-up,
And you sheilas out digging holes.

Just who do they think they are?
They want to be equal and more,
They'll sit on their bums with a can of beer,
While we have to mop up the floor.
I'm sick of this bloody packin' up,
And cookin' and cleanin' and stuff.
It's time us blokes started fightin' back,
And tell 'em we've all had enough.

Next time she says, 'I'm off to the pub
With the girls for a couple of beers,'
Tell her, 'Don't come whingin' to me when ya crook,
And there's an achin' between your ears.
Don't think I'm ironin' ya workin' clothes,
Or gettin' out to pack your food,
And if ya come home frisky again tonight,
Well, I'm not in the bloody mood!

Now I've seen you eye that barman off –
Yeah, that good-looking ironman jerk.
I know what you rowdy sheilas are like
When you've had a hard day down at work.
Well, remember who cleans up ya bloody mess,
And who rinses ya socks and your undies.
You think we'll be right with a pat on the bum,
And a kiss and a cuddle on Sundays.'

Now youse reckon we're right on the weekdays,
When we're watchin' the Midday show.
Then on Wednesday mornings there's bingo –
Yeah, me mates and me always go.
Most Fridays we'll meet down at K-Mart,
And we'll have a good gossip outside,
But we're startin' to feel that we're used and abused –
So us blokes have to salvage some pride.

So tell her she'll have to stop drinkin' and gamblin',
And stayin' out alone.
Stop taking us husbands for granted,
And spend some more time here at home.
And there's one ultimatum I'm givin' –
'Ere our marriage might get on the skids –
If she doesn't stop all this high livin' –
I just will not be havin' her kids!

Good Looker

Glenny Palmer

I have a place for everything
And all is in its place,
But when my hubby's searching
Things just vanish without trace.

He opens up the cupboard door
And says, 'It's not in here.'
I think he's waiting for the thing
To wave to him and cheer.

'It must be in there somewhere,
You just used it yesterday.'
'Nope,' he says with arms still folded . . .
'Not in here, no way.'

By now I'm getting crabby
'Cause I've got my job to do,
But for the sake of peace
I take up searching for it too.

I reach inside the cupboard
And I shift a tin or two.
Do you believe in miracles?
The thing comes into view.

And does he hug and kiss me
'Cause the flamin' thing is found?
Not on your life, that's when
He turns the situation round.

He accuses me of hiding it:
'You shouldn't shove it here.'
'I haven't shoved it anywhere –
At least not yet, my dear.'

So now I'm an inventor
And I'm working on a plan
To make a see-through cupboard
That will liberate my man.

The shelves are all transparent,
Things are set to wave and cheer
Automatically, when
Someone says, 'It's not in here.'

Platypus & Kookaburra

Beasts & Birds

*E*arly white settlers to this great old continent were so entranced by the strangeness and unique nature of the wildlife that they couldn't wait to introduce rabbits, foxes, sparrows, cats and a whole host of other feral animals to join the escaped domestic creatures such as pigs, horses, donkeys, camels and buffalo – all of which proceeded to help destroy the pristine and unique ecology that nurtured the strange creatures that had the scientific world of eighteenth-century Europe amazed!

Our unique marsupials are still amazing and continue to inspire writers and poets. In this section the native animals share the pages with 'new' Australian creatures, such as cattle dogs, extinct Aussie creatures like the *Muttaburrasaurus* and a couple of non-existent creatures that I've thrown in for good measure.

Platypus and Kookaburra

Rex Ingamells

Platypus and Kookaburra
sat on a stump of gum,
watching streaks of sunset glide
and hearing insects hum.
The streaks were blue and red and green;
the insects had a yellow sheen.

Said Platypus, 'If I but knew
the way to fly, I'd be
a Platyburrakookapus
and live up in a tree.'
Said Kookaburra, 'I'll be blowed;
the river-bank has overflowed.

'My feet,' he said, 'are getting wet;
the water's touching us.
O, how I wish that I could be
a Kookaplatyburrapus
so I could safely splash and scud
through pools of deep and gorgeous mud.'

Upon that instant Bunyip came
and said, 'Your will be done:
you'll both be what you want to be
by rising of the sun.'
At that the streaks of blue and red
were gone and stars were there instead.

The morning came, as mornings do;
but what a morning that!
A Platyburrakookapus,
with beak as flat as flat,
crouched on a gum-branch high aloft:
and when he tried to laugh he coughed.

And, flopping in the mud and water
of the riverside,
a Kookaplatyburrapus
tried and tried and tried,
but tried in vain, to show that he
was clever – for he couldn't be.

That night the Bunyip came and climbed
the highest gumtree limb,
and Platyburrakookapus
was soon inside of him;
and then he ate without a fuss
poor Kookaplatyburrapus.

Bell-birds

Henry Kendall

By channels of coolness the echoes are calling,
And down the dim gorges I hear the creek falling:
It lives in the mountain where moss and the sedges
Touch with their beauty the banks and the ledges.
Through breaks of the cedar and sycamore bowers
Struggles the light that is love to the flowers;
And, softer than slumber, and sweeter than singing,
The notes of the bell-birds are running and ringing.

The silver-voiced bell-birds, the darlings of daytime!
They sing in September their songs of the May-time:
When shadows wax strong, and the thunder-bolts hurtle,
They hide with their fear in the leaves of the myrtle;
When rain and the sunbeams shine mingled together,
They start up like fairies that follow fair weather;
And straightway the hues of their feathers unfolden
Are the green and the purple, the blue and the golden.

October, the maiden of bright yellow tresses,
Loiters for love in these cool wildernesses;
Loiters, knee-deep, in the grasses, to listen,
Where dripping rocks gleam and the leafy pools glisten:
Then is the time when the water-moons splendid
Break with their gold, and are scattered or blended
Over the creeks, till the woodlands have warning
Of songs of the bell-bird and wings of the morning.

Welcome as waters unkissed by the summer
Are the voices of bell-birds to thirsty far-comers.
When fiery December sets foot in the forest.
And the need of the wayfarer presses the sorest.
Pent in the ridges for ever and ever
The bell-birds direct him to spring and to river,
With ring and with ripple, like runnels whose torrents
Are toned by the pebbles and leaves in the currents.

Often I sit, looking back to a childhood,
Mixt with the sights and the sounds of the wildwood,
Longing for power and the sweetness to fashion,
Lyrics with beats like the heart-beats of Passion; –
Songs interwoven of lights and of laughters
Borrowed from bell-birds in far forest-rafters;
So I might keep in the city and alleys
The beauty and strength of the deep mountain valleys:
Charming to slumber the pain of my losses
With glimpses of creeks and a vision of mosses.

Native Companions Dancing

John Shaw-Neilson

On the blue plains in wintry days
The stately birds move in the dance.
Keen eyes have they, and quaint old ways
On the blue plains in wintry days.
The Wind, their unseen Piper, plays,
They strut, salute, retreat, advance;
On the blue plains, on wintry days,
These stately birds move in the dance.

Old Man Platypus

AB Paterson ('THE BANJO')

Far from the trouble and toil of town,
 Where the reed beds sweep and shiver,
Look at a fragment of velvet brown –
Old Man Platypus drifting down,
 Drifting along the river.

And he plays and dives in the river bends
 In a style that is most elusive;
With few relations and fewer friends,
For Old Man Platypus descends
 From a family most exclusive.

He shares his burrow beneath the bank
 With his wife and his son and daughter
At the roots of the reeds and the grasses rank;
And the bubbles show where our hero sank
 To its entrance under water.

Safe in their burrow below the falls
 They live in a world of wonder,
Where no one visits and no one calls,
They sleep like little brown billiard balls
 With their beaks tucked neatly under.

And he talks in a deep unfriendly growl
 As he goes on his journey lonely;
For he's no relation to fish nor fowl,
Nor to bird nor beast, nor to horned owl;
 In fact, he's the one and only!

The Kangaroo

Hal Gye (JAMES HACKSTON)

I am the kangaroo,
Slate-grey, and red;
And when, as oft I do,
I lift my head
Against the far-off blue
Of sky and earth,
I am a symbol, too,
Of this land's birth.

I am the rock and tree,
The wide plains dry,
The gorges wild and free
The blue-hot sky,
The blue-grey greenery –
Gully and rise,
The Aboriginal,
And his far eyes.

The silences am I,
The granite peak,
The flood, the river high,
The dried-up creek,
The hot white clouds that lie
Before the sun,
The breeze that rustles by
Where grasses run.

I lift my head, and so
Time there is writ,
Ages of long ago
Are held in it.
I am a statue, oh,
As old as stone:
Grey boulder stooping low,
Standing, alone.

I am the dry, hot land.
The sand, the clay,
The burning wind that fanned
Some far-off day:
I, kangaroo, as planned,
Still, still unspent,
The breath, the bone, the strand
Of our continent.

My Dinosaur

Jim Haynes

My dinosaur can cross the street,
He's very careful with his feet,
He doesn't squash the folk we meet,
'Cos that would just be awful!

He always crosses at the lights
When he goes out alone at nights,
I've told him, 'Don't get into fights,
And don't be loud and roarful!'

He usually comes back home by eight,
He tiptoes in through our back gate,
And sleeps in our backyard till late,
He's very very snoreful!

It's hard to hide a dinosaur
In our backyard and I'm not sure
If the neighbours mind, what's more –
I don't know if it's lawful!

When he wakes up it's time for lunch,
I give him Coco Pops to munch,
He eats them with a mighty crunch,
Without milk, by the clawful!

He gets sad sometimes 'cos he knows
His family are extinct I s'pose.
I give him hankies for his nose,
Good job I've got a drawerful!

Muttaburrasaurus

Milton Taylor

Where the swamp is green and slimy,
Where the ground is black and grimy,
That's where HE'LL be – Oh Blimey!
MUTTABURRASAURUS.

And if he comes to track us,
He'll use his tail to whack us,
He'll jump on us and crack us.
MUTTABURRASAURUS.

He'll use his teeth to gnaw us,
His long toe-nails will bore us,
He'll chew and chomp and claw us.
MUTTABURRASAURUS.

He's really so gi-normous,
His fiery breath will warm us,
Into blobs of glob he'll form us.
MUTTABURRASAURUS.

We'll quietly go a-creeping,
And hope he won't be peeping,
Then, roaring, come out leaping.
MUTTABURRASAURUS.

If we see him there before us,
Let's hope he'll just ignore us,
We'll say he never saw us.
MUTTABURRASAURUS.

The Ant Explorer

CJ Dennis

Once a little sugar ant made up his mind to roam –
To fare away, far away, far away from home.
He had eaten all his breakfast, and he had his Ma's consent
To see what he should chance to see and here's the way he went –
Up and down a fern frond, round and round a stone,
Down a gloomy gully where he loathed to be alone,
Up a mighty mountain range, seven inches high,
Through the fearful forest grass that nearly hid the sky,
Out along a bracken bridge, bending in the moss,
Till he reached a dreadful desert that was feet and feet across.
'Twas a dry, deserted desert, and a trackless land to tread;
He wished that he was home again and tucked-up tight in bed.
His little legs were wobbly, his strength was nearly spent,
And so he turned around again and here's the way he went –
Back away from desert lands feet and feet across,
Back along the bracken bridge bending in the moss,
Through the fearful forest grass, shutting out the sky,
Up a mighty mountain range seven inches high,
Down a gloomy gully, where he loathed to be alone,
Up and down a fern frond and round and round a stone.
A dreary ant, a weary ant, resolved no more to roam,
He staggered up a garden path and popped back home.

264

Flies

Joseph Tishler ('BELLERIVE')

When the wind doth cease to ripple and the blazing sun is high,
We are pestered by the families of Mr and Mrs Fly,
Buzzing here and buzzing there and buzzing o'er the table,
They must have populated since the days of Cain and Abel!

Fleas

Joseph Tishler ('BELLERIVE')

Only a Flea, a restless flea, a flea of the sultry night;
Only a flea, a diabolical flea, the flea that pranceth and bite;
'Twill boldly leap, deprive you of sleep, will cause you to wriggle and scratch;
Only a flea, a pest of a flea, but a deuced hard insect to catch!

Pensioned Off!

Carmel Randle

My farm is full of pensioners – the kind, four-legged type
That potter round my paddock, waiting 'till the time is ripe
To go to 'Horses' Heaven', or wherever horses go,
But every time one passes on, I'll shed a tear, I know!

My children loved these animals! I confess that I did, too!
I saw so many of them born – each miracle seemed new!
I watched my husband break them in with gentle, loving care,
And when each child acquired a mount, believe me – I was there!

Old Dixie, and fat Brigadoon had taught them all to ride,
But owning their own pony was the ultimate in pride!
And, black or bay or chestnut? What's a colour between friends?
The horse was theirs to love and care for! Sadly childhood ends!

Young folk grow up and marry, and not often have the chance
To live the life they might prefer, out where the pastures dance
In wind-swept orchestration – where the rain and sun combine
To grow a Horses' Heaven on this sunburnt land of mine.

And so I keep the pensioners – Sugar, Brigadoon,
Bee-Jay and old Frosty ... Freddy ... – now I'm making room
For ponies for the Grandchildren, and one – my husband's pet.
She's not too old to drop a foal – the line continues yet!

My farm is full of pensioners! I'm happy, you can see,
For they're my generation, and they're growing old with me!
They earn their quiet retirement! Each time I pause to look,
I read my children's childhood in our Family History Book!

'My Ute' (A Bit Of A Doggerel)

Milton Taylor

I'm a kelpie, a collie, a cattle dog blue,
Labrador, doberman, dalmatian too,
Poodle, retriever or foxie-pom cross,
In the back of my ute mate – I am the boss!
My ute is a Holden, a Datsun, a Ford,
Toyota or Mazda, when I spring aboard
I bask in the glory, the power one feels
When guiding my wonderful kingdom on wheels.
Be it brand new and shiny or battered and old
Black, white or purple or three shades of gold,
The colour's no problem, the brand name no sweat
As long as it gets me where I wish to get.
My ute is the best, creme de la creme
Ute and dog, dog and ute, oh boy what a team!
Surveying my realm I'm bursting with pride
Enjoying my wondrous triumphal ride.
You'll all hear my challenge, my bark of defiance
Commanding attention, demanding compliance
As my ute makes its progress, hear the sound ring
From the king of the ute, in the ute of the king.
Other dogs howl as they strain to compete
With my regal position, Lord of the street,
Their utes are quite nice, I bear them no malice
But compared to my marvellous travelling palace
They're damned insufficient for one of my stature,
They can't cause euphoria, bring about rapture
Like my splendid ute can, it's one of a kind,
Most noble of utes – that ute is mine!

On the footpath or street I'll do you no harm,
But dare touch my ute and I'll chew off your arm.
The eye of the tiger and lurking beneath
The heart of the lion with crocodile's teeth!
Docile no longer, ablaze with aggression
Guarding my treasured, most valued possession.
What causes this change, this strange transformation
From friend to all men to scourge of the nation?
If man's home is his castle, then a dog has one too,
Nought else can approach what a ute does for you,
And the pride, the contentment, I tell you it's beaut,
Just being a dog in your own bloody ute!

A Pig's Lament

Murray Hartin

People say I'm ugly, people say I'm fat,
People say a lot of things a damn sight worse than that.
They say I like to live in slop, they say my hygiene's crook,
They say my life is total filth – but I tell ya, they're mistook.

I may be just a pig to them who rolls in mud and sludge,
But who are they to criticise, who are they to judge?
If I'm given half a chance I'm really very clean,
I don't throw rubbish in the creek or breathe in nicotine.

I don't pump smoke into the air or sewage to the sea,
There's a lot of things that I don't do, but still they pick on me.
Well, it's only fair I get the chance to have a little dig,
You can keep your humans, 'cause I'd rather be a PIG!

Cats on the Roof

Ted Harrington

The street where I board is a forest of flats,
And it's cursed by a plague of most insolent cats.
As soon as the sun has sunk down in the west
They all sally forth on an amorous quest.
A tomcat will call from the top of a roof,
A second will answer from somewhere aloof;
Then others arrive, and the concert begins
As they slither and slide on the tiles and the tins.

Cats on the roof,
Cats on the roof,
Amorous, clamorous
Cats on the roof,
White ones and yellow ones,
Black-as-Othello ones,
Oh, the Devil's in league with the cats on the roof.

They talk of the need for our country's defence,
But it wouldn't involve a great deal of expense
To put on the market some new sort of bombs
To hurl at the tabs and the turbulent toms
Who gather in numbers that nightly increase
To shatter our slumber and slaughter our peace.
An inventor will surely make plenty of oof
Who can deal with the menace of cats on the roof,

They climb and they clamber, they hiss and they wail,
And they go up and down on the musical scale.
A shy young soprano will start on a note
While the ardent old tenor is clearing his throat.
Then off they will go on a dainty duet,
And the bass will come in when the tempo is set;
And any young student of sharps and of flats
Can learn quite a lot from a chorus of cats.

Then all of a sudden the tempo will change –
They really possess a most wonderful range
From alto, contralto, falsetto and bass;
Caruso and Melba are not in the race.
The tenor will rise on a note of his own
And the bass will die off to a horrible moan.
Oh, I doubt if the patience of Job would be proof
'Gainst amorous, clamorous cats on the roof.

A lull may occur when the midnight is past,
And you think you are set for some slumber at last,
But just as you're dozing, your face to the wall,
The concert will end in a general brawl.
And you'll turn on your pillow and mentally vow
To kill every cat that you meet with from now,
Till morning comes in with a dusting of mats,
And another night's rest has been ruined by cats.

Cats on the roof,
Cats on the roof,
Amorous, clamorous
Cats on the roof,
White ones and yellow ones,
Black-as-Othello ones,
Oh, the Devil's in league with the cats on the roof.

The Magpie Season

Bob Magor

It's that blasted magpie season
When for no apparent reason
These sweet gentle backyard creatures
    all become a killer force.
Crack attack – no time for details,
Clear the sky – from wrens to wedgetails.
And the earthbound feel their fury too
    from rabbit up to horse.

Do their hormones stir internal
When these birds become maternal
And these placid peaceful neighbours
    change from Jekyll into Hyde?
And you know your peace is erstwhile
When a fiery feathered missile
Makes you wish you'd worn a helmet
    if you journey far outside.

It's beyond my comprehension –
They reject my intervention
While perched sixty feet up skywards
    on a eucalyptus throne.
And their beaks snap close to ravage
Howling wings swoop past to savage
For where yesterday was peaceful
    now today's a battle zone.

269

Overnight the rooster moulted
Then the house cow up and bolted.
The poor cat's gone into hiding
   and the dog's got PMT.
Yes, that's Puppy Magpie Tension
And it's embarassing to mention.
That my farm's reduced to chaos
   by some birds up in a tree.

For they'll catch you unsuspecting
Like from chookhouse egg collecting
Even hanging out the washing
   soon becomes a risky chore.
And I s'pose they think it's funny
As I seek the outside dunny,
That they sometimes cause a mishap
   long before I reach the door.

But although these feathered fighters
Are annoying little blighters.
There's odd bonuses created
   sent to make a fellow glad.
The wife's mother copped a mauling
And Jehovahs ceased their calling
And I'm too scared to mow the lawn now
   – so you see it's not all bad.

Love Song to a Yabbie

Grahame Watt

We were sitting by a waterhole, my girl and I, one night,
When we heard a yabbie singing a love song clear and bright.
'If I could only hold your claw and gently touch your feeler,
I'd be yours for evermore and you would be my sheila.
I'd get down on my sixteen knees, for me it's just frustration,
I feel for you, my shell goes weak, you are my own crustacean.
You're the yabbie that I love, I've gone and flipped my flippers,
We could settle in the mud and raise lots of little nippers.'

Cricket Match!

Carmel Randle

There's a cricket in the loo
And I don't know what to do.
'Cause I've come here in a hurry and I really want to go ...
And I'm sure that if I sit
And try to do my little bit,
He'll get a fright and jump on me, I know!

Now, I know he's only small,
But that doesn't count at all!
It's the thought of something jumping on your bum!
'Cause a cricket looks quite prickly –
And my bum is rather tickly –
And I wish he'd take himself to Kingdom Come!

I suppose I ought to catch him,
Take him out, and then dispatch him
To join his cobbers in the Great Outdoors
Or I could call a mate
To come and save me from my fate –
But I don't think that would earn me much applause!

Now, if it was a snake,
All the household I could wake,
And they'd run with sticks and rakes to save my life,
But when it is a cricket,
They expect that you can lick it
Yourself – and save your Family all the strife!

So, whatever can I do
With this cricket in the loo
Who's causing all this mental flap and fluttin'?
Ah yes! I'm gonna win!
I'll just send him for a swim –
I'll reach across and quickly press the button!

There's a Daddy Longlegs at Work Somewhere

Greg Champion and Jim Haynes

There's one just here and one over there,
Spinnin' their webs and walkin' on air,
On the go, no time to spare,
There's a Daddy Longlegs at Work Somewhere.

In a bookcase by the phone,
That's a Daddy Longlegs' home,
Danglin' blissfully, unaware,
There's a Daddy Longlegs at Work Somewhere.

In the cupboard where we keep the broom,
In the laundry or in Mum's spare room,
Or in the space behind the stair,
There's a Daddy Longlegs at Work Somewhere.

Upside down and always busy,
You reckon that they'd get real dizzy,
Don't disturb them, have a care,
There's a Daddy Longlegs at Work Somewhere.

Station Songs & Droving Ditties

Cattle & Sheep

Many people think that this type of poetry is the only kind written in the traditional rhymed verse style by Australia's so-called 'bush' poets. Obviously not true, as you can see – only twenty or so out of almost three hundred poems! Bush verse for entertainment today is just as likely to be about contemporary life in suburbia; albeit with the traditional viewpoint and humour of the old verse style still intact.

Still, it is true that rhymed verse has documented rural life in Australia over two centuries and, consequently, this section could have filled the whole book. Therefore I tried very hard to make it a collection of the highest quality pieces that display the various styles and moods of traditional verse from the droving days and the era when Australia 'rode on the sheep's back'. The poems date from mid-nineteenth century to well into the twentieth century and most of the 'greats' are represented.

Station Songs and Droving Ditties

Harry Morant ('THE BREAKER')

'Station songs and droving ditties!'
Strung together on the track
Far away from coastal cities
In the droving days – outback;

Some on distant water-courses
'Neath the blazing Northern sun,
When returning with the horses
To a far North-western run;

Some were fashioned in the gloaming
While the morrow's damper cooked;
Some were penned by rivers roaming
Where the wily fish was hooked;

Ere the midday 'quart' was ready
And an hour was slow to pass
Whilst the nags were feeding steady
On the ripening Mitchell grass;

Or, when horse-bells chimed and tinkled
Where the feed was drenched with dew,
And the wintry white stars twinkled
High above in heaven's blue.

Then – of stockwhips' ring and rattle
In the range – some memory flashed;
Or of night-rides after cattle
When the gidya branches crashed.

And a rhyme perchance I've come by
Recollecting some past ride –
When we trapped the flying brumby
On the Southern Queensland side.

Jingles! – neither good nor clever –
Just a rover's random rhymes,
But they'll serve their turn if ever
They recall the old bush times,

When a bushman, in his leisure,
Reads them 'neath the shady pine;
Or they give one moment's pleasure
To some old bush mate o' mine!

Rain

Anon

What a friend we have in Jesus,
Sending all the lovely rain.
Fills the rousie's heart with pleasure,
Fills the shearer's heart with pain.

The Grass Stealers

JM Allison

In Australia where the cattle tracks
Are two miles wide,
And run from northern Queensland
To the Great Divide,
The drover and the shearer
And the rouseabouts, alas!
They wouldn't steal a penny,
But they all steal grass.

For the neddies never wander
If the going's good and sweet,
But stick around the fire
With the hobbles on their feet.
So Alf and Bill and Bendigo
And Harry of the Pass,
They wouldn't steal a copper,
But they all steal grass.

When the Overlanders gather
In the wide and dusty plain,
When tomorrow's never mentioned,
And they never speak of rain,
When the blazing sun is setting
Like a disc of shining brass,
They wouldn't steal a copper,
But they all steal grass.

They steal it from the squatter;
They steal it from his run.
They steal it from the cocky
And think it mighty fun.
They steal it from each other,
And nothing can surpass
The methods of the travellers
Who all steal grass.

It's sundown on the Darling,
There's water in the bend,
But not a blade of forage
Where the cattle musters end.
So it's nip the squatter's wire
And let the horses pass!
They'll take the track tomorrow
With their bellies full of grass.

Now stealing grass for horses
May be a horrid crime,
Especially to the squatter
With his paddocks lush and prime;
But a man who wouldn't steal
A bit of grass to feed his horse
Should be flung into the Darling
Or some other watercourse.

Saltbush Bill

AB Paterson ('THE BANJO')

Now this is the law of the Overland that all in the West obey –
A man must cover with travelling sheep a six-mile stage a day;
But this is the law which the drovers make, right easily understood,
They travel their stage where the grass is bad, but they camp where the grass is good;
They camp, and they ravage the squatter's grass till never a blade remains,
Then they drift away as the white clouds drift on the edge of the saltbush plains;
From camp to camp and from run to run they battle it hand to hand
For a blade of grass and the right to pass on the track of the Overland.

For this is the law of the Great Stock Routes, 'tis written in white and black –
The man that goes with a travelling mob must keep to a half-mile track;
And the drovers keep to a half-mile track on the runs where the grass is dead,
But they spread their sheep on a well-grassed run till they go with a two-mile spread.
So the squatters hurry the drovers on from dawn till the fall of night,
And the squatters' dogs and the drovers' dogs get mixed in a deadly fight;
Yet the squatters' men, though they hunt the mob, are willing the peace to keep,
For the drovers learn how to use their hands when they go with the travelling sheep.

But this is the tale of a jackaroo that came from a foreign strand,
And the fight that he fought with Saltbush Bill, the King of the Overland.
Now Saltbush Bill was a drover tough, as ever the country knew,
He had fought his way on the Great Stock Routes from the sea to the big Barcoo;
He could tell when he came to a friendly run that gave him a chance to spread,
And he knew where the hungry owners were that hurried his sheep ahead;
He was drifting down in the 'Eighty drought with a mob that could scarcely creep –
When kangaroos by the thousands starve, it is rough on the travelling sheep.

And he camped one night at the crossing-place on the edge of the Wilga run,
'We must manage a feed for them here,' he said, 'or half of the mob are done!'
So he spread them out when they left the camp wherever they liked to go,
Till he grew aware of a jackaroo with a station-hand in tow,
And they set to work on the straggling sheep, and with many a stockwhip crack
They forced them in where the grass was dead in the space of the half-mile track;
And William prayed that the hand of Fate might suddenly strike him blue
But he'd get some grass for his starving sheep in the teeth of that jackaroo.

So he turned and he cursed the jackeroo, he cursed him alive or dead,
From the soles of his great unwieldy feet to the crown of his ugly head,
With an extra curse on the moke he rode and the cur at his heels that ran,
Till the jackaroo from his horse got down and went for the droving man;
With the station-hand for his picker-up, though the sheep ran loose the while,
They battled it out on the saltbush plain in the regular prize-ring style.
Now, the new-chum fought for his honour's sake and the pride of the English race,
But the drover fought for his daily bread with a smile on his bearded face –

So he shifted ground and he sparred for wind and he made it a lengthy mill,
And from time to time as his scouts came in they whispered to Saltbush Bill –
'We have spread the sheep with a two-mile spread, and the grass it is something grand,
You must stick to him, Bill, for another round for the pride of the Overland.'
The new-chum made it a rushing fight, though never a blow got home,
Till the sun rode high in the cloudless sky and glared on the brick-red loam
Till the sheep drew in to the shelter-trees and settled them down to rest;
Then the drover said he would fight no more and gave his opponent best.

So the new-chum rode to the station straight, and he told them a story grand
Of the desperate fight that he fought that day with the King of the Overland.
And the tale went home to the Public Schools of the pluck of the English swell,
How the drover fought for his very life, but blood in the end must tell.
278   But the travelling sheep and the Wilga sheep were boxed on the Old Man Plain.

'Twas a full week's work ere they drafted out and hunted them off again;
With a week's good grass in their wretched hides, with a curse and a stockwhip crack,
They hunted them off on the road once more to starve on the half-mile track.

And Saltbush Bill, on the Overland, will many a time recite
How the best day's work that he ever did was the day that he lost the fight.

Andy's Gone with Cattle

Henry Lawson

Our Andy's gone with cattle now –
Our hearts are out of order –
With drought he's gone to battle now
Across the Queensland border.

He's left us in dejection now,
Our thoughts with him are roving;
It's dull on this selection now,
Since Andy went a-droving.

Who now shall wear the cheerful face
In times when things are slackest?
And who shall whistle round the place
When Fortune frowns her blackest?

Oh, who shall cheek the squatter now
When he comes round us snarling?
His tongue is growing hotter now
Since Andy crossed the Darling.

The gates are out of order now,
In storms the 'riders' rattle;
For far across the border now
Our Andy's gone with cattle.

Poor Aunty's looking thin and white;
And Uncle's cross with worry;
And poor old Blucher howls all night
Since Andy left Macquarie.

Oh, may the showers in torrents fall,
And all the tanks run over;
And may the grass grow green and tall
In pathways of the drover;

And may good angels send the rain
On desert stretches sandy;
And when the summer comes again
God grant 'twill bring us Andy.

Where the Pelican Builds

Mary Hannay-Foote

The horses were ready, the rails were down,
But the riders lingered still –
One had a parting word to say,
And one had his pipe to fill.
Then they mounted, one with a granted prayer,
And one with a grief unguessed.
'We are going,' they said as they rode away,
'Where the pelican builds her nest!'

They had told us of pastures wide and green,
To be sought past the sunset's glow;
Of rifts in the ranges by opal lit;
And gold 'neath the river's flow.
And thirst and hunger were banished words
When they spoke of the unknown West;
No drought they dreaded, no flood they feared,
Where the pelican builds her nest!

The creek at the ford was but fetlock deep
When we watched them crossing there;
The rains have replenished it thrice since then,
And thrice has the rock lain bare.
But the waters of Hope have flowed and fled,
And never from blue hill's breast
Come back – by the sun and the sands devoured –
Where the pelican builds her nest.

Those Who Dare

Anon

'Neath blazing skies beyond the farthest hut,
Beyond the gibber desert's stony glare,
Lie grassy leagues of pasture, wondrous lands,
That hold the rainbow's end for those who dare.

The Packhorse Drover

Bruce Simpson ('LANCEWOOD')

Oh the droving life is a life that's free,
   On the unfenced routes of the back country,
And a packhorse camp is the place to be,
   When they're bringing the store mobs over;
Oh life is happy with not a care,
   With the bush smells strong on the balmy air,
For a whiff of the cook would curl your hair,
   In the camp of the packhorse drover.

Now the drover's bed is a couch to please,
   On the stony ground mid the Bogan fleas,
Or in mud that is up to a horse's knees,
   when the wintry rains drift over;
But life is happy and life is sweet,
   Tho' there's never enough for a man to eat,
And losing weight is a simple feat,
   In the camp of a packhorse drover.

The sky is grey with a hint of rain,
   While the wind blows chill o'er the Rankine plain,
And a ringer swears that he'll drove again,
   When the ceiling of Hell frosts over;
But life is happy and life is good,
   'Round a cow dung fire when there is no wood,
When the damper tastes as it never should,
   In the camp of a packhorse drover.

We watch the mob and we sing the blues,
    And we'd sell our souls for a nip of booze,
As the hours drag by on their leaden shoes,
    And the Southern Cross turns over;
It's a rugged life but we never whine,
    For the mateship found in the bush is fine,
Tho' the boss of course is a hungry swine,
    And a typical packhorse drover.

Song of the Wave Hill Track

Bruce Simpson ('LANCEWOOD')

Our bullocks are fresh and the season is good,
    For we follow the yearly Wet.
The first mob back on the Wave Hill track,
    And the rain clouds gather yet.
We took our mob from the mustering camp,
    Just on a month ago,
Twelve hundred head and all scrub bred,
    They carry the 050.

Our horses are fat and the creeks are full,
    The feed is the very best;
We'll poke them along with a cheery song,
    And say goodbye to the West.
We camped last night past the timber's edge,
    Where the grasses grow like grain,
Behind our back is the timbered track,
    Before us – the blacksoil plain.

The blacksoil plain where mirages dance,
    And shimmer and then are gone,
Past Brady's grave where the grasses wave,
    The stockroute wanders on,
O'er the rolling downs that rise and fade,
    Past many a river bend,
O'er the tableland where the lone mills stand,
    And on to the journey's end.

But we are young and our hearts are light,
   And the life that we live is free,
With a cheque to spend at the journey's end,
   Not a care in the world have we,
For time and distance are nought to us,
   And the bullocks are feeding slow,
The first mob back on the Wave Hill track.
   Five hundred miles to go.

The Drover's Lament

Anon

There's the red kangaroo and the mad cockatoo,
That nests in the old gumtree,
And there's all those rabbits with engaging habits,
And they've all got a mate but me!
The emu on the flat, the little bush rat,
The wedgetail flying free,
Goanna lying still, wallaby on the hill –
They've all got a mate but me!

On Kiley's Run

AB Paterson ('THE BANJO')

The roving breezes come and go
   On Kiley's Run,
The sleepy river murmurs low,
And far away one dimly sees
Beyond the stretch of forest trees –
Beyond the foothills dusk and dun –
The ranges sleeping in the sun
   On Kiley's Run.

'Tis many years since first I came
   To Kiley's Run,
More years than I would care to name
Since I, a stripling, used to ride
For miles and miles at Kiley's side,
The while in stirring tones he told
The stories of the days of old
   On Kiley's Run.

I see the old bush homestead now
    On Kiley's Run,
Just nestled down beneath the brow
Of one small ridge above the sweep
Of river flat, where willows weep
And jasmine flowers and roses bloom,
The air was laden with perfume
    On Kiley's Run.

We lived the good old station life
    On Kiley's Run,
With little thought of care or strife.
Old Kiley seldom used to roam,
He liked to make the Run his home,
The swagman never turned away
With empty hand at close of day
    From Kiley's Run.

We kept a racehorse now and then
    On Kiley's Run,
And neighb'ring stations brought their men
To meetings where the sport was free,
And dainty ladies came to see
Their champions ride; with laugh and song
The old house rang the whole night long
    On Kiley's Run.

The station hands were friends I wot
    On Kiley's Run,
A reckless, merry-hearted lot –
All splendid riders, and they knew
The 'boss' was kindness through and through.
Old Kiley always stood their friend,
And so they served him to the end
    On Kiley's Run.

But droughts and losses came apace
    To Kiley's Run,
Till ruin stared him in the face;
He toiled and toiled while lived the light,
He dreamed of overdrafts at night:
At length, because he could not pay,
His bankers took the stock away
    From Kiley's Run.

Old Kiley stood and saw them go
 From Kiley's Run.
The well-bred cattle marching slow;
His stockmen, mates for many a day,
They wrung his hand and went away.
Too old to make another start,
Old Kiley died – of broken heart,
 On Kiley's Run.

The owner lives in England now
 Of Kiley's Run.
He knows a racehorse from a cow;
But that is all he knows of stock:
His chiefest care is how to dock
Expenses, and he sends from town
To cut the shearers' wages down
 On Kiley's Run.

There are no neighbours anywhere
 Near Kiley's Run.
The hospitable homes are bare,
The gardens gone; for no pretence
Must hinder cutting down expense:
The homestead that we held so dear
Contains a half-paid overseer
 On Kiley's Run.

All life and sport and hope have died
 On Kiley's Run.
No longer there the stockmen ride;
For sour-faced boundary riders creep
On mongrel horses after sheep,
Through ranges where, at racing speed,
Old Kiley used to 'wheel the lead'
 On Kiley's Run.

There runs a lane for thirty miles
 Through Kiley's Run.
On either side the herbage smiles,
But wretched trav'lling sheep must pass
Without a drink or blade of grass
Thro' that long lane of death and shame:
The weary drovers curse the name
 Of Kiley's Run.

The name itself is changed of late
   Of Kiley's Run.
They call it 'Chandos Park Estate'.
The lonely swagman through the dark
Must hump his swag past Chandos Park.
The name is English, don't you see,
The old name sweeter sounds to me
   Of 'Kiley's Run'.

I cannot guess what fate will bring
   To Kiley's Run –
For chances come and changes ring –
I scarcely think 'twill always be
Locked up to suit an absentee;
And if he lets it out in farms
His tenants soon will carry arms
   On Kiley's Run.

On Monday We've Mutton

F Lancelott

You may talk of the dishes of Paris renown,
Or for plenty through London may range,
If variety's pleasing, oh, leave either town,
And come to the bush for a change.

On Monday we've mutton, with damper and tea;
On Tuesday, tea, damper and mutton,
Such dishes I'm certain all men must agree
Are fit for peer, peasant, or glutton.

On Wednesday we've damper, with mutton and tea;
On Thursday tea, mutton and damper,
On Friday we've mutton, tea, damper, while we
With our flocks over hill and dale scamper.

Our Saturday feast may seem rather strange,
'Tis of damper with tea and fine mutton;
Now surely I've shown you that plenty of change
In the bush, is the friendly board put on.

But no, rest assured that another fine treat
Is ready for all men on one day,
For every bushman is sure that he'll meet
With the whole of the dishes on Sunday.

The Billy of Tea

Anon

You may talk of your whisky or talk of your beer,
I've something far better awaiting me here;
It stands on that fire beneath the gum-tree,
And you cannot much lick it – a billy of tea.
So fill up your tumbler as high as you can,
You'll never persuade me it's not the best plan,
To let all the beer and the spirits go free
And stick to my darling old Billy of Tea.

I wake in the morning as soon as 'tis light,
And go to the nosebag to see it's all right,
That the ants on the sugar no mortgage have got,
And immediately sling my old black billy-pot,
And while it is boiling the horses I seek,
And follow them down perhaps as far as the creek;
I take off the hobbles and let them go free,
And haste to tuck into my Billy of Tea.

And at night when I camp, if the day has been warm,
I give each of the horses their tucker of corn,
From the two in the pole to the one in the lead,
And the billy for each holds a comfortable feed;
Then the fire I start and the water I get,
And the corned beef and damper in order I set,
But I don't touch the grub, though so hungry I be,
I will wait till it's ready – the Billy of Tea.

Since the Country Carried Sheep

Harry Morant ('THE BREAKER')

We trucked the cows to Homebush, saw the girls, and started back,
Went West through Cunnamulla, and got to the Eulo track,
Camped a while at Gonybibil – but, Lord! you wouldn't know
It for the place where you and Mick were stockmen long ago.

Young Merino bought the station, fenced the run and built a 'shed',
Sacked the stockmen, sold the cattle, and put on sheep instead,
But he wasn't built for Queensland; and every blessed year
One hears of 'labour troubles' when Merino starts to shear.

There are ructions with the rouseabouts, and shearers' strikes galore!
The likes were never thought of in the cattle days of yore.
And slowly, round small paddocks now, the 'sleeping lizards' creep,
And Gonybibil's beggared since the country carried sheep.

Time was we had the horses up ere starlight waned away,
The billy would be boiling by the breaking of the day;
And our horses – by Protection – were aye in decent nick,
When we rode up the 'Bidgee where the clearskins mustered thick.

They've built *brush-yards* on Wild Horse Creek, where in the morning's hush
We've sat silent in the saddle, and listened for the rush
Of the scrubbers – when we heard 'em, 'twas wheel 'em if you can,
While gidgee, pine and mulga tried the nerve of horse and man.

The mickies that we've branded there! the colts we had to ride!
In Gonybibil's palmy days – before the old boss died.
Could Yorkie Hawkins see his run, I guess his ghost would weep,
For Gonybibil's beggared since the country carried sheep.

From sunrise until sunset through the summer days we'd ride,
But stockyard rails were up and pegged, with cattle safe inside,
When 'twixt the gloamin' and the murk, we heard the well-known note –
The peal of boisterous laughter from the kookaburra's throat.

Camped out beneath the starlit skies, the tree-tops overhead,
A saddle for a pillow, and a blanket for a bed,
'Twas pleasant, mate, to listen to the soughing of the breeze,
And learn the lilting lullabies which stirred the mulga-trees.

Our sleep was sound in those times, for the mustering days were hard,
The morrows might be harder, with the branding in the yard.
But did you see the station now! the men – and mokes – they keep!
You'd own the place was beggared – since the country carried sheep.

Shearing at Castlereagh

AB Paterson ('THE BANJO')

The bell is set aringing, and the engine gives a toot,
There's five and thirty shearers here are shearing for the loot,
So stir yourselves, you penners-up and shove the sheep along,
The musterers are fetching them a hundred thousand strong,
And make your collie dogs speak up – what would the buyers say
In London if the wool was late this year from Castlereagh?

The man that 'rung' the Tubbo shed is not the ringer here,
That stripling from the Cooma side can teach him how to shear.
They trim away the ragged locks, and rip the cutter goes,
And leaves a track of snowy fleece from brisket to the nose;
It's lovely how they peel it off with never stop nor stay,
They're racing for the ringer's place this year at Castlereagh.

The man that keeps the cutters sharp is growling in his cage,
He's always in a hurry and he's always in a rage –
'You clumsy-fisted muttonheads, you'd turn a fellow sick,
You pass yourselves as shearers? You were born to swing a pick!
Another broken cutter here, that's two you've broke today,
It's awful how such crawlers come to shear at Castlereagh.'

The youngsters picking up the fleece enjoy the merry din,
They throw the classer up the fleece, he throws it to the bin;
The pressers standing by the rack are waiting for the wool,
There's room for just a couple more, the press is nearly full;
Now jump upon the lever, lads, and heave and heave away,
Another bale of golden fleece is branded 'Castlereagh'.

Middleton's Rouseabout

Henry Lawson

Tall and freckled and sandy,
　　Face of a country lout;
This was the picture of Andy,
　　Middleton's Rouseabout.

Type of a coming nation,
　　In the land of cattle and sheep,
Worked on Middleton's station,
　　'Pound a week and his keep'.

On Middleton's wide dominions
　　Plied the stockwhip an' shears;
Hadn't any opinions,
　　Hadn't any 'idears'.

Swiftly the years went over,
　　Liquor and drought prevailed;
Middleton went as a drover,
　　After his station had failed.

Type of a careless nation,
　　Men who are soon played out,
Middleton was – and his station
　　Was bought by the Rouseabout.

Flourishing beard and sandy,
　　Tall and robust and stout;
This is the picture of Andy,
　　Middleton's Rouseabout.

Now on his own dominions
　　Works with his overseers;
Hasn't any opinions,
　　Hasn't any 'idears'.

Northward to the Sheds

Will Ogilvie

There's a whisper from the regions out beyond the Barwon banks;
There's a gathering of the legions and a forming of the ranks;
There's a murmur coming nearer with the signs that never fail,
And it's time for every shearer to be out upon the trail.
They must leave their girls behind them and their empty glasses, too,
For there's plenty left to mind them when they cross the dry Barcoo;
There'll be kissing, there'll be sorrow such as only sweethearts know,
But before the noon to-morrow they'll be singing as they go –

> For the Western creeks are calling,
> And the idle days are done,
> With the snowy fleeces falling
> And the Queensland sheds begun!

There is shortening of the bridle, there is tightening of the girth,
There is fondling of the idol that they love the best on earth;
Northward from the Lachlan River and the sun-dried Castlereagh,
Outward to the Never-Never ride the ringers on their way.
From the green bends of the Murray they have run their horses in,
For there's haste and there is hurry when the Queensland sheds begin;
On the Bogan they are bridling, they are saddling on the Bland;
There is plunging and there's sidling – for the colts don't understand

> That the Western creeks are calling
> And the idle days are done,
> With the snowy fleeces falling
> And the Queensland sheds begun!

They will camp below the station, they'll be cutting peg and pole,
Rearing tents for occupation till the calling of the roll;
And it's time the nags were driven, and it's time to strap the pack,
For there's never license given to the laggards on the track.
Hark the music of the battle! it is time to bare our swords;
Do you hear the rush and rattle as they tramp along the boards?
They are past the pen-doors picking light-woolled weaners one by one;
I can hear the shear-blades clicking and I know the fight's begun!

The Travelling Post Office

AB Paterson ('THE BANJO')

The roving breezes come and go, the reed beds sweep and sway,
The sleepy river murmurs low, and loiters on its way,
It is the land of lots o' time along the Castlereagh.

The old man's son had left the farm, he found it dull and slow,
He drifted to the great north-west where all the rovers go.
'He's gone so long,' the old man said, 'he's dropped right out of mind,
But if you'd write a line to him I'd take it very kind;
He's shearing here and fencing there, a kind of waif and stray,
He's droving now with Conroy's sheep along the Castlereagh.
The sheep are travelling for the grass, and travelling very slow;
They may be at Mundooran now, or past the Overflow,
Or tramping down the black soil flats across by Waddiwong,
But all those little country towns would send the letter wrong,
The mailman, if he's extra tired, would pass them in his sleep,
It's safest to address the note to 'Care of Conroy's sheep',
For five and twenty thousand head can scarcely go astray,
You write to "Care of Conroy's sheep along the Castlereagh".'

By rock and ridge and riverside the western mail has gone,
Across the great Blue Mountain Range to take that letter on.
A moment on the topmost grade while open fire doors glare,
She pauses like a living thing to breathe the mountain air,
Then launches down the other side across the plain away
To bear that note to 'Conroy's sheep along the Castlereagh'.

And now by coach and mailman's bag it goes from town to town,
And Conroy's Gap and Conroy's Creek have marked it 'further down'.
Beneath a sky of deepest blue where never cloud abides,
A speck upon the waste of plain the lonely mailman rides.
Where fierce hot winds have set the pine and myall boughs asweep
He hails the shearers passing by for news of Conroy's sheep.
By big lagoons where wildfowl play and crested pigeons flock,
By campfires where the drovers ride around their restless stock,
And past the teamster toiling down to fetch the wool away
My letter chases Conroy's sheep along the Castlereagh.

Station Life

WT Goodge ('THE COLONEL')

Oh, a station life is the life for me,
   And the cold baked mutton in the morning!
Oh, the glorious ride o'er the plains so free,
   And the cold baked mutton in the morning!
And the rising moon on the mountain's brow!
And the ringtailed 'possum on the gum tree bough!
And the leathery damper and the salted cow,
   And the cold baked mutton in the morning!

'Ard Tac

Anon

I'm a shearer, yes I am, and I've shorn 'em sheep and lamb,
From the Wimmera to the Darling Downs and back,
And I've rung a shed or two when the fleece was tough as glue,
But I'll tell you where I stuck the 'ardest tac.

I was down round Yenda way killin' time from day to day,
Till the big sheds started movin' further out;
When I struck a bloke by chance that I summed up in a glance
As a cocky from a vineyard round about.

Now it seems he picked me, too; well, it wasn't 'ard to do,
Cos I had some tongs, a-hangin' at the hip.
'I got a mob,' he said, 'a mob about two hundred head,
And I'd give a ten pun note to have the clip.'

I says: 'Right – I'll take the stand'; it meant gettin' in me hand;
And by nine o'clock we'd rounded up the mob
In a shed sunk in the ground – yeah, with wine casks all around.
And that was where I started on me job.

I goes easy for a bit while me hand was gettin' fit,
And by dinner time I'd done some half a score,
With the cocky pickin' up, and handing me a cup,
Of pinkie after every sheep I shore.

The cocky had to go away about the seventh day,
After showin' me the kind of casks to use;
Then *I'd* do the pickin' up, and manipulate the cup,
Strollin' round them wine casks, just to pick and choose.

Then I'd stagger to the pen, grab a sheep and start again,
With a noise between a hiccup and a sob,
And sometimes I'd fall asleep with me arms around the sheep,
Worn and weary from me over-arduous job.

And so, six weeks went by, until one day with a sigh,
I pushed the dear old cobbler through the door,
Gathered in the cocky's pay, then staggered on me way,
From the hardest bloody shed I ever shore.

It's Grand To Be a Squatter

AB Paterson ('THE BANJO')

It's grand to be a squatter
    And sit upon a post,
And watch your little ewes and lambs
    A-giving up the ghost.

It's grand to be a 'cockie'
    With wife and kids to keep,
And find an all-wise Providence
    Has mustered all your sheep.

It's grand to be a Western man,
    With shovel in your hand,
To dig your little homestead out
    From underneath the sand.

It's grand to be a shearer
    Along the Darling-side,
And pluck the wool from stinking sheep
    That some days since have died.

It's grand to be a rabbit
  And breed till all is blue,
And then to die in heaps because
  There's nothing left to chew.

It's grand to be a Minister
  And travel like a swell,
And tell the Central District folk
  To go to – Inverell.

It's grand to be a socialist
  And lead the bold array
That marches to prosperity
  At seven bob a day.

It's grand to be an unemployed
  And lie in the Domain,
And wake up every second day –
  And go to sleep again.

It's grand to borrow English tin
  To pay for wharves and docks,
And then to find it isn't in
  The little money-box.

It's grand to be a democrat
  And toady to the mob,
For fear that if you told the truth
  They'd hunt you from your job.

It's grand to be a lot of things
  In this fair Southern land,
But if the Lord would send us rain,
  That would, indeed, be grand!

Good Tales

Anon

We have our tales of other days,
When the bushmen meet and camp-fires blaze,
And round the ring of dancing light
The great dark bush with arms of night,
Folds every hearer in its spell . . .
Good tales the northern wanderers tell.

Buckalong

Charles Souter ('DR NIL')

They have cleared them 'ills down Jarvis way, where the great tall gum-trees grew;
An' where there was forests of she-oak once, you'll find but a scanty few.
Wire fences runs 'longside o' the roads where once there was posts and rails;
An' the old slab cottage 'as tumbled down an' so 'as the old cow-bails.
The blacksmith's forge on the Ad'laide road 'as been gone this many a year;
An' they've closed the pub McGonnigal kep', where we useter stop for a beer.

But when I was young at Buckalong,
When fust I come ter Buckalong,
There wasn't much in life we missed,
Nor many girls we hadn't kissed,
An' the best man there had the hardest fist,
When fust I come ter Buckalong!

I've galloped all over them 'ills meself, after emus and kangaroo,
On Sundays, after we'd been ter church – an' the Parson, 'e come too.
An' the Trooper come, an' the Doctor come, an' some o' the gals as well;
We reckoned as some of *us* coves could ride, but them *gals* could ride like Hell!
We used no dogs fer runnin' 'em down, just rode 'em to a stand.
An' the cove as got ahead o' them gals was the proudest cove in the land!

They was bushmen then at Buckalong,
When I was a lad at Buckalong,
We didn't squat in motor cars
An' swap blue yarns an' green cigars,
An' we never let down the slip-rail bars,
In them early days at Buckalong!

The roads is like some city street, all bitcherman and tar!
They don't make tracks fer the horseman now, only the motor car.
A team o' bullicks would bust themselves a-tryin' ter keep their feet,
An' there ain't no shade by the long wayside where a cove can spell in the heat.
The creeks is dry an' the paddicks bare, an' there ain't a patch o' scrub;
An' all yer can find is a petrol pump, when what yer want is a pub!

But when fust I come ter Buckalong,
When we was boys at Buckalong,
The bush WAS bush, an' the birds could sing,
An' a man could RIDE, an' an axe could ring,
An' yer life-blood flowed like a golden spring!,
When I was a lad ... at Buckalong!

We're All Australians Now

Proud & Patriotic

There's something about rhymed verse with a strong beat that lends itself to being a rallying call. You can feel the urge to march and chant and cheer and join in – like a national anthem, a war cry or a football club song – of which there are none in this volume (a possibly very un-Australian omission but one I'm happy to live with!!).

Having said that, the bulk of the poems in this section are reflective. Still, they serve as a reminder that 'us Aussies' tend to believe that we are the luckiest people on Earth. Whether native-born, like most of these poets, or Aussie by choice, like Eric Bogle, these writers repeatedly make the point that Australia's criteria for beauty and belonging are not those of Europe. Perhaps you can't really love a place until it feels sufficiently 'different' from other places. Perhaps you can't have a sense of true nationhood until you feel 'different' enough.

'We're All Australians Now'

AB Paterson ('THE BANJO')

Published as an open letter to the troops, 1915

Australia takes her pen in hand,
  To write a line to you,
To let you fellows understand,
  How proud we are of you.

From shearing shed and cattle run,
  From Broome to Hobson's Bay,
Each native-born Australian son,
  Stands straighter up today.

The man who used to 'hump his drum',
  On far-out Queensland runs,
Is fighting side by side with some
  Tasmanian farmer's sons.

The fisher-boys dropped sail and oar
  To grimly stand the test,
Along that storm-swept Turkish shore,
  With miners from the west.

The old state jealousies of yore
  Are dead as Pharaoh's sow,
We're not State children any more
  We're all Australians now!

Our six-starred flag that used to fly,
  Half-shyly to the breeze,
Unknown where older nations ply
  Their trade on foreign seas,

Flies out to meet the morning blue
  With Vict'ry at the prow;
For that's the flag the *Sydney* flew,
  The wide seas know it now!

The mettle that a race can show,
   Is proved with shot and steel,
And now we know what nations know
   And feel what nations feel.

The honoured graves beneath the crest
   Of Gaba Tepe hill,
May hold our bravest and our best,
   But we have brave men still.

With all our petty quarrels done,
   Dissensions overthrown,
We have, through what you boys have done,
   A history of our own.

Our old world diff'rences are dead,
   Like weeds beneath the plough,
For English, Scotch, and Irish-bred,
   They're all Australians now!

So now we'll toast the Third Brigade,
   That led Australia's van,
For never shall their glory fade
   In minds Australian.

Fight on, fight on, unflinchingly,
   Till right and justice reign.
Fight on, fight on, till Victory
   Shall send you home again.

And with Australia's flag shall fly
   A spray of wattle bough,
To symbolise our unity,
   We're all Australians now.

My Country

Dorothea Mackellar

The love of field and coppice,
　Of green and shaded lanes,
Of ordered woods and gardens
　Is running in your veins,
Strong love of grey-blue distance,
　Brown streams and soft, dim skies –
I know but cannot share it,
　My love is otherwise.

I love a sunburnt country,
　A land of sweeping plains,
Of rugged mountain ranges,
　Of droughts and flooding rains.
I love her far horizons,
　I love her jewel-sea,
Her beauty and her terror –
　The wide brown land for me!

The stark white ring barked forests
　All tragic to the moon,
The sapphire-misted mountains,
　The hot gold hush of noon.
Green tangle of the brushes,
　Where lithe lianas coil,
And orchids deck the tree-tops
　And ferns the warm dark soil.

Core of my heart, my country!
　Her pitiless blue sky,
When sick at heart, around us,
　We see the cattle die –
But then the grey clouds gather,
　And we can bless again
The drumming of an army,
　The steady soaking rain.

Core of my heart, my country!
　Land of the Rainbow gold,
For flood and fire and famine,
　She pays us back threefold –
Over the thirsty paddocks,
　Watch, after many days,
The filmy veil of greenness
　That thickens as we gaze ...

An opal-hearted country,
　A wilful lavish land –
All you who have not loved her,
　You will not understand –
Though earth holds many splendours,
　Wherever I may die,
I know to what brown country
　My homing thoughts will fly.

Shelter

Eric Bogle

I'm drowning in the sunshine as it pours down from the sky.
There's something stirring in my heart, bright colours fill my eye,
As from here to the far horizon your beauty does unfold,
And oh, you look so lovely dressed in green and gold.

I can almost touch the ocean, shimmering in the distant haze,
As I stand here on this mountain on this loveliest day of days.
Round half the world I've drifted, left no wild oats unsown,
But now my view has shifted and I think I've just come home.

To the homeless and the hungry may you always open doors.
May the restless and the weary find safe harbour on your shores.
May you always be our Dreamtime place, our spirit's glad release,
May you always be our shelter, may we always live in peace.

Sunny New South Wales

Anon

We often hear men boast about the land that gave them birth,
And each one thinks his native land the fairest spot on earth;
In beauty, riches, power, no land can his surpass;
To his, all other lands on earth cannot hold a glass.
Now, if other people have their boasts, then, say, why should not we?
For we can drink our jovial toast and sing with three times three;
For there's not a country in the world where all that's fair prevails,
As it does here in this our land, our Sunny New South Wales.
Then toast with me our happy land, where all that's fair prevails,
Our colour's blue, our hearts are true, in Sunny New South Wales.

Now let us take a passing glance at all that we possess.
That ours is such a wealthy land no stranger e'er would guess.
Our climate's good, that all admit, our flowers sweet and rare;
And scenes abound on every hand so marvellously fair.
Our native girls are fair and good, their hearts are pure and true,
And to their colour stick like bricks, the bright Australian blue.
Some never loved a roving life, nor blest the ocean's gales;
But they bless the breeze that blew them to a life in New South Wales.
Then toast with me our happy land, where all that's fair prevails,
Our colour's blue, our hearts are true, in Sunny New South Wales.

The Old Australian Ways

AB Paterson ('THE BANJO')

The London lights are far abeam
  Behind a bank of cloud,
Along the shore the gas lights gleam,
  The gale is piping loud:
And down the Channel, groping blind,
  We drive her through the haze
Towards the land we left behind –
The good old land of 'never mind',
  And old Australian ways.

The narrow ways of English folk
  Are not for such as we;
They bear the long-accustomed yoke
  Of staid conservancy:
But all our roads are new and strange
  And through our blood there runs
The vagabonding love of change
That drove us westward of the range
  And westward of the suns.

The city folk go to and fro
  Behind a prison's bars,
They never feel the breezes blow
  And never see the stars;
They never hear in blossomed trees
  The music low and sweet
Of wild birds making melodies,
Nor catch the little laughing breeze
  That whispers in the wheat.

Our fathers came of roving stock
  That could not fixed abide:
And we have followed field and flock
  Since e'er we learnt to ride;
By miner's camp and shearing shed,
  In land of heat and drought,
We followed where our fortunes led,
With fortune always on ahead
  And always further out.

The wind is in the barley grass,
   The wattles are in bloom;
The breezes greet us as they pass
   With honey-sweet perfume;
The parakeets go screaming by
   With flash of golden wing,
And from the swamp the wild ducks cry
Their long-drawn note of revelry,
   Rejoicing at the spring.

So throw the weary pen aside
   And let the papers rest,
For we must saddle up and ride
   Towards the blue hill's breast;
And we must travel far and fast
   Across their rugged maze,
To find the Spring of Youth at last,
And call back from the buried past
   The old Australian ways.

When Clancy took the drover's track
   In years of long ago,
He drifted to the outer back
   Beyond the Overflow;
By rolling plain and rocky shelf,
   With stockwhip in his hand,
He reached at last, oh lucky elf,
To Town of Come-and-Help-Yourself
   In Rough-and-Ready Land.

And if it be that you would know
   The tracks he used to ride,
Then you must saddle up and go
   Beyond the Queensland side –
Beyond the reach of rule or law,
   To ride the long day through,
In Nature's homestead – filled with awe:
You then might see what Clancy saw
   And know what Clancy knew.

Green and Gold Malaria

Rupert McCall

The day would soon arrive when I could not ignore the rash.
I was obviously ill and so I called on Doctor Nash.
This standard consultation would adjudicate my fate.
I walked into his surgery and gave it to him straight:
'Doc, I wonder if you might explain this allergy of mine,
I get these pins and needles running up and down my spine.
From there, across my body, it will suddenly extend –
My neck will feel a shiver and the hairs will stand on end.
And then there is the symptom that a man can only fear –
A choking in the throat, and the crying of a tear.'
Well, the Doctor scratched his melon with a rather worried look.
His furrowed brow suggested that the news to come was crook.
'What is it, Doc?' I motioned. 'Have I got a rare disease?
I'm man enough to cop it sweet, so give it to me, please.'
'I'm not too sure,' he answered, in a puzzled kind of way.
'You've got some kind of fever, but it's hard for me to say.
When is it that you feel this most peculiar condition?'
I thought for just a moment, then I gave him my position:
'I get it when I'm standing in an Anzac Day parade,
And I get it when the anthem of our native land is played,
And I get it when Meninga makes a Kiwi-crunching run,
And when Border grits his teeth to scrore a really gutsy ton.
I got it back in '91 when Farr-Jones held the Cup,
And I got it when Japan was stormed by Better Loosen Up.
I get it when the Banjo takes me down the Snowy River,
And Matilda sends me waltzing with a billy-boiling shiver.
It hit me hard when Sydney was awarded with the Games,
And I get it when I see our farmers fighting for their names.
It flattened me when Bertrand raised the boxing kangaroo,
And when Perkins smashed the record, well, the rashes were true blue.
So tell me, Doc,' I questioned. 'Am I really gonna die?'
He broke into a smile before he looked me in the eye.
As he fumbled with his stethoscope and pushed it out of reach,
He wiped away a tear and then he gave this stirring speech:
'From the beaches here in Queensland to the sweeping shores of Broome,
On the Harbour banks of Sydney where the waratah's in bloom.
From Uluru at sunset to the mighty Tasman Sea,
In the Adelaide cathedrals, at the roaring MCG.

From the Great Australian Bight up to the Gulf of Carpentaria,
The medical profession call it "green and gold malaria".
But forget about the text books, son, the truth I shouldn't hide.
The rash that you've contracted here is "good old Aussie pride".
I'm afraid that you were born with it and one thing is for sure –
You'll die with it, young man, because there isn't any cure.'

Come, Sing Australian Songs to Me!

PJ Hartigan (JOHN O'BRIEN)

Come, Little One, and sing to me
A song our big wide land to bless,
Around whose gentle parent-knee
We've twined the flowers of kindliness.

Your eyes are clear Australian blue,
Your voice like soft bush breezes blown;
Her sunshine steeps the heart of you,
Your tresses are the wattle's own.

What, no Australian song, my child,
No lay of love, no hymn of praise?
And yet no mother ever smiled
With our dear country's winsome ways:

You sing the songs of all the earth,
Of bower and bloom and bird and bee;
And has the land that gave you birth
No haunting, native melody?

Your poets' eager pens awake
The world-old themes of love and youth,
The pulse of life, the joy, the ache,
The pregnant line of earnest truth;

They dress you these in native guise,
And interweave with loving hand
The freshness of your rain-washed skies,
The colours of your sunlit land.

307

What, no Australian song, my dear?
And yet I've heard the cottage ring
With notes the world would pause to hear,
When at their work your sisters sing.

They sing the songs of all the earth,
Of tender sky and dimpling sea,
But all their strains have not the worth
Of one Australian song, for me.

I've heard the harp the breezes play
Among the wilding wilga-trees;
I've swept my world of care away
When bush birds lift their melodies;

I've seen the paddocks all ablaze
When spring in golden glory comes,
The purple hills of summer days,
The autumn ochres through the gums;

I've seen the bright folk riding in
O'er blooms that deck the clovered plain,
And neath the trees, when moonbeams spin
Their silver-dappled counterpane.

What, no Australian song, my pet?
No patriot note on native horn,
To bind the hearts in kindness met,
And link the leal Australian-born?

Yet every exile, wandering lone
Our happy careless homes among,
May live the best his heart has known
Whene're his country's songs are sung.

You sing the songs of all the earth,
Of alien flower and alien tree:
But no one, in my grief or mirth,
Will sing Australian songs to me.

You sing of every land but mine,
Where life is lilting neath the sun,
Still all its spirit seems ashine
In you, my little laughing one.

Your eyes are clear Australian blue,
Your face is towards the future set;
The bounding, gladsome heart of you
Is hers – and only hers, my pet.

Ah, Little One, what dreams would rise
If, nestled here upon my knee,
You'd flash those soft Australian eyes,
And sing your country's songs to me!

The Australian's Lament

Susan Nugent Wood

Far away, in sweet Australia,
   Now the summer's shining fair;
Now the wattle's flowery branches,
   Scent the glad bush everywhere.
On the home I love so fondly,
   Brightly now the sunbeams play;
All is warmth, and light, and beauty,
   In my own land far away!

In these cold and gloomy regions,
   Life is sad and dark to me;
Not a blossom, not a sunbeam,
   Not a leaf upon the tree.
O'er my haunted spirit ever,
   Voices of the summer day,
Tell me of the happy sunshine
   In my bright land far away!

Sadly breaks on me the morning,
   All the day is lone and drear;
Evening wraps my heart in shadow,
Night alone to me is dear.
Dreaming then of sweet Australia,
   Once again I freely stray,
'Neath the wattle's scented branches,
   In my bright land far away!

The Thong

Col Wilson ('BLUE THE SHEARER')

Let's talk about the Icons that are worshipped by us Aussies.
Akubra hats, the Opera House, meat pies, Speedo Cossies.
Some would say our Icon is that famous waltzing song,
I reckon that it's something else. I reckon it's the thong.

I've thought a thousand thoughts of thongs, and I think that the thong,
Is more an Aussie Icon, than the swagman's billabong.
Just as real men don't eat quiche, the dinkum Aussie male,
Will wear his dinkum Aussie thong, come rain, or sleet, or hail.

You can keep your Nikes and Reeboks. It's the thong that should be put,
With Aussie pride and dignity, on every Aussie foot.
I'm going to start a business. Like Bond, I can't go wrong,
I'll market it throughout the world, as Blue's designer thong.

A thong for each occasion. It's just sound commonsense
To make a tough, all purpose thong, to wear to all events.
Simple, sturdy, comfortable, my Blue's designer thong,
Will let the foot breathe evenly, and dissipate the pong.

It's good for killing blowflies on the barbecue or stove,
And it's great for crushing garlic. Just belt it on the clove,
And wipe the garlic laden thong on chicken, beef, or pork,
Inhale the pure aroma of that garlic when you walk.

A thong for early evening, to wear with hipster tights,
I can see the jingle in my mind, as though it were in lights.
Just a thong at twilight, when the tights are low.
With a string of diamantes, 'twined artistic around each toe.

A thong to wear to worship. I'd call it eventhong,
The strap is very holy, and the soul, so very strong.
A thong to wear to football, to cricket, or the shops,
To shearing sheds, to factories. Steel-capped thongs for cops.

I'd move away from footwear, create a new design,
For a chocolate-coated thong, to give my valentine,
And way into the future, when the years have moved along,
She will show her grandkids, love's old sweet thong.

And when we go republic, and we're looking for a song
To celebrate our Icon, let's hear it for the thong.
Forget Waltzing Matilda, Advance Australia Fair,
A brand new National Anthem will be wafting through the air:

God save our gracious thong.
Make our feet safe and strong,
And free from pong.
Wear them instead of shoes,
To pubs and barbecues.
Health, happiness to all of youse,
God save our thong.

How Australian Are You?

Jim Haynes

How Australian are you?
Can you play the didgeridoo?
Could you go naked in the bush and still survive?
Can you cook a kangaroo?
Spear a barramundi too?
Do you know which plants to eat to stay alive?

Was dad a shearer or a drover?
Or did your family come over
From Europe or Asia just last year?
How Australian can you get?
Can you ride a surfboard yet?
When we beat the Poms at cricket do you cheer?

How Australian are you?
Can you make a wallaby stew?
Did your great-great-granddad come on that first fleet?
Was he a convict? Is it true?
Was he a redhaired bloke called 'Blue'?
Did he hop around with chains upon his feet?

How Australian am I?
I'll drink a beer and eat a pie
And me granddad owned some cattle, and some sheep.
How Australian was yours?
Did he fight in any wars?
Did he die at Gallipoli or in his sleep?

Was your granddad true blue?
Was your dad a digger too?
Any explorers in your family tree?
A pioneer or two?
Just a bushranger will do.
Does that make you more Australian than me?

What's your Aussie claim to fame?
Do you have an Aussie name?
'Oodgeroo Noonuccal', 'Namatjira', oh, they're easy.
But 'Victor Chang' and 'Jenny Kee',
They sound Australian to me.
Like 'Ettingshausen', 'Dipierdomenico' and 'Campese'.

So how Australian are you?
Are you Aussie through and through?
If you can't do all these things are you an Alien?
Well maybe we should start
With how you feel, inside your heart,
'Cos there are eighteen million ways to be Australian.

Our Own Flag

AB Paterson ('THE BANJO')

They mustered us up with a royal din,
　In wearisome weeks of drought.
Ere ever the half of the crops were in,
　Or the half of the sheds cut out.

'Twas down with saddle and spurs and whip
　The swagman dropped his swag.
And we hurried us off to an outbound ship
　To fight for the English flag.

The English flag – it is ours in sooth
　We stand by it wrong or right.
But deep in our hearts is the honest truth
　We fought for the sake of a fight.

And the English flag may flutter and wave
　Where the World-wide Oceans toss,
But the flag the Australian dies to save
　Is the flag of the Southern Cross.

If ever they want us to stand the brunt
　Of a hard-fought, grim campaign,
We will carry our own flag up to the front
　When we go to the wars again.

Past Carin'

Sighs & Sorrows

*T*hese are poems about those times when the human spirit is broken by the unbearable and unfair burdens life has placed upon it. The inherent contradiction here, of course, is that the very fact that poets can find words to express their feelings at such times represents a triumph of the human spirit in the face of the worst that fate can throw at us.

In this section you will find that unfairness, suffering, degradation, sorrow and loss have inspired some of the strongest and most emotional poems and verses in the whole collection. Then, of course, there are the poems that deal with death itself – and the sorrow it leaves behind.

I've included Barcroft Boake's poem 'Jim's Whip' here. This poem is a well-crafted, evocative and extremely sentimental example of Australian rhymed verse. It is also sadly ironic as Boake suicided in bushland at Middle Harbour, Sydney, by hanging himself with his own stockwhip – perhaps the ultimate Australian bush poet's suicide. He was twenty-six years old and his collected verse was published posthumously. Paterson said, 'In his best pieces the spirit of the bush took hold of him, and he spoke as one possessed.' He also said, in light of Boake's tragic premature death, 'The bush is not a good home for melancholics.' I wonder if he also had Lawson in mind!

315

Past Carin'

Henry Lawson

Now up and down the siding brown
  The great black crows are flyin',
And down below the spur, I know,
  Another 'milker's' dyin';
The crops have withered from the ground,
  The tank's clay bed is glarin',
But from my heart no tear nor sound,
  For I have gone past carin' –
    Past worryin' or carin',
    Past feelin' aught or carin';
    But from my heart no tear nor sound,
    For I have gone past carin'.

Through Death and Trouble, turn about,
  Through hopeless desolation,
Through flood and fever, fire and drought,
  And slavery and starvation;
Through childbirth, sickness, hurt, and blight,
  And nervousness an' scarin',
Through bein' left alone at night,
  I've got to be past carin'.
    Past botherin' or carin',
    Past feelin' and past carin';
    Through city cheats and neighbours' spite,
    I've come to be past carin'.

Our first child took, in days like these,
    A cruel week in dyin',
All day upon her father's knees,
    Or on my poor breast lyin';
The tears we shed – the prayers we said
    Were awful, wild – despairin'!
I've pulled three through, and buried two
    Since then – and I'm past carin'.
        I've grown to be past carin',
        Past worryin' and wearin';
        I've pulled three through and buried two
        Since then, and I'm past carin'.

'Twas ten years first, then came the worst,
    All for a dusty clearin',
I thought, I thought my heart would burst
    When first my man went shearin';
He's drovin' in the great North-west,
    I don't know how he's farin';
For I, the one that loved him best,
    Have grown to be past carin'.
        I've grown to be past carin'
        Past lookin' for or carin';
        The girl that waited long ago,
        Has lived to be past carin'.

My eyes are dry, I cannot cry,
    I've got no heart for breakin',
But where it was in days gone by,
    A dull and empty achin'.
My last boy ran away from me,
    I know my temper's wearin',
But now I only wish to be
    Beyond all signs of carin'.
        Past wearyin' or carin',
        Past feelin' and despairin';
        And now I only wish to be
        Beyond all signs of carin'.

Lament

Sarah Collins

They chain us two by two, and whip and lash along,
They cut off our provisions, if we do the least thing wrong,
They march us in the burning sun, until our feet are sore,
So hard's our lot now we are got upon Van Diemen's shore.
We labour hard from morn to night, until our bones do ache,
Then every one, they must obey, their mouldy beds must make;
We often wish, when we lay down, we ne'er may rise no more,
To meet our savage governors upon Van Diemen's shore.
Every night when I lay down, I wash my straw with tears,
While wind upon this horrid shore whistles in our ears;
Those dreadful beasts upon this land around our cots do roar;
Most dismal is our doom upon Van Diemen's shore.
Come all young men and maidens, bad company forsake,
If tongue can tell our overthrow, it would make your heart to ache;
You girls, I pray, be ruled by me, your wicked ways give o'er,
For fear, like us, you spend your days upon Van Diemen's shore.

Moreton Bay

Anon

One Sunday morning as I went walking, by Brisbane waters I chanced to stray;
I heard a prisoner his fate bewailing, as on the sunny river bank he lay:
'I am a native of Erin's island, and banished now from my native shore;
They tore me from my aged parents and from the maiden whom I do adore.

'I've been a prisoner at Port Macquarie, at Norfolk Island and Emu Plains,
At Castle Hill and at cursed Toongabbie, at all those settlements I've worked in
    chains;
But of all places of condemnation and penal stations of New South Wales,
To Moreton Bay I have found no equal; excessive tyranny each day prevails.

'For three long years I was beastly treated, and heavy irons on my legs I wore;
My back with flogging is lacerated and often painted with my crimson gore.
And many a man from downright starvation lies mouldering now underneath
    the clay;
And Captain Logan he had us mangled at the triangles of Moreton Bay.

'Like the Egyptians and ancient Hebrews we were oppressed under Logan's
    yoke,
Till a native black lying there in ambush did give our tyrant his mortal stroke,
My fellow prisoners, be exhilerated that all such monsters such a death may
    find!
And when from bondage we are liberated our former suffering shall fade from
    mind.'

Labouring with the Hoe

Frank McNamara ('FRANK THE POET')

I was convicted by the laws of England's hostile crown,
Conveyed across those swelling seas in slavery's fettered bound,
For ever banished from that shore where love and friendship grow,
That loss of freedom to deplore and work the labouring hoe.

Despised, rejected and oppressed, in tattered rags I'm clad –
What anguish fills my aching breast and almost drives me mad
When I hear the settler's threatening voice say, 'Arise! to labour go;
Take scourging, convicts, for your choice or work the labouring hoe.'

Growing weary from compulsive toil beneath the noontide sun
While drops of sweat bedew the soil my task remains undone;
I'm flogged for wilful negligence, or the tyrants call it so –
Ah what a doleful recompense for labouring with the hoe.

Behold yon lofty woodbine hills where the rose in the morning shines,
Those crystal brooks that do distil and mingle through those vines –
There seems to me no pleasures gained, they but augment my woe
Whilst here an outcast doomed to live and work the labouring hoe.

You generous sons of Erin's isle whose heart for glory burns,
Pity a wretched exile who his long-lost country mourns;
Restore me, Heaven, to liberty whilst I lie here below;
Untie that clue of bondage and release me from the hoe.

The Last of His Tribe

Henry Kendall

He crouches, and buries his face on his knees,
    And hides in the dark of his hair;
For he cannot look up to the storm-smitten trees,
    Or think of the loneliness there –
    Of the loss and the loneliness there.

The wallaroos grope through the tufts of the grass,
    And turn to their coverts for fear;
But he sits in the ashes and lets them pass
    Where the boomerangs sleep with the spear –
    With the nullah, the sling, and the spear.

Uloola, behold him! The thunder that breaks
    On the tops of the rocks with the rain.
And the wind which drives up with the salt of the lakes
    Have made him a hunter again –
    A hunter and fisher again.

For his eyes have been full with a smouldering thought;
    But he dreams of the hunts of yore,
And of foes that he sought, and of fights that he fought
    With those who will battle no more –
    Who will go to the battle no more.

It is well that the water which tumbles and fills,
    Goes moaning and moaning along;
For an echo rolls out from the sides of the hills,
    And he starts at a wonderful song –
    At the sound of a wonderful song.

And he sees, through the rents of the scattering fogs,
    The corroboree warlike and grim,
And the lubra who sat by the fire on the logs,
    To watch, like a mourner, for him –
    Like a mother and mourner for him.

Will he go in his sleep from these desolate lands,
    Like a chief, to the rest of his race,
With the honey-voiced woman who beckons and stands,
    And gleams like a dream in his face –
    Like a marvellous dream in his face?

Lament for A Dialect

Mary Duroux

Dyirringan is lost to the tribes of
    the Yuin,
I am filled with remorse
    and I weep at the ruin.
Of beautiful words
    that were softly spoken,
Now lay in the past,
    all shattered and broken.
We forgot it somehow
    when English began,
The sweet sounding dialect
    of Dyirringan.
If we're to be civilized
    whom can we blame,
To have lost you,
    my language,
      is my greatest shame.

The Drover's Boy

Ted Egan

They couldn't understand why the drover cried
As they buried the drover's boy
For the drover had always seemed so hard
To the men in his employ.
A bolting horse, a stirrup lost
And the drover's boy was dead.
The shovelled dirt, a mumbled word
And it's back to the road ahead,
And forget about the drover's boy.

They couldn't understand why the drover cut
A lock of the dead boy's hair.
He put it in the band of his battered old hat.
As they watched him standing there,
He told them: 'Take the cattle on,
I'll sit with the boy a while,'
A silent thought, a pipe to smoke,
And it's ride another mile,
And forget about the drover's boy.

They couldn't understand why the drover and the boy
Always camped so far away,
For the tall white man and the slim black boy
Had never had much to say.
And the boy would be gone at break of dawn,
Tail the horses, carry on,
While the drover roused the sleeping men,
'Daylight, hit the road again,
And follow, the drover's boy.'
Follow the drover's boy.

In the Camooweal Pub they talked about
The death of the drover's boy,
They drank their rum with a stranger who'd come
From a Kimberley run, FitzRoy,
And he told of the massacre in the west
Barest details, guess the rest,
Shoot the bucks, grab a gin,
Cut her hair, break her in,
Call her a boy, the drover's boy
Call her a boy, the drover's boy.

So when they build that Stockman's Hall of Fame.
And they talk about the droving game,
Remember the girl who was bedmate and guide,
Rode with the drover side by side,
Watched the bullocks, flayed the hide,
Faithful wife, never a bride,
Bred his sons for the cattle runs.
Don't weep ... for the drover's boy
Don't mourn ... for the drover's boy
But don't forget ... the drover's boy.

Knocking Around

Henry Lawson

Weary old wife, with the bucket and cow,
'How's your son Jack? and where is he now?'
Haggard old eyes that turn to the west –
'Boys will be boys, and he's gone with the rest!'
Grief without tears and grief without sound;
'Somewhere up-country he's knocking around.'

Knocking around with a vagabond crew,
Does for himself what a mother would do;
Maybe in trouble and maybe hard-up,
Maybe in want of a bite or a sup;
Dead of the fever, or lost in the drought,
Lonely old mother! he's knocking about.

Wiry old man at the tail of the plough,
'Heard of Jack lately? and where is he now?'
Pauses a moment his forehead to wipe,
Drops the rope reins while he feels for his pipe,
Scratches his grey head in sorrow or doubt:
'Somewheers or others he's knocking about.'

Knocking about on the runs of the west,
Holding his own with the worst and the best
Breaking in horses and risking his neck,
Droving or shearing or making a cheque;
Straight as a sapling – six-foot and sound,
Jack is all right when he's knocking around.

Since Then

Henry Lawson

I met Jack Ellis in town to-day –
Jack Ellis – my old mate, Jack –
Ten years ago, from the Castlereagh,
We carried our swags together away
To the Never-Again, Out Back.

But times have altered since those old days,
　　And the times have changed the men.
Ah, well! there's little to blame or praise –
Jack Ellis and I have tramped long ways
　　On different tracks since then.

His hat was battered, his coat was green,
　　The toes of his boots were through,
But the pride was his! It was I felt mean –
I wished that my collar was not so clean,
　　Nor the clothes I wore so new.

He saw me first, and he knew 'twas I –
　　The holiday swell he met.
Why have we no faith in each other? Ah, why? –
He made as though he would pass me by,
　　For he thought that I might forget.

He ought to have known me better than that,
　　By the tracks we tramped far out –
The sweltering scrub and the blazing flat,
When the heat came down through each old felt hat
　　In the hell-born western drought.

He took my hand in a distant way
　　(I thought how we parted last),
And we seemed like men who have nought to say
And who meet – 'Good-day,' and who part – 'Good-day,'
　　Who never have shared the past.

I asked him in for a drink with me –
　　Jack Ellis – my old mate, Jack –
But his manner no longer was careless and free,
He followed, but not with the grin that he
　　Wore always in days Out Back.

I tried to live in the past once more –
　　Or the present and past combine,
But the days between I could not ignore –
I couldn't help notice the clothes he wore,
　　And he couldn't but notice mine.

He placed his glass on the polished bar,
    And he wouldn't fill up again;
For he is prouder than most men are –
Jack Ellis and I have tramped too far
    On different tracks since then.

He said that he had a mate to meet,
    And 'I'll see you again,' said he,
Then he hurried away through the crowded street
And the rattle of buses and scrape of feet
    Seemed suddenly loud to me.

And I almost wished that the time were come
    When less will be left to Fate –
When boys will start on the track from home
With equal chances, and no old chum
    Have more or less than his mate.

Scots of the Riverina

Henry Lawson

The boy ran away to the city from his home at Christmas time –
They were Scots of the Riverina, and to run from home was a crime.
The old man burned his letters, the first and last he burned,
And he scratched his name from the Bible when the old woman's back was turned.

A year went past, and another; and the fruit went down the line.
They heard the boy had enlisted, but the old man made no sign.
His name must never be mentioned on the farm by Gundagai –
They were Scots of the Riverina with ever the kirk hard by.

The boy came home on his 'final', and the township's bonfire burned.
His mother's arms were about him, but the old man's back was turned.
The daughters begged for pardon till the old man raised his hand –
A Scot of the Riverina who was hard to understand.

The boy was killed in Flanders, where the bravest heroes die.
There were tears at the Grahame homestead, and grief in Gundagai;
But the old man ploughed at daybreak and the old man ploughed till the mirk –
There were furrows of pain in the orchard while his housefolk went to the kirk. 325

The hurricane-lamp in the rafters dimly and dimly burned,
And the old man died at the table when the old woman's back was turned.
Face down on his bare arms folded he sank with his wild grey hair
Outspread o'er the open Bible and a name re-written there.

Sayonara Nakamura

Ted Egan

When the luggers all sailed away
From Roebuck Bay on that fateful day
The diver on the B 19 was Nakamura
Not yet twenty-one
From the Land of the Rising Sun
His homeland was the island Okinawa.

In the deepest holes of the Lacepede Shoals
To fulfil the pearling master's goals
Went the diver from the B 19, Nakamura
His quest for the lustrous pearl
As strong as his love for the beautiful girl
He'd wed when he returned to Okinawa.

From the West came a tropical squall
And the mercury began to fall
Forty fathoms deep was Nakamura
'Set sail' – no time to stage
For the storm began to rage
And they dragged to the surface the boy from Okinawa.

The agony's in his eyes
An old Malayman cries
He knows that the bends have got young Nakamura
Helplessly they cursed
As the diver's lungs near burst
And he died on the deck the boy from Okinawa.

To the diver's cemetery at Broome
Bearing gifts all deep in gloom
They walked with the body of the diver, Nakamura
Headstones face the west
A thousand divers lie at rest
And they're joined today by the boy from Okinawa.

But it's goodbye now, farewell
Say goodbye to Okinawa
For today we'll bury you
In West Australia
You will never be as one
With the Land of the Rising Sun
Sayonara. Sayonara Nakamura.

Jim's Whip

Barcroft Boake ('SURCINGLE')

Yes, there it hangs upon the wall
And never gives a sound,
The hand that trimmed its greenhide fall
Is hidden underground,
There, in that patch of sally shade,
Beneath that grassy mound.

I never take it from the wall,
That whip beloned to *him*,
The man I singled from them all,
He was my husband, Jim;
I see him now, so straight and tall,
So long and lithe of limb.

That whip was with him night and day
When he was on the track;
I've often heard him laugh, and say
That when they heard its crack,
After the breaking of the drought,
The cattle all came back.

And all the time that Jim was here
A-working on the run
I'd hear that whip ring sharp and clear
Just about set of sun
To let me know that he was near
And that his work was done.

327

I was away that afternoon,
Penning the calves, when, bang!
I heard his whip, 'twas rather soon –
A thousand echoes rang
And died away among the hills,
As toward the hut I sprang.

I made the tea and waited, but,
Seized by a sudden whim,
I went and sat outside the hut
Watching the light grow dim –
I waited there till after dark,
But not a sign of Jim.

The evening air was damp with dew;
Just as the clock struck ten
His horse came riderless – I knew
What was the matter *then*.
Why should the Lord have singled out
My Jim from other men?

I took the horse and found him where
He lay beneath the sky
With blood all clotted on his hair;
I felt too dazed to cry –
I held him to me as I prayed
To God that I might die.

But sometimes now I seem to hear –
Just when the air grows chill –
A single whip-crack, sharp and clear,
Re-echo from the hill.
That's Jim, to let me know he's near
And thinking of me still.

My Father-in-Law And I

Henry Lawson

My father-in-law is a careworn man,
  And a silent man is he:
But he summons a smile as well as he can
  Whenever he meets with me.
The sign we make with a silent shake
  That speaks of the days gone by –
Like men who meet at a funeral –
  My father-in-law and I.

My father-in-law is a sober man
  (And a virtuous man, I think);
But we spare a shilling whenever we can,
  And we both drop in for a drink.
Our pints they fill, and we say, 'Ah, well!'
  With the sound of the world-old sigh –
Like the drink that comes after a funeral –
  My father-in-law and I.

My father-in-law is a kindly man –
  A domestic man is he.
He tries to look cheerful as well as he can
  Whenever he meets with me.
But we stand and think till the second drink
  In a silence that might imply
That we'd both get over a funeral.
  My father-in-law and I.

Shoulda Been a Champion

Denis Kevans

Ah, you shoulda seen him, when he was just a kid,
Nobody could believe it, the things that Jimmie did,
Now, with his mates around him, and a beanie on his nut,
He's pouren' down the schooners, he's builden' up his gut.

Ah, shoulda been a champion, shoulda been a king,
Jimmie, mate, ah, Jimmie, coulda been anything,
Knocken' back the schooners, leanen' on a broom,
Down at the early opener, tryen' to find some room.

When he was just a junior, you shoulda seen him, son,
Slicen' through the centres, like a shot out of a gun,
Swerve and dodge and sidestep, head like a balloon,
Finished playen' seconds with a team at Bundanoon.

If he'd 've only listened, but he never could be told,
No worries in the world, he woulda worn the green 'n gold,
Bleary-eyed, and beery, out on the strip he struts,
Hands, as safe as ever, ah, but look at his 'comic cuts'.

There, we leave 'em drinken', listen to 'em laugh,
Jimmie, with his schooner, like a pregnant, Pommy half,
When he hitches up his stubbies, there's somethin' in his eyes,
Even fifty schooners can never quite disguise.

Second Class Wait Here

Henry Lawson

On suburban railway stations – you may see them as you pass –
There are sideboards on the platforms saying, 'Wait here second class';
And to me the whirr and thunder and the cluck of running gear
Seem to be for ever saying, saying 'Second class wait here' –
    'Wait here second class,
    Second class wait here.'
Seem to be for ever saying, saying 'Second class wait here'.

And the second class were waiting in the days of serf and prince,
And the second class are waiting – they've been waiting ever since.
There are gardens in the background, and the line is bare and drear,
Yet they wait beneath a signboard, sneering 'Second class wait here'.

I have waited oft in winter, in the mornings dark and damp,
When the asphalt platform glistened underneath the lonely lamp.
Ghastly on the brick-faced cutting 'Sellum's Soap' and 'Blower's Beer';
Ghastly on enamelled signboards with their 'Second class wait here'.

And the others seemed like burglars, slouched and muffled to the throats,
Standing round apart and silent in their shoddy overcoats,
And the wind among the wires, and the poplars bleak and bare,
Seemed to be for ever snarling, snarling 'Second class wait here'.

Out beyond the further suburb, 'neath a chimney stack alone,
Lay the works of Grinder Brothers, with a platform of their own;
And I waited there and suffered, waited there for many a year,
Slaved beneath a phantom signboard, telling our class to wait here.

Ah! a man must feel revengeful for a boyhood such as mine.
God! I hate the very houses near the workshop by the line;
And the smell of railway stations, and the roar of running gear,
And the scornful-seeming signboards, saying 'Second class wait here'.

There's a train with Death for driver, which is ever going past,
And there are no class compartments, and we all must go at last
To the long white jasper platform with an Eden in the rear;
And there won't be any signboards, saying 'Second class wait here'.

Old Tunes

Henry Lawson

When friends are listening round me, Jack, to hear my dying breath,
And I am lying in a sleep they say will end in death,
Don't notice what the doctor says – and *let* the nurse complain –
I'll tell you how to rouse me if I'll ever wake again.

Just you bring in your fiddle, Jack, and set your heart in tune,
And strike up 'Annie Laurie', or 'The Rising of the Moon';
And if you see no token of a rising in my throat,
You'll need to brace your mouth, old man – I'm booked by Charon's boat.

And if you are not satisfied that I am off the scene,
Strike up 'The Marseillaise', or else 'The Wearing of the Green';
And should my fingers tremble not, then I have crossed the line,
But keep your fingers steady, Jack, and strike up 'Auld Lang Syne'.

No Foe Shall Gather Our Harvest

Service & Sacrifice

For a nation that has no borders with any other nation, Australia has a remarkably 'war-conscious' heritage. This is mainly due to the fact that the Boer War and World War I occurred just before and after we achieved nationhood. The Boer War was the first time we thought of our soldiers as 'Australian' rather than residents of separate colonies. World War I was the first time we really struggled with many concepts of independent nationhood. (Elsewhere in this book, AB Paterson's poem, 'We're All Australians Now!', deals with this idea. It really also belongs here in this section but you can easily flick back and read it again!)

The experience at Anzac Cove has been called a defining moment for our nation. This baptism of blood and fire gave birth to the concept of an Australia that was no longer a British colony, but a nation apart whose needs and best interests could be quite different to those of Britain. Some Australians felt our troops were cynically betrayed by British strategy in the Dardanelles.

The Anzac experience was also an heroic opportunity for the young men of this nation, especially the bushmen. Later, in Palestine, the skills of the Aussie bushman would be exactly what was needed to take Beersheba and win a desert war on horseback, creating another legend of which a young nation could be proud.

In World War II the threat of invasion emphasised our geographical distance from Europe and forced us to accept the idea that we are also culturally different from Britain.

Mary Gilmore's powerful poem, which gives this section its title, was published in the *Women's Weekly* as a feature article in mid-1940. I find it interesting that it begins by acknowledging the white ethnic cultural links to Britain but then proceeds, with distinctly Australian imagery, to make its fiercely nationalistic point. Keith McKenry's poem seems a fitting one to end this collection.

No Foe Shall Gather Our Harvest
Mary Gilmore

Sons of the mountains of Scotland, clansmen from correl and kyle,
Breed of the moors of England, children of Erin's green isle.
We stand four-square to the tempest whatever the battering hail,
No foe shall gather our harvest or sit on our stockyard rail.

Our women shall walk in honour, our children shall know no chain,
This land that is ours forever the invader shall strike at in vain.
Anzac! Bapaume! and the Marne! Could ever the old blood fail?
No foe shall gather our harvest or sit on our stockyard rail.

So hail-fellow-met we muster and hail-fellow-met fall in,
Wherever the guns may thunder or the rocketing 'air mail' spin!
Born of the soil and the whirlwind – though death itself be the gale,
No foe shall gather our harvest or sit on our stockyard rail.

We are the sons of Australia, of the men who fashioned the land,
We are the sons of the women who walked with them, hand in hand;
And we swear by the dead who bore us, by the heroes who
    blazed the trail,
No foe shall gather our harvest or sit on our stockyard rail.

The Last Parade

AB Paterson ('THE BANJO')

With never a sound of trumpet,
    With never a flag displayed,
The last of the old campaigners
    Lined up for the last parade.

Weary they were and battered,
    Shoeless, and knocked about;
From under their ragged forelocks
    Their hungry eyes looked out.

And they watched as the old commander
    Read out, to the cheering men,
The Nation's thanks and the orders
    To carry them home again.

And the last of the old campaigners,
    Sinewy, lean, and spare –
He spoke for his hungry comrades:
    'Have we not done our share?

'Starving and tired and thirsty
  We limped on the blazing plain;
And after a long night's picket
  You saddled us up again.

'We froze on the windswept kopjes
  When the frost lay snowy white.
Never a halt in the daytime,
  Never a rest at night!

'We knew when the rifles rattled
  From the hillside bare and brown,
And over our weary shoulders
  We felt warm blood run down.

'As we turned for the stretching gallop,
  Crushed to the earth with weight;
But we carried our riders through it –
  Carried them p'raps too late.

'Steel! We were steel to stand it –
  We that have lasted through,
We that are old campaigners
  Pitiful, poor, and few.

'Over the sea you brought us,
  Over the leagues of foam:
Now we have served you fairly
  Will you not take us home?

'Home to the Hunter River,
  To the flats where the lucerne grows;
Home where the Murrumbidgee
  Runs white with the melted snows.

'This is a small thing, surely!
  Will not you give command
That the last of the old campaigners
  Go back to their native land?'

They looked at the grim commander,
But never a sign he made.
'Dismiss!' and the old campaigners
Moved off from their last parade.

Boots

'The Australian boots were the best of any issued to the Allied forces.'

AB Paterson ('THE BANJO')

We've travelled per Joe Gardiner, a humping of our swag
In the country of the Gidgee and Belar.
We've swum the Di'mantina with our raiment in a bag,
And we've travelled per superior motor car,
But when we went to Germany we hadn't any choice,
No matter what our training or pursuits,
For they gave us no selection 'twixt a Ford or Rolls de Royce
So we did it in our good Australian boots.

They called us 'mad Australians'; they couldn't understand
How officers and men could fraternise,
They said that we were 'reckless', we were 'wild, and out of hand',
With nothing great or sacred to our eyes.
But on one thing you could gamble, in the thickest of the fray,
Though they called us volunteers and raw recruits,
You could track us past the shell holes, and the tracks were all one way
Of the good Australian ammunition boots.

The Highlanders were next of kin, the Irish were a treat,
The Yankees knew it all and had to learn,
The Frenchmen kept it going, both in vict'ry and defeat,
Fighting grimly till the tide was on the turn.
And our army kept beside 'em, did its bit and took its chance,
And I hailed our newborn nation and its fruits,
As I listened to the clatter on the cobblestones of France
Of the good Australian military boots.

The Austral-Bloody-aise

CJ Dennis

Fellers of Australier,
　　Blokes an' coves an' coots,
Shift yer bloody carcases,
　　Move yer bloody boots.
Gird yer bloody loins up.
　　Get yer bloody gun.
Set the bloody enermy
　　An' watch the bugger run.

Get a bloody move on.
　　Have some bloody sense.
Learn the bloody art of
　　Self de-bloody-fence.

Have some bloody brains be-
　　Neath yer bloody lids.
An' swing a bloody sabre
　　Fer the missus an' the kids.
Chuck supportin' bloody posts.
　　An' strikin' bloody lights.
Support a bloody fam'ly an'
　　Strike fer yer bloody rights.

Joy is bloody fleetin',
　　Life is bloody short.
Wot's the use uv wastin' it
　　All on bloody sport?
Hitch yer bloody tip-dray
　　To a bloody star.
Let yer bloody watchword be
　　'Australi-bloody-ar!'

'Ow's the bloody nation
　　Goin' to ixpand
'Lest us bloody blokes an' coves
　　Lend a bloody 'and?
'Eave yer bloody apathy
　　Down a bloody chasm:
'Ump yer bloody burden with
　　Enthusi-bloody-asm.

W'en the bloody trouble
   Hits yer native land
Take a bloody rifle
   In yer bloody 'and.
Keep yer bloody upper lip
   Stiff as stiff kin be,
An' speed a bloody bullet for
Pos-bloody-terity.

W'en the bloody bugle
   Sounds 'Ad-bloody-vance'
Don't be like a flock uv sheep
   In a bloody trance
Biff the bloody foeman
   Where it don't agree.
Spifler-bloody-cate him
   To Eternity.

Fellers of Australier,
   Cobbers, chaps an' mates,
Hear the bloody enermy
   Kickin' at the gates!
Blow the bloody bugle,
Beat the bloody drum,
Upper-cut and out the cow
   To kingdom-bloody-come!

Get a bloody move on,
   Have some bloody sense
Learn the bloody art of
   Self de-bloody-fence!

Anzac Cove

Leon Gellert

There's a lonely stretch of hillocks;
There's a beach asleep and drear;
There's a battered broken fort beside the sea.
There are sunken, trampled graves;
And a little rotting pier:
And winding paths that wind unceasingly.

There's a torn and silent valley:
There's a tiny rivulet
With some blood upon the stones beside its mouth.
There are lines of buried bones:
There's an unpaid waiting debt:
There's a sound of gentle sobbing in the South.

War!

Leon Gellert

When my poor body died – Alas!
I watched it topple down a hill
And sink beside a tuft of grass.
... I laughed like mad,
... And laughing still
I bowed and thanked the bit of shell
That set me free and made me glad.
Then, quietly,
I strolled into Hell.

The Jester in the Trench

Leon Gellert

'That just reminds me of a yarn,' he said;
  And everybody turned to hear his tale.
He had a thousand yarns inside his head.
  They waited for him, ready with their mirth
And creeping smiles – then suddenly turned pale,
  Grew still, and gazed upon the earth.

They heard no tale. No further word was said.
  And with his untold fun,
  Half leaning on his gun,
They left him – dead.

The Digger

Anon

He went over to London and straight away strode,
Into army headquarters in Horseferry Road.
And he saw all the bludgers who dodge all the strafe,
By getting soft jobs on the headquarters' staff.
A lousy lance-corporal said, 'Pardon me please,
You've mud on your tunic and blood on your sleeve!
You look so disgraceful that people will laugh!'
Said the lousy lance-corporal on headquarters' staff.

The Digger then shot him a murderous glance;
He said, 'We've just come back from that balls-up in France,
Where bullets are flying and comforts are few,
And good men are dying for bastards like you!
We're shelled from the left and we're shelled from the right,
We're bombed all the day and we're bombed all the night,
And if something don't happen, and that pretty soon,
There'll be nobody left in the bloody platoon!'

The story soon got to the ears of Lord Gort,
Who gave the whole matter a great deal of thought,
And awarded the Digger a VC and two bars,
For giving that corporal a kick up the arse.
Now, when this war's over and we're out of here,
You'll see him in Sydney town, begging for beer.
He'll ask for a deener to buy a small glass . . .
But all that he'll get is a kick in the arse!

The Ragtime Army

Anon

We are the ragtime army, the A.N.Z.A.C.,
We cannot shoot, we won't salute,
What bloody good are we?
And when we get to Berlin Old Kaiser Bill says he:
'Hoch, hoch, mein Gott, what a lousy rotten lot,
Are the A.N.Z.A.C.'

And the Band Played Waltzing Matilda

Eric Bogle

When I was a young man I carried a pack
And I lived the free life of a rover,
From the Murray's green banks to the dusty outback,
I waltzed my matilda all over.
Then in 1915, the country said, 'Son,
There's no time for rovin', there's work to be done,'
And they gave me a tin hat, and gave me a gun,
And they sent me away to the war.
And the band played Waltzing Matilda,
As our ship pulled away from the quay
And amidst all the cheers, the flag-waving and tears,
We sailed off for Gallipoli.

How well I remember that terrible day
When our blood stained the sand and the water,
And how in that hell that they called Suvla Bay,
We were butchered like lambs at the slaughter.
Johnny Turk he was waiting, he'd primed himself well,
He showered us with bullets, and rained us with shell,
And in ten minutes flat, he'd blown us to hell:
Nearly blew us right back to Australia.
And the band played Waltzing Matilda,
As we stopped to bury the slain.
We buried ours and the Turks buried theirs,
Then we started all over again.

And those that were left, well, we tried to survive
In that mad world of death, blood and fire,
And for ten weary weeks I kept myself alive,
Though around me the corpses piled higher,
Then a big Turkish shell knocked me arse over head,
And when I woke up in my hospital bed
I saw what it had done, and I wished I was dead,
Never knew there were worse things than dying.
For I'll go no more waltzing Matilda
All around the wild bush far and free,
To hump tent and pegs, a man needs both legs,
No more waltzing Matilda for me.

They collected the crippled, the wounded and maimed
And they shipped us back home to Australia,
The armless, the legless, the blind and insane,
All the brave wounded heroes of Suvla.
And when our ship pulled into Circular Quay,
And I looked at the place where my legs used to be,
I thanked Christ there was nobody waiting for me –
To grieve, and to mourn and to pity.
And the band played Waltzing Matilda
As they carried us down the gangway,
But nobody cheered, they just stood there and stared –
And then turned their faces away.

So now every April I sit on my porch,
And I watch the parade pass before me,
And I see my old comrades how proudly they march,
Reliving old dreams and past glories.
But the old men march slowly their bones stiff and sore –
Tired old men from a tired old war,
And the young people ask what are they marching for,
And I ask myself the same question.
But the band plays Waltzing Matilda
And the old men still answer the call,
But year by year those old men disappear
Soon no one will march there at all.

The Wells of Beersheba

Ted Egan

The soldiers ate their breakfast
Bully beef and biscuits
They'd ridden for the last two days and nights
Their faithful horses ground their oats
Through bitted mouths in nosebags
Veterans of a hundred desert fights.

It's through the Sinai Desert, boys
On the way to Gaza
Jerusalem is in our sights
But first we need Beersheba
The waters of Beersheba.

Australian guns were blazing
On the slopes of Tel el Saba
The British fought the action to the west
But the Turks and Germans grimly
Manned the ramparts of Beersheba
Determined to withstand another test.

Come on! Come on infantry
Hit 'em hard artillery
If this operation's to succeed
Beersheba must be captured
We must take the town by nightfall
Beersheba's water is our greatest need.

The day dragged on, the fight was grim
Sunset just an hour away
Chauvel could see the only way to go,
'We'll charge their bloody trenches
With the Fourth and Twelfth Light Horse
It's the only way to win this little show.'

Mount up! Fourth and Twelfth Light Horse!
Fix bayonets for the charge
Say your prayers and wave your mates goodbye
For you must ride those three long miles
And take the Turkish trenches
Beersheba boys, you must do or die.

Across the rocky plain they rode
A trot to form a line
A canter for another mile or more
Eight hundred wild colonial boys
Then thundered to a gallop
Riding as they'd never done before.

Shells are bursting round them
Sheets of flame and dust
Horses and their riders blown apart.
Still they charge relentlessly
A mile ahead and they can see
The trenches where the fight will really start.

Machine guns fired and rifles spat
Their message at the horses that
Began to jump the trenches one by one
Then the fighting's hand to hand,
The enemy could not withstand,
Cold steel, and then the fighting's done.

The canvas troughs are then unrolled
The horses slake their thirst
Girths are slackened by Beersheba's gate.
The tired Australian horseman
Strokes the neck of his old waler,
'Well done, well bloody done, my dear old mate.'

It's through the Sinai Desert, boys
On the way to Gaza
Jerusalem is in our sights
For now we've won Beersheba
The waters of Beersheba.

Middle East Song

Anon

Oh they took us out to Egypt, that God-forsaken land,
It's filled with bloody nothing and covered up with sand.
They fed us on stale biscuits, camel piss and stew,
And we wandered round in circles with bugger-all to do.

The generals that they sent us had not a bloody clue,
They ought to round the bastards up and put them in a zoo.
They said, 'Keep your eye on Rommel, don't let the bastard pass.'
But he'd sneak around behind them and kick them in the arse!

Then out came Montgomery, his prayerbook in his hand.
He said, 'Now men, the time has come to make a bloody stand.
We've got the Lord on our side and Rommel's cupboard's bare.
Now then men, down on your knees and say a bloody prayer!'

And we prayed, 'Oh Jesus save us, 'tis not the Hun we fear,
Save us from the crazy bastards Churchill sends out here!'

Beach Burial

Kenneth Slessor

Softly and humbly to the Gulf of Arabs
The convoy of dead sailors come;
At night they sway and wander in the waters far under,
But morning rolls them in the foam.

Between the sob and clubbing of the gunfire
Someone, it seems, has time for this,
To pluck them from the shallows and bury them in burrows
And tread the sand upon their nakedness;

And each cross, the driven stake of tidewood,
Bears the last signature of men,
Written with such perplexity, with such bewildered pity,
The words choke as they begin –

'Unknown seaman' – the ghostly pencil
Wavers and fades, the purple drips,
The breath of the wet season has washed their inscriptions
As blue as drowned men's lips.

Dead seamen, gone in search of the same landfall,
Whether as enemies they fought,
Or fought with us or neither; the sand joins them together,
Enlisted on the other front.
El Alamein.

El Alamein

John Jarmain

There are flowers now, they say, at Alamein;
Yes, flowers in the minefields now.
So those that come to view that vacant scene
Where death remains and agony has been
Will find the lilies grow –
Flowers, and nothing that we know.

So they rang the bells for us and Alamein,
Bells which we could not hear:
And to those who heard the bells what could it mean,
That name of loss and pride, El Alamein?
– Not the murk and harm of war,
But their hope, their own warm prayer.

It will become a staid historic name,
That crazy sea of sand!
Like Troy or Agincourt its single fame
Will be the garland for our brow, our claim,
On us a fleck of glory to the end:
And there our dead will keep their holy ground.

And this is not the place that we recall,
The crowded desert crossed with foaming tracks.
The one blotched building, lacking half a wall,
The grey-faced men, sand powdered over all;
The tanks, the guns, the trucks,
The black, dark-smoking wrecks.

So be it: none but us has known that land:
El Alamein will still be only ours
And those ten days of chaos in the sand.
Others will come who cannot understand,
Will halt beside the rusty minefield wires
And find there – flowers.

Men in Green

David Campbell

Oh, there were fifteen men in green,
Each with a tommy-gun,
Who leapt into my plane at dawn;
We rose to meet the sun.

We set our course towards the east
And climbed into the day
Till the ribbed jungle underneath
Like a giant fossil lay.

We climbed towards the distant range
Where two white paws of cloud
Clutched at the shoulders of the pass;
The green men laughed aloud.

They did not fear the ape-like cloud
That climbed the mountain crest
And hung from twisted ropes of air
With thunder in their breast.

They did not fear the summer's sun
In whose hot centre lie
A hundred hissing cannon shells
For the unwatchful eye.

And when on Dobadura's field
We landed, each man raised
His thumb towards the open sky;
But to their right I gazed.

For fifteen men in jungle green
Rose from the kunai grass
And came towards the plane. My men
In silence watched them pass;
It seemed they looked upon themselves
In Time's prophetic glass.

Oh, there were some leaned on a stick
And some on stretchers lay.
But few walked on their own two feet
In the early green of day.

They had not feared the ape-like cloud
That climbed the mountain crest;
They had not feared the summer's sun
With bullets for their breast.

Their eyes were bright, their looks were dull,
Their skin had turned to clay.
Nature had met them in the night
And stalked them in the day.

And I think still of men in green
On the Soputa track
With fifteen spitting tommy-guns
To keep a jungle back.

Remember the Waltzing

Jim Haynes

She was Tilly, the funny old lady,
She lived at the end of our street –
And I'd always stop
When I went to the shop
And she'd give me a smile and a treat.

One day we sat in her kitchen,
I asked why she lived alone.
That was when she
Showed his photo to me,
And read me his last letter home.

'Remember the Waltzing Matilda?
Remember the old one-two-three?
A Barndance and then a Varso Vienna,
Remember your arms around me?

Remember the Waltzing Matilda?
And if this war ever should end,
The very first chance,
The first Town Hall Dance,
I'll waltz my Matilda again.'

He never returned from Kokoda
To dance in our little Town Hall.
She never went there,
She couldn't bear
To see his name up on the wall.

Tilly, the funny old lady,
She lived a lifetime alone –
Reading the page,
Watching them fade,
The words of his last letter home.

'Remember the Waltzing Matilda?
Remember the old one-two-three?
A Barndance and then a Varso Vienna,
Remember your arms around me?

Remember the Waltzing Matilda?
And if this war ever should end,
The very first chance,
The first Town Hall Dance,
I'll waltz my Matilda again.'

Mothers, Daughters, Wives

Judy Small

The first time it was fathers
The last time it was sons
And in between your husbands
Marched away with drums and guns
And you never thought to question
You just went on with your lives
'Cos all they taught you who to be
Was mothers, daughters, wives.

You can only just remember
The tears your mothers shed
As they sat and read their papers
Through the lists and lists of dead
And the gold frames held the photographs
That mothers kissed each night
And the door frames held the shocked
And silent strangers from the fight.

And it was twenty-one years later
With children of your own
The trumpets sounded once again
And the soldier boys were gone
And you drove their trucks
And made their guns and tended to their wounds
And at night you kissed the photographs
And prayed for safe returns.

And after it was over
You had to learn again
To be just wives and mothers
When you'd done the work of men
So you worked to help the needy
And you never trod on toes
And the photos on the piano
Struck a happy family pose.

And then your daughters grew to women
And your little boys to men
And you prayed that you were dreaming
When the call-up came again
But you proudly smiled and held your tears
As they bravely waved goodbye
And the photos on the mantelpiece
Always made you cry.

And now you're getting older
And in time the photos fade
And in widowhood you sit back
And reflect on the parade

Of the passing of your memories
As your daughters change their lives
Seeing more to our existence
Than just mothers, daughters, wives.

But the first time it was fathers
The last time it was sons
And in between your husbands
Marched away with drums and guns
And your never thought to question
You just went on with your lives
'Cos all they taught you who to be
Was mothers, daughters, wives –
And you believed them.

I Was Only Nineteen

John Schumann

Mum and Dad and Denny saw the passing out parade at Puckapunyal,
It was a long march from cadets
The 6th Battalion was next to tour and it was me who drew the card,
We did Kanungra and Shoalwater before we left.

And Townsville lined the footpaths as we marched down to the quay.
There's a clipping from the paper – shows us young and strong and clean.
And there's me in me slouch hat with me SLR and greens,
God help me – I was only nineteen.

From Vung Tau riding Chinooks to the dust of Nui Dat,
I'd been in and out of choppers now for months,
But we made our tents a home, VB and pinups on the lockers,
And an Asian orange sunset through the scrub.

And can you tell me doctor why I still can't get to sleep?
And night time's just a jungle dark and a barking M16?
And what's this rash that comes and goes?
Can you tell me what it means?
God help me – I was only nineteen.

A full week operation when each step can mean your last one
On two legs – it was a war within yourself.
But you wouldn't let your mates down till they had you dusted off,
So you closed your eyes and thought of something else.

Then someone yelled out, 'Contact!' and the bloke behind me swore.
We looked in there for hours, then a God Almighty roar!
Frankie kicked a mine the day that mankind kicked the moon.
God help me – he was going home in June.

I can still see Frankie drinking tinnies in the Grand Hotel,
On a 36-hour rec leave in Vung Tao.
And I can still hear Frankie lying screaming in the jungle,
Till the morphine came and killed the bloody row.

And the Anzac legends didn't mention mud and blood and tears,
And the stories that my father told me never seemed quite real,
I caught some pieces in my back that I didn't even feel.
God help me – I was only nineteen.

And can you tell me doctor why I still can't go to sleep?
And why the Channel Seven chopper chills me to my feet?
And what's this rash that comes and goes?
Can you tell me what it means?
God help me – I was only nineteen.

The Last Gallipoli Veteran

Keith McKenry

The last Gallipoli veteran is marching alone today;
His comrades from the Great War have fallen by the way.
Two hundred yards in his best suit, his medals, and his braid,
He marches in a line of *one* along Anzac Parade.
The last link with Gallipoli, Cape Helles, and Lone Pine,
He is Australian legend going down the line.
He listens to the service and stands for the 'Last Post';
The last of the Anzacs, he is less a man ... than ghost.

353

Index by Title

Index by Author